THE CALL OF THE CREEK

The Art & Soul of Fly Fishing for Wild Trout

James Salas

Headwaters Publishing

What These Great Americans Say About the Creek

(And Would Likely Have Something to Say About This Book, Too.)

I could have done what big-name authors do—chased down Fortune 500 CEOs, influencers, and paid blurbs to tell you how great this book is. But instead, I went with something better: timeless words from those who truly understood the creek, the fish, and the water that calls to all of us.

"Many go fishing all their lives without knowing that it is not fish they are after."
— **Henry David Thoreau** (American philosopher, poet, and naturalist best known for Walden and his reflections on nature, solitude, and simplicity.)

"A trout is a moment of beauty known only to those who seek it."
— **Arnold Gingrich** (Writer, editor, and fly fishing enthusiast; founder of Esquire magazine and author of The Well-Tempered Angler,)

"To go fishing is the chance to wash one's soul with pure air, with the rush of the brook, or with the shimmer of the sun on blue water."
— **Herbert Hoover** *(31st President of the United States and avid fisherman who found solace in nature and trout streams.)*

"The mountains are calling and I must go."
— **John Muir** *(Naturalist, founder of the Sierra Club, and advocate for the U.S. National Parks.)*

"A river seems a magic thing. A magic, moving, living part of the very earth itself."
— **Laura Gilpin** *(Photographer and writer known for capturing the beauty of the American West.)*

The Call of the Creek: The Art & Soul of Fly Fishing for Wild Trout

© 2025 James Salas

All rights reserved. No part of this book may be reproduced, stored, or shared without written permission from the author, except for brief quotations used in book reviews.

ISBN: 979-8-9929225-1-6

First Edition, 2025

Published by Headwaters Publishing
Printed in the United States of America
Cover Design by Headwaters Publishing
Editing by Headwaters Publishing

Safety Disclaimer: Fishing and outdoor activities involve inherent risks. Readers are encouraged to follow local laws, regulations, and safety guidelines when engaging in these activities. The author and publisher assume no responsibility for any injury, loss, or damages resulting from the application of techniques or advice contained in this book.

General Disclaimer: This book is based on the author's personal experiences and research. While every effort has been made to ensure accuracy, the author and publisher make no guarantees regarding the completeness or reliability of the information. The content is provided "as is" and should not be considered professional advice. The author and publisher disclaim any liability for any decisions made based on the information presented in this book.

Amazon Disclaimer: This book is independently published and is not affiliated with, sponsored by, or endorsed by any brands, companies, or organizations mentioned within.

Fictional Disclaimer: This book contains personal stories and recollections. Some events, names, and conversations have been altered or combined for storytelling purposes. Any resemblance to actual persons, living or dead, is purely coincidental.

Headwaters Publishing

To Katie and David—
Some of the best days are the ones spent
knee-deep in a cold mountain stream,
chasing trout and adventure.
I hope the creek always calls you.

Author's Note

By the time you turn these pages, you'll be stepping into the world of trout streams—casting into shadowed pools, imagining the rush of cold water against your legs, and anticipating the telltale flash of a rising fish. And yet, you may have already noticed something: this book contains no glossy photographs—only words, and a handful of simple illustrations.

I wrestled with that decision for a long time. My hard drives—and let's be honest, my maxed-out cloud storage—are filled with images from years spent wandering rivers. Snapshots of breathtaking landscapes, fish held briefly in wet hands before release, and old rods leaning against cabin walls, their cork grips darkened by the touch of time. But none of them tell the whole story. None of them could ever measure up to the actual experience of being there. If they could, I wouldn't keep going back.

A photograph might show a perfect bend in a mountain stream, but it cannot capture the sound of water tumbling over stone, the scent of pine drifting through the canyon, or the way the river's voice changes as the day unfolds. It cannot convey the slow-building anticipation before a cast, the way the light shifts across the surface, or the silent reverence of standing alone in the wild.

That is why I chose to let most of the imagery live in your mind. The few illustrations in these pages are not meant to define the experience but to serve as waypoints—reminders of the world we enter when we step into moving water. The rest is yours to create. Because fly fishing isn't about a single moment captured—it's about the way the river lingers in your mind long after you've left it. It's about how the water calls you back, how the weight of the rod in your hand becomes second nature, how every trout caught or lost is part of something bigger than itself.

So take these words and let them create their own pictures in your mind. Fill in the gaps with your own memories, or with the ones you hope to make. Because in the end, the real beauty of a trout stream—and of this book—is not in seeing, but in feeling.

Introduction

Trout fishing isn't just a sport; it's a connection—to nature, to the wild, and to something deeper within ourselves. For many of us, life can become a blur of responsibilities and routines, leaving little time to pause and reflect. This book offers a reminder of what can be found when we step away from the noise and immerse ourselves in the rhythm of a flowing stream.

Fly fishing is both an art and a meditation. It's a craft that demands patience, skill, and an understanding of the water and its inhabitants. It's about more than catching fish—it's about being present in the moment. It's about observing the way the current moves, the way insects dance on the surface, and the way trout rise to feed. These experiences anchor us in the present, offering clarity and peace in a world that often feels overwhelming.

This book is for everyone who has ever felt drawn to the water—whether you're an experienced angler looking to refine your skills, or someone who has never held a fly rod before. If you've ever dreamed of standing in a pristine mountain stream, watching a trout rise to a perfectly placed fly, then this book is for you. It's for those who seek not just the catch, but the entire experience—the calm before the cast, the exhilaration of a take, and the satisfaction of releasing a fish back into the current.

Throughout these pages, you'll find practical guidance on how to become a more confident and capable angler. You'll learn about reading water, understanding trout behavior, and selecting the right fly patterns. You'll also discover the beauty of different trout waters across the country, from the quiet streams of the Appalachian Mountains to the rugged rivers of the West and the storied waters of the Northeast. Each place offers its own challenges and rewards, and each helps us grow as anglers and as people.

But this book isn't just about techniques and destinations—it's about a philosophy. Trout fishing teaches us to slow down, to pay attention, and to adapt. It reminds us that success is not always measured in numbers, but in the quality of the experience. It's about the joy of learning a new skill, the thrill of discovery, and the stories we create along the way. These are the moments that stay with us—the ones we carry home and share with friends and family, the ones that become part of who we are.

For beginners, this book provides a road map to starting your journey. It guides you through the basics of casting, choosing equipment, and finding your first trout waters. It offers encouragement to step outside your comfort zone, to embrace the learning curve, and to savor the process. Fly fishing is not about instant gratification; it's about the slow, steady progress that comes with practice and patience.

For seasoned anglers, this book is a chance to revisit the fundamentals and deepen your understanding of the sport. Even the most experienced fly fishers can learn something new—a subtle adjustment to a cast, a new approach to reading water, or a fresh perspective on the places we fish. The more we learn, the more we appreciate the complexity and beauty of the sport.

Beyond the practical advice, this book explores the emotional and spiritual rewards of fly fishing. The creek has a way of healing us, of helping us see the world differently. Standing in moving water, we become part of something larger—something timeless. The creek doesn't care who we are or where we come from. It doesn't care about our accomplishments or our failures. It simply flows, and in doing so, it reminds us to let go of what doesn't matter and focus on what does.

Trout fishing also teaches us respect—for the fish, for the environment, and for the legacy of those who came before us. The rivers we fish today are a gift, preserved through the efforts of conservationists, passionate anglers, and organizations like Trout Unlimited. By understanding the delicate balance of these ecosystems, we become stewards of the waters we love. This book will show you not only how to fish, but how to fish responsibly—so that future generations can experience the same joy and wonder that we do.

Finally, this book is a celebration of the stories we collect along the way. Fly fishing is rich with humor, adventure, and unexpected moments. From the fish that got away to the perfect cast that landed the catch of a lifetime, these stories shape our relationship with the water and with each other. They remind us why we keep coming back—why the call of the creek is so hard to ignore.

So, whether you're standing in a quiet mountain stream, wading through a wide western river, or simply dreaming of the next time you'll cast a line, this book is for you. It's an invitation to experience the magic of fly fishing—to embrace the challenges, to cherish the beauty, and to answer the call of the creek.

A Note on the Word "Creek"

I use the word creek throughout this book, but let's get something straight—it could just as well be a river, a stream, a brook, or any moving body of water that holds trout. The names change, the water flows, but the essence remains the same.

I chose creek because there's something romantic, intimate, and raw about it. A river has grandeur, a stream has movement, but a creek? A creek is personal. It whispers instead of roars. It's where you find yourself alone with the water, the rocks, and the trout that seem to materialize from the shadows. It's the kind of place where you can kneel in the shallows, feel the current press against your fingers, and lose track of time.

You don't just fish a creek—you listen to it. You follow its bends, learn its rhythm, and, if you're lucky, you disappear into it.

So if you fish rivers, tailwaters, or sprawling freestone streams, know that every time I say creek, I mean all of them. Because in the world of moving water, names don't matter. The trout don't care what you call it. They only care that you showed up.

Table of Contents

Part 1: The Soul of Fly Fishing 1
Chapter 1: The First Cast 1
Chapter 2: A Sport Like No Other 4
Chapter 3: Why a Good Guide Changes Everything 7
Chapter 4: Ther River's Endless Call 10
Chapter 5: Born to Fish: The Instinct that Never Fades 14

Part 2: The Art & Science of Fly Fishing 17
Chapter 6: Essential Gear (and What You Can Skip) 18
Chapter 7: The Fly Shop 21
Chapter 8: The Seven Must-Have Flies & Nymphs 26
Chapter 9: The Six Essential Fly-Fishing Setups 30
Chapter 10: Tying Your Own Fly 35
Chapter 11: The Unspoken Rules of Fly Fishing 38
Chapter 12: Perfecting Your Cast Without Water 43
Chapter 13: The Hidden Power of Lag in Your Cast 47
Chapter 14: The Art of the Drift 51

Part 3: Chasing Trout: The Waters We Fish 55
Chapter 15: Trout Waters: The Key Differences You Need to Know 56
Chapter 16: The Beauty of Trout Waters 60
Chapter 17: Reading the Water 64
Chapter 18: How Trout Use Cover and Camouflage 67
Chapter 19: The Ephemeroptera 71
Chapter 20: Hatch Cycles and Feeding Frenzies 75
Chapter 21: Chasing the Hatch 79
Chapter 22: Trout Only Live in Beautiful Places 83
Chapter 23: Who Lives in a Trout Stream? 86

Chapter 24: Big Trout, Big Secrets 90

Chapter 25: What I learned About Trout While Snorkeling in a Waterfall Pool 93

Chapter 26: Hatchery Waters: The Pros, Cons, and Reality 98

Chapter 27: Spring Creeks vs. Freestone Rivers 103

Chapter 28: High-Elevation Streams and Lakes 107

Chapter 29: Urban Trout Waters 112

Chapter 30: The Blue Lines on the Map 117

Chapter 31: 50 Blue Ribbon Streams 122

Chapter 32: The Underrated Trout Streams 127

CHAPTER 33: THE HIDDEN POWER OF UNDERGROUND SPRINGS 131

Chapter 34: Trout, Seasons, and the Unpredictable Mood Swings of the River 139

Part 4: The Fly Fisher's Journey 142

Chapter 35: Short Trips vs. All-Day Adventures 143

Chapter 36: Snacks, Drinks, and Trail Food 147

Chapter 37: Capturing the Story: How to Document & Share Your Journey 151

Chapter 38: Filming and Recording Your Experience 155

Chapter 39: Then vs. Now 159

Chapter 40: Trout Fishing in the Dead of Winter 163

Chapter 41: Fly Fishing vs. Spinning Rod 166

Chapter 42: Brush, Branches, and Broken Leaders 169

Chapter 43: Solo Fishing vs. Fishing with a Buddy 172

Chapter 44: Why Catching a Big Trout is More Mental Than Physical 178

Chapter 45: The Hardest Skill: Knowing When to Walk Away 182

Part 5: Trout Behavior & Underwater Truth 186

Chapter 46: The World Through a Tout's Senses 187

Chapter 47: The Science of the Rise 191

Chapter 48: How Water Temperature Shapes Trout Behavior
.... 196

Chapter 49: Coweeta: Guardian of the Flowing Waters 201

Chapter 50: Why a Trout is Too Valuable to Catch Just Once
.... 205

Part 6: The Heart of the Stream: Fly Fishing's Deeper Meaning **208**

Chapter 51: The Essence of Trout Fishing 209

Chapter 52: What Trout Teach Us About Time 215

Chapter 53: The Unwritten Code of the River 218

Chapter 54: The Ritual of Fly Fishing 221

Chapter 55: Fishing with Kids and Passing It On 225

Chapter 56: The Hatchery 228

Chapter 57: Why We Keep Chasing Trout 233

Chapter 58: The Magic of Returning to a Stream 236

Chapter 59: Why Fly Fishing is a Lifetime Pursuit 240

Chapter 60: Final Cast: The Stream Keeps Flowing 243

Part 7: Exploring New Waters: Adventures Beyond Home
.... **247**

Chapter 61: The Top 10 National Parks for Fly Fishing 248

CHAPTER 62: THE 15 BEST STATES FOR TROUT FISHING 252

Chapter 63: Exploring International Fly Fishing 257

Chapter 64: The Legends of Fly Fishing 261

Part 8: The Past, Present and Future of Fly Fishing **265**

Chapter 65: Rediscovering the Forgotten Streams 266

Chapter 66: Can Trout Remember? The Science of Trout Memory 269

Chapter 67: Why Rivers Heal Us 273

Chapter 68: The Impact of Conservation Laws on Fly Fishing 277

Chapter 69: Success Stories of Rivers That Were Nearly Lost but Brought Back 281

Chapter 70: The Rise of Fishing in the Digital Age 284

Chapter 71: The Evolution of Fly Rods 288

Chapter 72: Fly Fishing Myths 292

Chapter 73: Reviving The Lost Art of Wet Fly Fishing 296

Chapter 74: The Bare Necessities 300

Appendix: 303

Part 1: The Soul of Fly Fishing

Chapter 1: The First Cast

Answering the Call of the Creek

I had no idea one cast would change everything.

The fly smacked the water. Ripples shot outward, a signal sent into the current. I held my breath. I was fishing. And I was about to be hooked for life.

That's the power of fly fishing. The second the line unfurls, the fly lands, and the water tightens around it, you're in. It doesn't matter if it's a perfect loop or a tangled disaster. That first cast marks the beginning of something bigger. And before you know it, that first cast becomes a lifetime pursuit.

What This Book Offers You

My goal with The Calling of the Creek is simple: get you on the water more.

If you already fish, I want to deepen your experience, help you see the stream differently. If you're just starting, I want to pull you into something that will shift the way you see nature, time, and yourself. And if you've fished for years but find yourself going less and less, let this be a reminder—your season isn't over. The stream keeps flowing. The fish are still waiting.

Fly fishing isn't just about trout. It's about answering the call of the creek.

The First Cast That Changed Everything

I remember my first trout like it happened yesterday.

The cast? It didn't matter. The fly hit the water, and I was fishing.

After a few awkward attempts, I got the fly to drift in the right seam. Then—a tug. My heart pounded as I lifted the rod like I'd hooked a monster. The fish shot out of the water, its shimmering body catching the light. A giant, surely.

My friend watched, waiting for the reveal. I reeled it in, hands shaking, heart racing... and held up an 8-inch rainbow trout.

Laughter erupted.

"That's it?" he smirked. "All that drama for a creek chub?"

I didn't care. That little trout was my first. My hands trembled as I slipped it back into the stream, watching it vanish into the current.

That tiny trout didn't just take my fly—it took me. And I followed.

The Art of Spotting Trout

Before you even cast, learn to see them. Spotting trout can be just as thrilling as catching them. They blend in, vanish into the current, become part of the river itself. But if you know what to look for, they reveal themselves.

Watch the water. A trout won't always make itself obvious, but the river gives away its secrets.

Sometimes, it's a flash beneath the surface—a trout turning on its side, catching light as it feeds. Other times, it's just a dark shape on the bottom, a shadow that stays put while everything else drifts by.

Look for the signs. A swirl in the current where a fish just rose. A tail flicking, barely perceptible. A break in the flow behind a rock—that's where they sit, just outside the fast water, waiting for an easy meal. It takes time. But once you train your eyes, you'll see them everywhere. And the best part? The best fly fishers see fish before they cast.

More Than Just a Fish

Whether it's an eight-inch rainbow or a twenty-inch brown, the real reward isn't the fish—it's the moment. The feel of the stream, the rhythm of the water, the tension of the line.

That first cast and tiny trout hooked me. But I had no idea what was coming next.

Fly fishing wasn't just another way to catch fish—it was something deeper, something primal.

And that leads to the big question: What is it about fly

fishing that sets it apart? Let's dive into that next.

Chapter 2: A Sport Like No Other

Fly Fishing: More Than a Hobby

Fly fishing isn't just a pastime—it's an obsession. A way of life. Those who answer its call don't just fish; they pursue something deeper. It transcends generations, social status, and skill levels.

Why do some of the most powerful people in the world dedicate their time to it? Not for proof or prestige. Not to convince you to try it. They do it because they know something many don't. They've felt something that keeps them coming back—something the rest of the world is missing.

Fly Fishing Isn't About Status—It's About the Water

U.S. presidents have done it. Hollywood icons, world-class athletes, Fortune 500 CEOs. Some of the busiest, most accomplished people on the planet choose to spend their time knee-deep in a river, fly rod in hand.

Dwight D. Eisenhower, Herbert Hoover, and Ronald Reagan turned to fly fishing to escape political chaos. Theodore Roosevelt and Calvin Coolidge found peace casting a fly into America's wild rivers.

Paul Newman, Harrison Ford, and Henry Winkler all discovered solace in the rhythm of the water. Emma Watson, drawn to the sport for its environmental connection, has spoken about its ability to reset the mind. Michael Keaton? You'll find him far from the Hollywood lights, somewhere in the backcountry, quietly chasing trout.

Even athletes and tech moguls—people addicted to performance, data, and results—know there's something different about the river. NBA legend Jerry West. NFL quarterback Brett Favre. Ex-Google CEO Eric Schmidt. They unplug, step into the current, and leave the world behind.

No cell service. No distractions. Just the river, the cast, and the moment at hand.

These aren't people looking to impress anyone. They're

people who could do anything, go anywhere, yet they choose fly fishing. The question is—why?

Fly Fishing: A Lifelong Pursuit

It's not a hobby. It's not a sport. It's a journey.

A lifelong pursuit of solitude, adventure, and connection. A craft you can embrace as a child and still be refining when you're old.

Native Americans understood this long before graphite rods and hand-tied flies. To them, fishing wasn't about leisure—it was survival, respect, and tradition.

They used handwoven nets and fish traps, catching trout in shallow waters without disrupting the ecosystem. Spears carved from bone, hooks made from sharpened rock, stone weirs built to funnel fish into the perfect strike zone. Ingenious methods, passed down through generations, ensuring the rivers would always provide.

To many tribes, trout weren't just food; they were sacred. The rivers weren't just water—they were life itself. And they fished with the kind of patience, understanding, and reverence that modern anglers spend a lifetime trying to recapture.

A Different Kind of Catch

One of my most memorable days on the water had nothing to do with the fish I caught. It had everything to do with the fish I didn't.

I was stalking a perfect rainbow trout in a crystal-clear pool. Watching, waiting, my cast lined up, heart pounding. But something stopped me.

Instead of casting, I reached for my camera. I watched through the lens as the trout hovered in the current, effortless, its every move in perfect sync with the water. Its delicate fins adjusting to the smallest shift, its silver body flashing in the light.

I filmed it for what felt like hours. Studied its rhythm, its patience, its quiet existence in a world most never see.

That day, I never made a cast. I never set the hook. And yet, it remains one of the most profound fishing experiences of my life.

Eventually, every angler asks themselves the same question. Is there just as much joy in finding a trout as there is in catching one?

Why Fly Fishing is Unlike Any Other Pursuit

In a world obsessed with instant gratification, fly fishing forces you to slow down. It doesn't give you easy wins. It doesn't hand out trophies just for showing up.

It demands patience. The kind of patience that turns frustration into obsession.

It's a moving meditation. The rhythmic casting, the sound of rushing water, the brief moment of connection when a trout takes your fly—it's mindfulness in motion.

It's a journey, not a destination. No two days on the river are the same. You're always learning—about the fish, the water, the insects, and yourself.

It teaches humility. Even the most skilled anglers get skunked. The river doesn't care who you are. It rewards patience, respect, and adaptability.

And in the end, it's never been about the fish. It's about what fishing pulls out of you. The places it takes you, the people you meet, the stories you collect along the way.

The river is the greatest teacher. But sometimes, you need a guide to help you hear its lessons. Some of the most valuable wisdom in fly fishing doesn't come from books or videos—it comes from those who've spent a lifetime on the water.

And that's where we're headed next.

Chapter 3: Why a Good Guide Changes Everything

The Fastest Way to Master Fly Fishing

If there's one secret to accelerating your success in fly fishing, it's this: hire a guide. A good guide is more than just someone who takes you to a fishing spot—they are the gatekeepers to the best waters, the ultimate shortcut to mastering the sport. Their knowledge of local waters, trout behavior, seasonal hatches, and reading the river is worth triple whatever they charge.

Most guides don't do this for the money. They guide out of a deep love for the sport. They aren't getting rich—most of their fees go toward covering expenses like permits, gas, and maintaining gear, with only a small portion supporting their livelihood. They take pride in sharing their expertise, and when you land your first trout under their guidance, they often get just as excited as you do.

A Guided Trip That Changed Everything

I'll never forget the first time I hired a guide. I had fished for trout plenty of times before, but I wanted to explore a remote stretch of the Middle Prong of the Little River in the Smoky Mountains. I could have gone alone, sure—but I had no idea where the best pools were, how the local hatches worked, or where the biggest trout held their ground.

That's when I met Jeff, a guide who had spent years fishing the Middle Prong, knowing every bend, every submerged log, and every hidden pocket where the trout liked to hold—a seasoned guide with a quiet confidence, sharp eyes, and a deep reverence for the river.

We met before sunrise. Mist hovered above the water like a veil, and the only sounds were the quiet hum of the river and the occasional splash of a rising trout. Jeff moved like he belonged there, effortlessly stepping over slick rocks, reading the water with the precision of a seasoned hunter.

I, on the other hand, was a mess. Within minutes, my fly was tangled in the creekside brush—gnarled mountain laurel, rhododendron, and alder saplings lining the banks, just waiting to snatch an unpracticed cast. I lost another fly trying to drop my line too close to a submerged boulder. And when I finally did get a clean drift, I set the hook too late—four times in a row—watching in frustration as big trout flashed and disappeared.

Jeff didn't laugh. He didn't roll his eyes. Instead, he quietly stepped beside me and said, "Patience. The river moves at its own pace. Follow it."

He angled my body slightly upstream for better reach, and showed me how to let the current do half the work. He pointed out how trout hold behind rocks and in soft seams, waiting for an easy meal. With each cast, I learned to work with the river instead of against it.

Then it happened. The fly landed perfectly in the current, drifted downstream naturally, and a monster brown trout erupted from the depths. The rod bent, the reel screamed, and my heart pounded as I fought to keep control. My hands were shaking, my breathing was shallow, but Jeff stayed calm, coaching me through every movement.

This was the fight I had dreamed of.

And after what felt like forever—but was likely only a minute—I brought the trout to the net.

As we released the fish back into the water, Jeff gave me a nod. "Now you understand."

I was soaked from head to toe, having stepped a little too deep into the creek during the fight. But in the heat of the moment, the freezing water didn't even register. It wasn't until I was driving home, heater blasting, that I started feeling the damp chill settle into my bones. My boots squelched with every press of the gas pedal, and my fingers, still stiff from gripping the rod, ached from the lingering cold.

But none of that mattered.

That monster brown, the wisdom I had gained, and the rush of the fight made it all worth it.

Why You Should Hire a Guide

If you're serious about improving your fishing skills and finding the best, most productive waters, hiring a guide—even once a year—can transform your experience. Whether you're in Montana's Madison Valley, North Carolina's Pisgah National Forest, or Wyoming's Platte Valley, guides know where the fish are, what they're feeding on, and how to approach them. Instead of wasting time figuring things out on your own, a good guide accelerates your learning curve and gives you insights that would take years to develop alone.

I highly recommend supporting a local guide at least once a year. Not only does it help sustain their work, but it also gives you an unparalleled fishing experience that you'll never forget. The investment in a guide is an investment in your love for the sport, and the lessons they provide will stay with you for a lifetime.

If you're lucky, you'll walk away with more than just a trophy fish. You'll leave with a deeper understanding of the water, a fresh perspective on the sport, and maybe even a guide's wisdom that stays with you long after the trip is over. And that, in itself, is priceless.

A great guide doesn't just teach you how to catch fish—they teach you how to see the river in a way you never have before.

And just as a guide opens your eyes to the river's secrets, the water itself begins to call you back. The river becomes more than a place to fish—it becomes a part of you, an ever-flowing reminder that nature's rhythm can soothe, teach, and inspire.

Chapter 4: Ther River's Endless Call

The Creek That Calls You Back

There is something about a creek that keeps calling me back. The way the water moves—never pausing, never stagnant—an endless journey toward a destination it may never reach. I've spent hours, days, even years, mesmerized by these winding ribbons of water, and I know I'm not alone. Creeks speak to us in ways we struggle to put into words. They symbolize movement, life, change, and constancy all at once.

The Never-Ending Flow

What impresses me most about a creek is its persistence. No matter how many times I sit by the water, no matter how often I return to the same bend in the stream, the water is never the same. It is constantly renewed, carrying with it bits of leaves, twigs, silt—memories of places it has been and places it will go. That movement is hypnotic, a reminder that life, too, is in perpetual motion.

I've got hours of creek footage saved—because when I can't fish, watching a trout stream on repeat is the next best thing. It's like a screensaver for my soul. I have numerous paintings of creeks adorning my home. Not because I am an art collector in the traditional sense, but because I can't get enough of them. Each one captures a different angle, a different moment in time, yet they all share that same constant flow. I have seen creeks in the early morning mist, when the water seems to whisper secrets only the dawn can hear. I have watched them under the full light of day, reflecting the blue sky like a shattered mirror. I have stood beside them at dusk, when the last embers of the sun turn the water to molten gold.

The Power and Fury of the Creek

At our mountain cabin in western North Carolina, we have a creek that transforms dramatically with the weather. On most days, it surges and flows with restless energy, its clear waters weaving through moss-covered rocks and tumbling over gentle waterfalls. But after a heavy rainstorm, it becomes an entirely different force—an untamed, raging torrent. The water turns cloudy, thick with silt and debris, carrying tree branches and anything else caught in its path. It is both mesmerizing and terrifying, a reminder of nature's raw power. Then, just as quickly as it swells, within 24 hours, the creek returns to its peaceful self—clear, calm, and inviting once again. This cycle of rage and serenity, destruction and beauty, is part of what makes creeks so captivating.

The Stories Creeks Tell
A creek is never silent. It gurgles, it babbles, it roars. It tells stories if you listen closely enough. I remember one evening in the Appalachian foothills, following the sound of running water through thick woods until I came to a secluded creek. The water ran cold and clear over smooth stones, and there, in the fading light, I saw the flick of a brook trout's tail. I cast my line, and the fish took the fly with a swirl. For a moment, we were connected—me, the trout, the water that had shaped this place long before I arrived and would continue long after I left.

And then, as quickly as it had begun, it was over. The trout slipped free, vanishing back into the current. I sat on the bank for a long while, listening to the creek's steady hum. It felt like it was trying to tell me something, but I wasn't sure what. Maybe it was reminding me that no moment lasts forever, that everything flows on.

A Life in the Creek's Reflection

Creeks have been a part of my life for as long as I can remember. As a child, I stacked rocks and wedged sticks trying to tame the current, if only for a moment, marveling at how the water always found a way around them. As a teenager, I would escape to the woods, letting the creek drown out the noise of the world. Now, as an adult, I return to creeks not to escape, but to remember—to reconnect with something elemental and true.

I think of the famous naturalists and fishermen who understood this pull. John Muir, who wrote about the music of mountain streams. Norman Maclean, whose words in A River Runs Through It captured the poetry of moving water. Lee Wulff, who knew that to understand a stream was to understand the fish that lived within it. They all felt what I feel—that undeniable call of the creek.

The Creek as a Teacher

A creek teaches patience. It teaches observation. It teaches humility. I have stood on the banks of many creeks, casting flies with hope and anticipation, only to be met with rejection. I have watched trout rise just inches from my fly, only to refuse it at the last second. I have learned that success in fishing—and in life—often comes not from force, but from understanding. The water moves on its own terms. So do the fish. So must we.

One autumn afternoon, I found myself beside a narrow, fast-moving creek. The leaves had begun to turn, their reds and golds reflecting in the water. I had spent the better part of the day fishing without luck. Frustrated, I sat on a moss-covered rock and simply watched the water flow. And then, as if rewarding my patience, I saw it—a trout, perfectly camouflaged against the riverbed, darting between the shadows. It had been there all along, unnoticed in my haste. I tied on a smaller fly, cast gently, and this time, the trout took it without hesitation.

Always Flowing Forward

The creeks I fish today are not the same creeks I fished years ago, yet they are. The water is different, the landscape shifts, but the essence remains unchanged. Life moves forward, but some things—some places—continue to call us back.

I will always be drawn to creeks. I will always stop to watch the water move, to listen to its song, to lose myself in its endless journey. Because in the creek's constant motion, I find a kind of stillness. And that, I think, is why I will never get enough of them.

Creeks don't just teach us about movement and patience—they reveal something deeper about the fish that live within them. Because understanding a creek means understanding how trout think, how they see, and how they survive. If you truly want to master the art of fly fishing, you have to learn to see the world as a trout does.

But before we can think like a trout, we need to understand

why we're drawn to the water in the first place.

Chapter 5: Born to Fish: The Instinct that Never Fades

Why We Cast

From the beginning of time, humans have been drawn to water. Not just for survival, but for something deeper—something instinctual. Rivers, lakes, and oceans have always pulled at us, calling us to their shores. And when we arrive, it's almost inevitable that we reach for a fishing rod, a net, or just our bare hands.

But why? Why do we fish? Why does the act of casting a line across a moving current feel so deeply ingrained in us? It's not just about sport. It's not just about food. It's something more.

Science calls it the "blue mind effect"—the idea that being near water calms the brain, reduces stress, sharpens focus. But long before psychologists had a name for it, people felt it. For thousands of years, fishing was necessity and ritual. Ancient civilizations cast their lines from wooden canoes, waded through streams with woven baskets, speared fish from the edges of waterfalls. There was no debate about "catch and release." No discussion of fly patterns or casting techniques. Fishing was life.

And yet, even then, there must have been moments—when a hunter stood still, watching the water swirl, waiting for the right strike—where it became something more than survival. It became an art. A meditation. A connection.

No matter where you go in the world, you'll find fishermen. In the Amazon, native tribes still fish with hand-carved spears. In Japan, traditional anglers cast delicate flies with bamboo rods passed down through generations. In Alaska, families read the rivers like books, knowing exactly when and where the salmon will run. In the Appalachian foothills, a child stands beside a creek, holding a rod for the first time, feeling the same anticipation his ancestors felt before him.

Fishing doesn't belong to one class, one country, one kind of person. The trout doesn't care if you're a CEO, a schoolteacher, or a farmhand. The river doesn't grant special privileges to the wealthy. Out on the water, we are all the same.

And every angler remembers the moment they felt it. Not just the tug of a fish on the line, but the deeper pull—the realization that this was something they were meant to do.

Maybe it was standing knee-deep in a creek, feeling the rush of cold water against their legs. Maybe it was watching the rings of a rising trout, heart pounding, knowing they had chosen the right fly. Maybe it was the first time they set the hook and felt a living force fight back, sending a shock of adrenaline straight to their core.

Whatever it was, it changed them. Because after that moment, fishing was no longer just an activity. It was part of them.

Ask any fisherman what they're looking for, and they'll give you a different answer. Some say they're chasing the perfect cast. Others say they're after the fish of a lifetime. Some are just looking for peace, an escape from the noise of the world.

But the truth? We're all searching for something just out of reach. That's why we keep coming back. Because there's always another pool to fish, another perfect drift to attempt, another moment of connection waiting just beyond the next bend in the river.

Understanding the instinct to fish is just the beginning. To truly master the art, you have to go deeper—into the mechanics of casting, the science of water, the behavior of the fish themselves. Fly fishing isn't just standing in a stream. It's learning to move with the river, to match the hatch, to think like a trout.

But before you can read the water, before you can anticipate a trout's next move, you have to start with something even more fundamental—your tools. The right gear won't make you a great angler. But the wrong gear can hold you back.

In the next section, we'll separate what's essential from what's unnecessary, focusing on the tools that matter and the myths that don't. Because mastery doesn't begin with the fish. It begins with preparation.

Part 2: The Art & Science of Fly Fishing

Chapter 6: Essential Gear (and What You Can Skip)

The Truth About Fly Fishing Gear

Fly fishing gear can be as simple or as complicated as you make it. Walk into any fly shop, and it's easy to get lost in the walls of rods, the endless fly selections, the newest gadgets promising to improve your cast or increase your catch rate.

But the truth? You don't need much to get started. A rod, a few flies, and a place to fish. That's it.

Everything else is just extra—helpful, maybe, but not necessary. The real key is knowing what matters and what doesn't.

The Essentials

If you're stepping onto the water for the first time, here's what actually matters:

A fly rod and reel—nothing fancy, just balanced. A 9-foot, 5-weight rod is the workhorse of trout fishing, the setup that can handle everything from tiny dries to small streamers. Pair it with a simple reel. It won't make or break your fishing, but it keeps your line in check.

A floating fly line, backing, and leader—without them, your rod is just a stick. Floating line is the best place to start. It's versatile and forgiving, perfect for learning the rhythm of casting.

A handful of flies—not an entire fly shop's worth, just a selection of dry flies, nymphs, and streamers that match your local water. If you don't know what works, ask at a shop. A few well-chosen flies will outfish a hundred bad ones.

Waders and boots—if you plan on stepping into the water, comfort matters. Breathable waders keep you dry, and felt or rubber-soled boots give you stability. Slipping on wet rocks is part of the learning curve, but a good pair of boots can make the difference between a stumble and a swim.

Nippers and forceps—small tools, but crucial ones. Nippers trim line, forceps remove hooks cleanly.

A landing net—not just for convenience, but for the fish. A good net makes catch-and-release safer for trout and easier for you.

A small pack or vest—just enough to carry what you need. Flies, tippet, tools. Anything more is extra weight.

That's it. The rest? That depends on how deep you want to go.

The Nice-to-Haves

Once you get comfortable, a few extra pieces of gear can make life easier.

Polarized sunglasses help you see through the glare, revealing fish beneath the surface. A wading staff gives extra stability in strong currents. Fly floatant keeps dries from sinking, while strike indicators make nymphing more effective.

A well-organized fly box saves you the frustration of digging through a mess of tangled hooks.

None of these are essential, but each one has its moment.

The Stuff You Can Skip (At Least for Now)

Not everything marketed to fly anglers is necessary. In fact, most of it isn't.

High-end rods might feel nice, but an entry-level rod will serve you well for years. No need to own a different setup for every possible condition—one good rod and reel is enough to start.

Some anglers carry hundreds of flies, but in reality? A few reliable patterns matched to your water are all you need.

And then there are the gadgets—some useful, some unnecessary, some pure marketing. Keep it simple. The best lessons in fly fishing come from time on the water, not from gear catalogs.

A Lesson in Simplicity

I still remember the first time I stepped into a fly shop. The walls were packed with gear, the counters lined with reels that cost more than a month's rent. I could've spent a fortune and still walked out feeling unprepared.

An old-school angler—someone who'd been fishing long before fly rods came with tech specs—saw the overwhelmed look on my face and laughed.

"James," he said, "you don't need all that junk. All you need is a rod, a handful of flies, and a place to fish."

He was right. That day, I left the shop with only the basics. And it was the best decision I ever made.

I caught my first trout on a borrowed rod. Learned, the hard way, that a knotted leader can turn into a nightmare if you don't store it properly. Pulled out my line more than once only to find a coiled disaster that needed straightening before I could even make a cast.

It wasn't the gear that made me a better angler. It was time on the water.

And that's the truth about fly fishing. It's not about the latest rod, the most expensive reel, or owning every piece of gear on the market. It's about the experience—the river, the fish, the cast.

The Drift Ahead

Start simple. Refine your technique. Let experience guide your gear choices, not the other way around.

The pull of the fly shop is real. Walk into one, and it's easy to forget what actually matters. The rods, the handcrafted flies, the endless gadgets—some of it useful, some of it just a clever sales pitch.

In the next chapter, we step into that world. The fly shop isn't just a store—it's the heart of the fly fishing community. A place where wisdom is traded over coffee, where myths are born, and where every angler, no matter their experience, feels the pull of possibility.

Chapter 7: The Fly Shop

Fly fishing is an art, a science, and—let's be honest—a bit of an obsession

You can read books, watch videos, and spend years on the water honing your craft. But there's one resource that can accelerate your learning faster than anything else: your local fly shop.

More Than Just a Store

Walk into a fly shop, and you'll realize it's not just a place to buy gear—it's a hub of knowledge, a watering hole for anglers, and a classroom where lessons happen over the counter. The best fly shops aren't just businesses; they are communities. The people behind the counter aren't just salesmen—they're guides, storytellers, and, more often than not, damn good anglers.

Why You Need a Fly Shop (Even If You Think You Don't)

In an age where you can order anything online, from rods to fly-tying materials, some might wonder why they should bother visiting a fly shop. The answer? Because you can't order local knowledge off Amazon. A good fly shop gives you what no website can: up-to-the-minute information on hatches, water conditions, and what's actually working on your home waters.

The Real-Time Intel Advantage

Fly shops are like command centers. They know what's hatching, what flies are working, and where the fish are holding right now. When you walk in and ask, "What's been fishing well?" you're getting insights that would take you weeks of trial and error to figure out yourself.

Want to know which section of the river is fishing best? The guy behind the counter probably fished it yesterday. Need advice on what weight tippet to use? They've probably helped twenty other anglers solve the same problem this week.

Fly Selection: The Difference Between a Guess and a Sure Thing

Sure, you can scroll through pages of flies online, but nothing beats holding the fly in your hand, feeling the materials, and getting advice from someone who knows exactly why it works. If you're new to fly fishing, this is even more critical. The best fly shop employees will not only point you to the right flies but will teach you why they work.

And let's be honest—fly bins are like candy displays for anglers. You walk in thinking you'll buy three flies, and before you know it, you're walking out with two dozen, a new leader, and probably a hat you didn't need but now absolutely love.

The Lessons You Didn't Know You Needed

Fly shops are full of free lessons if you know how to listen. Watch the guy demonstrating how to tie a knot behind the counter. Listen when someone starts talking about how the river is flowing higher than normal and what that means for presentation. Absorb the stories being told, because somewhere in those stories are lessons—about reading water, timing a hatch, or working a drift—that will take years to learn on your own.

Fly Shops as Matchmakers: Finding the Right Rod for You

Fly rods aren't just tools—they are extensions of how you cast, how you fight fish, and how you feel the water. Picking the right rod goes beyond length and weight—it's about feel, action, and balance. A good fly shop will put a rod in your hand and let you cast it before you buy.

That $900 rod you've been eyeing online? It might feel dead in your hands. That mid-range rod you hadn't considered? It might feel like an extension of your arm. The only way to know is to try it—and the only place to do that is a fly shop.

A Personal Story: The Day the Fly Shop Saved My Trip

I once drove three hours to fish a legendary stretch of river, convinced I had everything I needed. I had studied the hatches, picked the right flies, and even prepped my gear the night before. But when I got to the river, something was wrong.

The water was higher than expected. The flies I had tied weren't working. I had that sinking feeling every angler knows—the one where you realize you're about to get skunked.

Out of desperation, I stopped at a small fly shop in the nearest town. The guy behind the counter didn't just sell me a few flies. He explained why the river was fishing differently, showed me how to adjust my rig, and mentioned that black Woolly Buggers and Pheasant Tail Nymphs were working best—no bright colors, just natural tones that matched the conditions. I walked out feeling like I had been handed a cheat code.

An hour later, I was into fish. Big fish. The kind that make you rethink everything you thought you knew. And it wasn't because of some miracle fly—it was because someone who knew that river better than I did gave me the right information at the right time.

The Community You Didn't Know You Needed

A fly shop is more than just a store—it's a gathering place. Regulars come in to swap stories, share photos, and talk about what's happening on the water. If you visit often enough, you become part of that network.

And here's the thing—if you support your fly shop, they'll support you. You'll start getting insider tips, invites to events, maybe even a heads-up when a new rod comes in that you need to try.

The Art of Asking Good Questions

Fly shop employees love to help, but they love it even more when you ask the right questions. Instead of just saying, "What's working?" try:

"What's the best time of day to fish this week?"

"Are fish feeding more on emergers or duns right now?"

"What adjustments should I make based on water levels?"

When you ask smart questions, you get detailed, useful answers. It's the difference between getting generic advice and getting insights tailored to your trip.

The Ethics of Supporting Your Fly Shop

Let's be real—fly shops are up against online retailers. But they offer something Amazon never can: a living, breathing, human connection to the sport. If you use their knowledge, their expertise, and their community, do the right thing—buy your gear there when you can. It keeps them open, keeps them sharing knowledge, and keeps the local fishing culture alive.

If you want to get better at fly fishing, you don't always need more gear. You don't need to spend thousands on a guided trip. Sometimes, all you need to do is walk through the doors of your local fly shop.

Inside, you'll find more than just flies and rods. You'll find experience. You'll find community. And, if you're paying attention, you'll find the kind of knowledge that turns good anglers into great ones.

Casting Forward

Of course, knowing where to buy flies is one thing. Knowing which flies to buy is another. A well-stocked fly box isn't about quantity—it's about having the right patterns for the right moments.

In the next chapter, we'll break it down to the essentials: the seven must-have flies and nymphs every angler should carry. Because when the trout are rising, the last thing you want is to be guessing.

Chapter 8: The Seven Must-Have Flies & Nymphs

The Seven Essential Flies

Fly fishing can be as simple or as complex as you make it. Thousands of patterns exist, each with its own history, purpose, and place in the river. It's easy to get overwhelmed. But when it comes down to it, trout fishing isn't about carrying an encyclopedia of flies. It's about understanding the few essential insects trout eat and the flies that best imitate them.

You could fill boxes with endless variations, but if you had to carry only seven flies, these are the ones that will serve you well in almost any trout stream in the country.

The Adams Dry Fly

There's a reason the Adams Dry Fly has stood the test of time. It's been fooling trout for over a century. Originally designed by Leonard Halladay in the 1920s, the Adams is the answer when trout are rising, and you have no idea what they're eating. Its grey and brown coloration sits somewhere between reality and suggestion—close enough to match a variety of mayflies, yet vague enough to work even when no hatch is obvious. If the water is calm, if the evening light is low, if you see rises but can't quite place the pattern—tie on an Adams.

The Pheasant Tail Nymph

Below the surface, it's a different game. The Pheasant Tail Nymph is the undisputed workhorse of subsurface flies. Originally developed by Frank Sawyer, it's slender, realistic, and deadly effective. Whether trout are aggressively feeding or barely interested, a well-presented Pheasant Tail gets results. It's the fly you reach for when dries go ignored, when the fish are sitting deeper, when the river looks empty but you know the trout are there.

The Elk Hair Caddis

If there's a single dry fly that can handle a little chaos, it's the Elk Hair Caddis. Al Troth designed it for a reason—caddisflies don't land softly. They skitter, bounce, dance across the surface, triggering aggressive strikes. The rough elk hair wing gives it buoyancy and movement, making it the perfect choice for riffles, pocket water, or anywhere the current adds a little turbulence. When caddis are bouncing, when summer evenings bring trout to the surface, when you need a dry fly that refuses to sink—this is the one.

The Hare's Ear Nymph

But when the trout aren't looking up, it's time to go subsurface again. The Hare's Ear Nymph is the ultimate imitator. It doesn't mimic a single insect—it mimics them all. Caddis larvae, mayfly nymphs, stoneflies—it's buggy, scruffy, and effective. In cold water, when trout are sluggish. In slow pools, when they're being selective. When nothing else seems to match the hatch, a Hare's Ear fills the gap.

The Woolly Bugger

Then there's the Woolly Bugger, a fly that defies classification. Baitfish? Leeches? Giant nymphs? The trout don't seem to care. All they know is that it's food, and they're going to eat it. Strip it, drift it, swing it—there's no wrong way to fish a Bugger. Murky water? Big, hungry trout? A day when nothing else seems to be working? Tie one on and hold on.

The Copper John

Some flies just work because they get down fast, and that's exactly what the Copper John was made for. Designed by John Barr in the 1990s, its bead head and wire body send it straight to the strike zone. In fast-moving runs where slower nymphs struggle to sink, the Copper John gets there first. When the river is running high, when trout are hugging the bottom, when you need to reach deep fish quickly—this fly does the job.

The Zebra Midge

And finally, there's the Zebra Midge. Simple. Small. Deadly. Trout eat midges year-round, especially in tailwaters and clear, slow-moving rivers. When nothing else works, when the fish are spooky, when the surface and midwater columns seem empty, a Zebra Midge fished deep can turn a dead stretch of water into a feeding lane.

The Masters of the Past and Their Flies

Every great fly fisher has a go-to pattern. Theodore Gordon, the father of American dry fly fishing, swore by the Quill Gordon. Lee Wulff, who pioneered modern catch-and-release ethics, designed the Royal Wulff, a high-floating dry fly that still fools trout today. Joe Brooks, one of the men who helped popularize fly fishing in America, loved the Grey Ghost, a streamer built for big, aggressive fish.

The best flies stick around for a reason. They work. They survive generations of anglers, adjustments in technique, changes in materials. They remain because trout never stop eating them.

My Go-To Flies

Every angler has that one fly they trust when nothing else seems to work. For me, it's a Pheasant Tail Nymph. One morning in the Smokies, the river was running low, and the fish were finicky. I tried dries, streamers, even a few soft hackles—nothing. Finally, I tied on a size 16 Pheasant Tail and fished it on a slow drift through a deep run. A subtle strike, then another. The bite was on.

For dries, I always carry an Adams. One summer at sunset, I found myself on a backcountry stream as the light faded behind the ridgeline. The trout were rising, but I couldn't see what they were taking. No obvious hatch. Just dimples on the surface, barely perceptible in the evening glow. I tied on a size 14 Adams and let it drift into the slow water at the tail of a pool. A brook trout took it without hesitation.

I fumbled with my net. The fish slipped free before I could bring it in. Some trout are meant to be caught. Some are meant to be remembered.

Next Up: Dialing in Your Setup

Flies alone won't catch fish. It's how you present them that matters. The right leader, the right drift, the right line.

In the next chapter, we'll break down the six essential fly fishing setups every angler should master. The difference between an empty net and a successful day on the water isn't just choosing the right fly—it's knowing exactly how to fish it.

Chapter 9: The Six Essential Fly-Fishing Setups

Mastering the Six Fly Fishing Setups

Fly fishing is both an art and a science. The romance of casting a dry fly onto a glassy stream captures the imagination, but reality tells a different story. Different waters, different conditions, and different trout behaviors demand specific approaches.

It's why the best anglers don't rely on just one method. They adapt, shifting between six fundamental setups—dry fly, nymphing, dry-dropper, dropper rig, streamer fishing, and Euro nymphing. Mastering all six is the difference between a frustrating day and a successful one.

The Dry Fly Setup: The Purist's Game

Nothing beats the rush of watching a trout rise to take a dry fly off the surface. A perfect cast, a flawless drift, the moment of connection—pure fly fishing. But purity doesn't mean easy. If the drift is off, the imitation flawed, or the presentation unnatural, the fish won't hesitate to refuse.

The best conditions for dry fly fishing? Still water. Low wind. Rising fish. The kind of morning where the river is a mirror, and you can see the rings of trout sipping insects before the sun burns off the mist.

It's a game of patience, precision, and perfect timing. The trout may only be feeding for a small window—sometimes minutes, not hours—and if you're not ready, you'll miss it.

A dry fly rig is built for surface takes. A single dry fly is tied to the end of the leader, floating naturally on the water. For added reach, a tapered leader (9–12 feet) connects to 4X–6X tippet, ensuring a delicate presentation. The key is a drag-free drift, letting the fly move naturally with the current while watching for the slightest rise

Nymphing: Fishing Below the Surface

There was a time when I refused to nymph. Dry flies were the real way to catch trout, or so I told myself.

That was until one summer on a small tailwater, where the surface stayed eerily quiet, no matter how perfect the conditions seemed. I watched other anglers hook fish after fish, while my dries floated by untouched.

I finally broke down. Tied on a pheasant tail. Let it drift deep.

The take was subtle, barely noticeable. The line hesitated, just for a second. I lifted the rod and felt that unmistakable weight. The kind that makes you realize how many fish you've been missing.

That was the day I learned what every seasoned fly fisher already knows—trout feed below the surface 80% of the time. Nymphing isn't just an option; it's the backbone of fly fishing.

The Setup: A nymph rig is designed to get flies deep where trout feed. A weighted nymph (or two) is tied at the end of fluorocarbon tippet attached to a 9–12 ft leader. To control depth, anglers use a strike indicator (for traditional nymphing) or a sighter (for Euro nymphing). Split shot can be added above the fly for extra weight. The goal? Get down fast, stay in the zone, and detect the subtlest takes.

The Dry-Dropper Setup: Covering Both Worlds

A dropper rig typically uses two flies—a dry fly and a nymph (or two nymphs). The dry fly (or lead fly) is tied to the end of the main leader, acting as a floating strike indicator. Below it, a dropper fly (usually a nymph) is tied 12–24 inches below to a piece of fluorocarbon tippet extending from the bend of the dry fly's hook or from a tag above it. This setup allows you to fish both the surface and subsurface, covering multiple feeding zones.

A dry fly on top, a nymph suspended below—the best of both worlds. When trout are feeding in multiple depths, this setup doubles your odds. The dry serves as both an offering and an indicator, letting you see the take without the need for a strike indicator.

It's the go-to when conditions are uncertain—when fish are rising but not fully committing, when the water is changing, when you need versatility over precision.

The Dropper Rig: The Two-Nymph Advantage

The set up: A dropper rig covers multiple depths at once. The lead fly (usually a buoyant dry fly or a heavier nymph) is tied at the end of the leader. The dropper fly is attached 12–24 inches below via a short tippet section tied to the bend of the lead fly's hook (or to a tag above it for more movement). This setup allows you to fish both surface and subsurface or run two nymphs at different levels, increasing your chances of hooking up

I was fishing a deep, slow bend in the Toccoa, watching my line glide through the current, the soft tick of my indicator bouncing as the flies drifted below.

Then, just a hesitation. A tiny shift. Almost nothing. But I lifted the rod tip, and suddenly, the water erupted—a wild rainbow, taken on the bottom fly.

That's the beauty of the dropper rig. It's not about guessing where the fish are. It's about letting the river tell you. One fly rides higher, one runs deep, and with every cast, you learn where the trout are feeding.

If the river is running high, add weight. If the trout are holding near the surface, adjust the length. The dropper rig isn't just a setup—it's a conversation with the water.

Streamer Fishing: Hunting for Aggressive Fish

Streamer fishing isn't about finesse. It's about triggering a reaction. Big fish. Big flies. A chase instead of a drift.

After a heavy rain, the water was up, murky and fast. I knew the trout wouldn't be sipping tiny mayflies—they'd be hunting. I tied on a woolly bugger, let it sink, and started stripping it back.

Halfway through the retrieve, a brown trout slammed it. No hesitation. No subtlety. Just an explosion of power, the kind of take that doesn't ask permission.

That's streamer fishing. You're not waiting—you're making the fish come to you.

Euro Nymphing: The Tactical Approach

A Euro nymphing rig is designed for maximum sensitivity and control. It uses two flies—an anchor fly and a dropper fly.

The anchor fly, typically a heavy tungsten bead nymph, is tied at the end of the tippet to sink quickly and maintain contact with the riverbed. 12–20 inches above it, the dropper fly is attached to a 6-inch tag off the main leader, allowing it to drift more freely in the current. This tight-line setup eliminates slack, keeping you in direct contact with your flies, so every subtle take is felt, not just seen.

It was a pressured tailwater, the kind where trout see a hundred bad casts a day. The usual setups weren't working. The fish were deep, refusing anything presented the old way.

I switched to a Euro nymphing rig. A long leader, a perdigon fly, no strike indicator. First drift—bam. The connection was instant, direct. No slack, no guessing. Just pure feel.

Euro nymphing isn't just another way to fish. It's a different game entirely. No bobbers, no traditional casting—just precision.

Mastering All Six Setups

A good angler doesn't rely on just one approach. Conditions change. Trout move. The river shifts. The best fishermen are the ones who can read the water and adjust.

If the trout are sipping mayflies? Dry fly time.

If they're holding deep, out of sight? Nymphing.

If they're feeding in multiple depths? Dry-dropper.

If they're near the bottom, feeding on the drift? Dropper rig.

If the water is high and fast? Streamers.

If traditional setups fail? Euro nymphing.

It's not about having a favorite technique. It's about having the right tool for the right moment.

From the Water to the Vise—If You Choose

Some fly fishers never tie their own flies. Others swear by it. There's no right or wrong answer.

Some love the craft, the precision, the satisfaction of fooling a trout with something they made by hand. Others just want to fish. Both are valid.

But for those who take up the vise, fly tying becomes more than just another skill. It becomes another way to understand the fish, the water, and the sport itself.

And that's where we're headed next.

Chapter 10: Tying Your Own Fly

There's nothing quite like catching a trout on a fly you tied yourself. The moment it happens, something shifts. Fly fishing stops being just a pursuit and becomes something more—an art, a craft, a personal connection to the water.

A fly you tie is different. It carries something extra. A store-bought fly is just a tool, but one you crafted with your own hands holds the memory of the vise, the thread, the tiny details you got right—or wrong. And when a trout rises to take that fly, the moment is yours in a way nothing else in fishing can match.

That's why so many anglers, even those who swore they'd never tie their own, eventually find themselves at the vise.

Why Tie Your Own Flies?

Some tie flies to match the hatch exactly, adjusting colors, sizes, and materials to fit the conditions. Some do it to save money, even though the first dozen flies might come out looking like something a bird coughed up. Others just enjoy the process—the quiet focus, the hands-on connection to the sport.

But it's more than that. Tying flies changes the way you see the river. Suddenly, you're not just looking at the water; you're watching for the bugs drifting in the current. You're seeing the details—the way a mayfly's wings shimmer, the subtle shades in a caddis's body, the exact moment a trout decides to rise.

It deepens everything.

The Tools You Need—And Nothing More

Some fly tiers have entire workbenches cluttered with gadgets, drawers full of materials they'll never use. But the truth? You don't need much.

A vise—that's the foundation. A bobbin to hold your thread. Sharp scissors. A whip finisher for clean knots. A bodkin for small adjustments. Maybe some hackle pliers to handle delicate feathers.

That's it. A few tools, a few materials, and you're ready.

The materials are just as simple. Hooks, beads, thread, a few feathers, a little wire. Some peacock herl for that natural iridescence trout can't resist. A pinch of dubbing to shape the body. You don't need a hundred different colors or every pattern under the sun. Just the basics.

Because the best flies aren't complicated.

The First Fly—And the First Lesson

I still remember the first fly I tied. It wasn't pretty. If anything, it looked like it had been through a bar fight. Uneven wraps, too much dubbing, hackle sticking out at weird angles.

I called it the Mike Tyson Nymph—scrappy, ugly, but somehow still dangerous.

And then something happened.

I tied it on, cast into a slow-moving seam, and watched my indicator hesitate. I lifted the rod. The line went tight. The fish wasn't big, but it didn't matter. It had fallen for my fly.

That was it. I was hooked—not just on fly fishing, but on tying.

There's a thrill in that first fish. A fly you created, one that exists only because you sat down and built it, just fooled a trout. That moment stays with you.

Tying as a Way of Seeing

The more flies you tie, the more you start noticing things. The way insects move. The way trout react. The way the color of a fly matters less than its silhouette.

It's like learning a new language. Suddenly, the river isn't just water—it's a conversation. You read the surface, watch for the signals, and choose your fly not because a guidebook told you to, but because you understand what the trout are eating.

That's the shift. Fly tying doesn't just make you a better fisherman. It makes you a better observer, a better thinker, a better problem solver.

The Tying Mentality

Some anglers tie flies because they have to. They fish remote waters where the exact patterns aren't sold in shops. Others tie because they love it, because they find peace in the repetition, in the slow, deliberate craft.

Some get obsessed. They chase perfection, working and reworking the same pattern until every wrap is flawless. Some don't care about perfection—they just want something that works.

There's no right way to do it. Just like fly fishing itself, tying is personal.

But there's one truth: a fly you tie yourself is different. It carries more weight. More meaning.

And when the trout takes it, you'll know exactly why it matters.

The Silent Lessons of the Stream

Tying flies is one thing. Fishing them is another. The moment you step into the river, a different set of rules applies—the unspoken code of fly fishing.

There are things no one tells you, things you only learn through time on the water. How to share a stretch of river. When to offer advice and when to keep quiet. Why some spots should be left unmentioned.

Fly fishing has its own etiquette, a silent rhythm that good anglers understand. In the next chapter, we dive into those unspoken rules—the ones that separate the casual fisherman from the true angler.

Chapter 11: The Unspoken Rules of Fly Fishing

Fly fishing, like any pursuit deeply connected to nature, is built on an unspoken code of ethics. It's a tradition passed down from one angler to the next—not through rules etched in stone, but through quiet gestures of respect: a nod of acknowledgment on the riverbank, a shared glance when the water is alive with rising fish, a knowing smile when a perfect cast is rewarded with nothing but silence.

This unspoken etiquette isn't about regulations; it's about preserving the experience, ensuring that the river—and the sport—remains just as sacred for those who come after us.

Knowing the Laws and Licensing Requirements

Before setting foot in a stream, every fly fisher has a responsibility to know the local laws and licensing requirements. These rules aren't arbitrary—they exist to protect fish populations, maintain water quality, and ensure the sustainability of the sport.

Catch-and-release restrictions, seasonal closures, and fly-only waters all serve a purpose, preserving the delicate balance between angler and environment.

Every state, every region, has its own regulations. Some rivers require barbless hooks, some prohibit live bait, some limit the number of fish that can be taken home. Ignoring these rules isn't just a violation of the law—it's a betrayal of the very waters we claim to love.

A good angler knows that a fishing license isn't just a piece of paper; it's a pledge to fish responsibly, to respect the resource, and to ensure that the next generation can wade into the same waters and find the same magic.

Respecting Private Property

Not all water is public, and not all land is ours to roam. Some of the most pristine trout streams wind through private lands, accessible only by permission or by knowing where public access begins and ends.

Trespassing is one of the surest ways to damage the reputation of fly anglers and erode the goodwill that allows many of us to fish these waters in the first place.

If a stream crosses private property, it's always worth asking permission before assuming access. A knock on a rancher's door, a friendly conversation with a landowner, a show of respect for fences and signage—these small gestures go a long way. More often than not, a polite request is met with generosity. And even if permission is denied, walking away with respect ensures that the next angler who asks might have better luck.

Respecting Other Fishermen

The river is wide, but sometimes, the fish are only in a few key places. A deep pool at the bend, a slow-moving eddy, a stretch of riffles filled with feeding trout—these spots draw anglers like moths to a flame. And yet, the mark of a seasoned fisherman isn't how many fish he catches; it's how well he shares the water.

Giving space is fundamental. No one likes to be crowded. If another angler is already fishing a stretch of river, it's respectful to give them room to work. That might mean moving upstream or downstream, finding a different pool, or simply waiting until they've finished their drift before stepping in.

A good rule of thumb: if you wouldn't want someone casting into your water, don't do it to them.

But etiquette goes beyond just distance—it's also about opportunity. If there's only one prime spot to fish, sometimes the best thing to do is step aside and let someone else have a turn.

A Story of Giving Up the Perfect Spot

I remember the day I found the perfect fishing spot. It was a hidden gem, the kind of place you dream about finding but never expect to stumble upon.

I had been driving along a back road, winding through the mountains, when I saw it—a narrow bridge spanning a deep, slow-moving pool, shaded by the thick overhang of trees. I pulled over, stepped onto the old bridge, and peered down.

Beneath the shadows, a school of trout darted in and out of the light, moving like ghosts in the deep water.

This was it. The perfect spot.

I wasted no time. I set up my gear, carefully choosing a fly that matched the season. My first cast was a little off. The second, closer. By the third, I had the perfect drift, the fly landing just right, dancing in the current. I could see the fish watching, hesitant, interested but uncertain.

And then, out of nowhere, I heard footsteps behind me. A small boy, no older than eight, was standing there, gripping a fishing rod. His tackle box was nothing more than an old coffee can, filled with corn and worms he had gathered himself.

He looked at me, then looked at the water. His eyes were full of hope.

I didn't think twice. I reeled in, stepped back, and handed him my spot.

He didn't say much—just nodded and scrambled into place, his whole body brimming with excitement. I watched as he fumbled with his gear, his enthusiasm more important than his technique. He cast out, and within moments, a trout took the bait.

That was his moment, not mine.

And I wouldn't have traded it for anything.

A Conversation with Bob, the Old-Timer

One of the most humbling lessons I ever learned about fly fishing came not from the river, but from a conversation with an old fisherman named Bob. Bob is gone now, but his quiet wisdom stays with me. He was the kind of man whose presence alone commanded respect—weathered hands, a quiet demeanor, and an unmistakable reverence for the sport.

I asked him, almost casually, if he used circle hooks or barbed hooks.

He looked at me, his expression gentle, and simply said, "I've heard of them." That was it.

But his answer shot through me like an arrow to the heart. In that moment, I understood something deeper—Bob would never use a barbed hook, even if it was allowed. Not because the law said so, but because of something more sacred. He fished in a way that was fair, ethical, and deeply respectful of the fish. It wasn't just about catching; it was about the way he moved through the world, the way he honored the river, the way he left nothing but ripples behind.

There was something profound in that, something that stayed with me long after our conversation ended. Because in the end, fly fishing isn't just defined by what you catch; it's the way you fish and the mark you leave behind.

The Unspoken Code

Fly fishing is a solitary pursuit, but it is also a shared one. Whether we are fishing alone in a remote mountain stream or shoulder to shoulder in a famous river, we are part of something bigger than ourselves.

The etiquette of fly fishing isn't about rules—it's about respect.

Because in the end, it's not just about the fish we catch. It's about the ones we leave behind—for the next angler, for the next generation. And sometimes, it's about stepping back from the perfect spot, handing over the rod, and letting someone else feel the pull of the river for the first time.

Sharpening Your Skills Off the Water

But respect extends beyond how we behave on the river—it's also reflected in how we prepare. The best anglers don't wait until they're waist-deep in a stream to refine their technique. They train for it.

In the next chapter, we'll explore how to perfect your cast without even touching the water. Whether you're stuck at home, in your backyard, or in a park, there are ways to sharpen your skills so that when the moment comes, your cast is as natural as the river itself.

Chapter 12: Perfecting Your Cast Without Water

Practice on Land, Fish on Water

There's an old saying in fly fishing: You don't practice on the water—you train off the water, so you can fish on the water.

Most anglers don't think about their casting until they're waist-deep in a river, struggling to hit a target. But by then, it's too late. The wind is against you, the current is moving, and the trout aren't going to wait while you sort out your double haul.

That's why the best fly anglers practice on dry land.

The First (and Last) Time I Practiced With a Hooked Fly

It was early spring, and I hadn't fished in months. My casting arm felt stiff, my timing was off, and everything felt clunky. The rivers were still too high to fish, but I figured I could at least knock the rust off with some practice.

I grabbed my rod, tied on a fly, and headed to an open field.

That was mistake number one. I used a real fly with a hook.

At first, it went well. I worked on my false casts, played with my loop control, and felt my form starting to come back. Then I got ambitious. I tried a longer cast, really leaned into it—and bam.

Before I even registered what had happened, I felt a sharp tug on my shirt. I looked down. The fly was buried deep, right in the fabric over my ribs.

No big deal, right? Just unhook it.

Except I had been using a barbed hook.

Now, instead of practicing my casting, I was performing minor surgery on myself in the middle of a public park. After five minutes of swearing, sweating, and considering whether I should just cut my shirt off, I finally worked it free.

Lesson learned.

From that day forward, I never practiced with a real fly again.

The Right Way to Practice Without Water

You don't need a river to improve your cast. You just need space. A backyard, an open field, a park—anywhere with room to work.

Avoid power lines, trees, fences, and anything else that might grab your line. And for the sake of everyone involved, make sure no one is standing behind you. A tight loop with a nine-foot leader can snap hard if it connects with skin.

On grass, your line won't shoot as smoothly as it does on water. The added resistance forces you to refine your mechanics, tightening your loops and cleaning up your stroke. If you can cast well on land, you'll cast even better on the river.

The Yarn Trick

Instead of a hooked fly, tie a small piece of yarn to the end of your leader. It mimics the weight of a dry fly, lands like a real fly would, and removes the risk of impaling yourself in the process.

Brightly colored yarn makes it even easier to see where your fly would land, letting you dial in your accuracy.

Drills That Make You a Better Caster

Practicing on land removes distractions. No current, no rising trout, no rush to get your line in the water. It's just you and the cast.

The 10 and 2 Drill locks in loop control and muscle memory. Imagine your rod as a clock hand. The backcast stops at ten o'clock, the forward cast stops at two. Slow and controlled. No wrist flicks. No tailing loops.

The Accuracy Challenge forces precision. Place a target—hula hoop, frisbee, anything—twenty-five feet away. Land your yarn inside it. Three times in a row? Move the target back five feet. Keep going.

The Wind Fighter prepares you for the reality of fly fishing. Stand in front of a fan or cast into the wind. Keep the loops tight. Drop the rod lower and slice the cast under the gusts. Learn to make the wind work for you, not against you.

The Fifty-Foot Bomb builds distance. Strip out fifty feet of fly line and shoot it with one or two false casts. Let the rod do the work. Trust the energy transfer. Power comes from timing, not force.

Ten Minutes a Day

Most anglers only cast when they're on the water. That's like a golfer only swinging a club during tournaments. You'll never improve that way.

The best fly casters practice consistently, even when they're nowhere near a river.

Just ten minutes before each season. That's all it takes to step into the water with confidence.

Or at least, that's the theory. In reality, I do ten minutes once every season, and that seems like plenty.

Train on Land, Fish on Water

After my fly-in-the-shirt disaster, I learned something important: casting practice doesn't need water to be effective.

You don't have to wait for perfect river conditions. You don't have to wait for trout season. With a yarn fly, a little space, and a few minutes a day, you can sharpen your skills, fine-tune your accuracy, and make sure that the next time you step into the river, your cast is the last thing you have to worry about.

So don't waste time waiting for the water to be right. Pick up your rod. Start training today.

Just remember—leave the barbed hooks at home.

Mastering the Lag: The Secret to a Powerful Cast

But practice alone isn't enough. You have to practice the right things.

The biggest difference between a beginner's cast and a master's isn't strength, or speed, or even precision. It's something most anglers overlook—the lag in the cast.

The best fly casters don't force the rod forward. They wait. They let the line load, let the energy build, then unleash it at the perfect moment. Timing is everything.

In the next chapter, we break down what lag in the cast really means, why it matters, and how to harness it for a smoother, more powerful stroke.

Because sometimes, the secret to casting farther isn't doing more—it's waiting just a little longer.

Chapter 13: The Hidden Power of Lag in Your Cast

The Snap of a Perfect Cast

There's a moment in a perfect fly cast when everything just clicks. The rod loads, the line tightens, and for a split second, energy moves through the system like a slingshot pulled to full tension. The cast fires forward—effortless, precise, powerful.

It's hard to explain, but once you experience it, you never forget it.

I spent years muscling my way through my cast, swinging harder, pushing faster, convinced that power came from force. Every instructor told me to let the rod do the work. I nodded, pretended to understand, then went right back to overpowering the rod.

It wasn't until I picked up a golf club that it finally made sense.

What Golf Taught Me About Fly Casting

In golf, the key to a powerful swing isn't brute force—it's how well you store and release energy. Watch a pro swing, and you'll see it: a lag between the hands and the clubhead, a perfect buildup of tension that explodes through the ball.

A fly rod works the same way. If you don't load it properly—if you rush the cast, overpower it, or don't give it time to bend—you lose that stored energy. The line falls limp, the loop collapses, and instead of a tight, controlled cast, you get a sloppy mess.

The best fly casters aren't the strongest; they're the smoothest. They wait. They feel the rod bend. They time their release. When they finally let go, the line unrolls with effortless precision.

Hearing the Snap

For the longest time, I never felt it. I was either too fast or too slow, too aggressive or too hesitant.

Then, one day on the river, it happened. A sharp, clean snap as the line unrolled in the air. Not the dreaded whip crack of a broken loop, but a crisp, perfect release.

I stopped mid-river, blinking in surprise. Was that me? Had I actually done it?

I tried again, this time focusing on the feel. I waited for the rod to load, held just a fraction longer on the backcast, then let the weight of the line pull everything forward.

Snap.

That was the moment it all changed. The cast wasn't about force—it was about timing. About trust.

Just like a golf swing, if you rush it, you kill the power. But if you wait—just a little longer than you think you should—the rod delivers all the energy for you.

The Flow of a Cast

A proper fly cast follows a precise rhythm. Start slow. Let the rod bend. Pause. Release at just the right moment.

The lift comes first—gentle, deliberate. The line peels off the water without disturbance. The rod flexes. The backcast accelerates smoothly, stopping abruptly at just the right angle. For a moment, everything is suspended.

Then comes the pause.

It's the most important part. Too soon, and the line has no time to extend. Too late, and the energy bleeds away.

The forward cast follows—clean, confident, unforced. The rod uncoils, the loop tightens, the line fires forward.

And then—the stop. A high rod tip, a controlled finish. Like a golfer's follow-through, it's where the energy transfers, where all the work comes together.

Roll Casts and Water-Loaded Casts—Fishing in Tight Spaces

Not every river gives you the luxury of a full backcast. Thick trees, fallen logs, steep banks—they all conspire against you. That's where the roll cast and water-loaded cast come in.

The roll cast is all about anchoring the line on the water, using surface tension to help load the rod. Lift, form a D-loop, drive the rod forward, and let the energy roll the line out. Tight quarters? Overhanging brush? No room to work? The roll cast is your best friend.

The water-loaded cast takes it a step further. Instead of lifting the line cleanly, you let the current create tension against the rod. A small lift, a controlled flick forward, and the energy transfers with almost no extra movement. It's a game-changer in pocket water, when you need to reposition without false casting.

Master these, and you'll fish water most anglers walk right past.

The Real Secret to a Powerful Cast

A great fly caster doesn't just master one technique. They adjust. They adapt. They cast for the conditions, the river, the moment.

But at the core of every cast—whether it's a full-looped distance bomb or a subtle roll under a low-hanging branch—is one fundamental truth:

Power comes from patience.

That's what golf taught me.

A rushed golf swing kills distance. A rushed fly cast kills the loop. The secret isn't swinging harder—it's waiting just long enough to let the energy build.

But here's the thing—casting is only half the equation. A perfect cast means nothing if the fly doesn't drift naturally.

The moment the fly touches the water, everything changes. The game shifts from power to finesse, from mechanics to instinct.

Because in the end, trout don't care how beautiful your cast is. They care about one thing—the drift.

In the next chapter, we move from the cast to the drift,

breaking down what makes a fly move naturally, why drag kills the presentation, and how to read the currents like a seasoned angler.

    Because fly fishing isn't just about getting the fly there—it's about making it move like something alive.

Chapter 14: The Art of the Drift

Fly fishing is full of myths. One of the biggest? That success depends entirely on picking the right fly.

It's an easy trap to fall into—pouring over fly boxes, obsessing over colors, worrying about whether the hatch is a Blue-Winged Olive or a Pale Morning Dun. But the truth is, trout care far more about how a fly drifts than what it is.

An imperfect fly with a perfect drift will fool more trout than the most exact imitation dragging unnaturally across the current.

Why Drift Matters More Than Fly Choice

Trout are tuned into the rhythm of the water. They see insects floating downstream, moving at the same speed as the current. The second something looks "off"—a fly skating across the surface, moving faster than the water, or behaving stiffly—they reject it instantly.

A perfect drift isn't about the fly. It's about movement. It's about matching the river's flow so well that the trout never question it.

Once you start seeing a river from this perspective, fly selection becomes secondary. If your fly doesn't behave naturally in the water, no amount of realism will make up for it.

The Silent Bite Killer: Drag

Drag is the enemy of every fly angler. It happens when your fly line moves at a different speed than your fly, creating tension that makes the fly behave unnaturally. Even the subtlest drag can cause a trout to refuse.

Micro-drag is almost invisible to the angler, but trout pick up on it instantly. Cross-current drag happens when your fly lands in one speed of water and your line in another, pulling the fly unnaturally. Upstream line drag forces the fly ahead of the current, speeding up its drift when it should be floating naturally.

The solution? Mending.

Mending is the art of adjusting your line mid-drift to

eliminate drag and keep your fly moving naturally. A well-placed upstream mend slows a fly that's moving too fast. A downstream mend helps when the current is holding the fly back. A reach cast sets your line in the right position before the fly lands, preventing drag before it even starts.

A small, well-timed mend can be the difference between a trout striking and a trout ignoring your fly altogether.

The Dead Drift vs. The Swing

Most of the time, you want a dead drift—your fly moving naturally with the water, like a real insect. But there are exceptions. Sometimes, movement triggers aggression. Swinging a soft hackle. Skating a caddis. Stripping a streamer. Knowing when to let the fly drift naturally versus when to give it life can make all the difference.

Dead drifts excel in slow to moderate currents, when trout are sipping mayflies or midges, when they're selective, cautious, and unwilling to chase. But there are moments when a swung wet fly or a twitched caddis draws a strike when nothing else will.

The river doesn't follow hard rules. Knowing when to drift and when to move the fly is part of learning its language.

The Angle of the Cast

Presentation doesn't start when the fly lands—it starts the moment you cast. A perfect drift from the wrong angle will still result in drag.

An upstream cast keeps your line behind the fly, avoiding unnatural tension. An across-and-down cast works for swinging flies but increases drag risk. A high-stick or tuck cast keeps the leader off the water, perfect for pocket water where drag happens fast.

Sometimes, the simplest fix for a poor drift isn't a mend—it's changing where you stand.

The Lesson I Learned the Hard Way

One day on the Oconaluftee River, I learned just how much drift matters.

The water was crystal clear. I could see everything—every

rock, every submerged log, every trout ignoring my fly.

I knew I was in the right spot. I watched trout feeding just beneath the surface, making slow, deliberate movements. I tied on a Blue-Winged Olive, the exact size and shade of the hatch. I made my cast. Nothing. Not even a look.

I switched flies. Nothing. I changed tippet size. Still nothing.

Frustrated, I stopped casting and just watched. That's when I noticed it—my fly was dragging, just slightly. It was subtle, almost imperceptible, but it wasn't drifting naturally. The trout knew.

I adjusted my cast, added an upstream mend, and tried again.

First drift—nothing.

Second drift—nothing.

Third drift—a flash, a take, and a deep bend in my rod.

It wasn't the fly that had been wrong—it was my drift all along.

The river doesn't lie. If trout aren't taking your fly, there's a reason. Maybe it's the drift. Maybe it's the angle. Maybe it's the approach. But if you stop, watch, and adjust, the water will tell you everything you need to know.

It's tempting to think the answer is in a different fly, a different color, a different pattern. And sometimes, it is. But more often than not, it's about presentation. Master the drift, and you'll catch more fish. Get it wrong, and it won't matter if you're throwing the most perfect imitation in the world.

Because the river only rewards what looks real.

The Water Shapes the Fish

But not all rivers are the same. A perfect drift in a spring creek won't look the same as one in a freestone river. A tailwater trout sees the world differently than a wild brook trout in a mountain stream.

To become a truly skilled angler, you need to do more than just read the water—you need to understand how different types of trout water shape the fish that live in them.

In the next chapter, we break down spring creeks, freestones, tailwaters, and more—what makes each unique, how they influence trout behavior, and how to adjust your approach to match the environment.

Because if you want to catch more trout, you need to start by knowing the water they call home.

Part 3: Chasing Trout: The Waters We Fish

Chapter 15: Trout Waters: The Key Differences You Need to Know

The Language of the River

Somewhere, deep in the backcountry or just beyond a winding road, a trout stream whispers its secrets. To the untrained eye, it might all look the same—a ribbon of water tumbling over rocks, bending through valleys, or gliding past grassy banks. But to an angler, every stream tells a story.

Its shape, speed, and temperature dictate everything. Where trout hide. How they feed. Whether your fly will tempt them or be ignored.

Understanding the different types of trout waters isn't just about knowing where to fish. It's about seeing the water the way a trout does.

Spring Creeks: The Gentle Giants

Spring creeks are born from underground sources, bubbling up from limestone aquifers and flowing with a steady, year-round consistency. The water is clear, cold, and rich with minerals, feeding an endless buffet of aquatic insects.

These streams demand precision. Trout in spring creeks are selective and wary, conditioned by the constant clarity and a lifetime of inspecting tiny mayflies, caddis, and midges.

I remember my first spring creek challenge—Armstrong Spring Creek in Montana. The water was gin-clear, so clear I could see every trout before they saw me.

A hefty brown hovered near a patch of swaying weeds, sipping emergers so softly that only the slightest ripple gave him away. I tied on a size 22 Blue-Winged Olive and crouched low, creeping up like a predator.

First cast? Rejected.

Second? Same.

It took four adjustments—a longer leader, finer tippet, and a softer presentation—before that brown finally rose to my fly.

That's spring creek fishing. A chess match, not a brawl.

These streams don't reward force. They reward patience, finesse, and a deep understanding of the drift.

Freestone Rivers: The Wild Runners

Freestone rivers are the wild horses of trout water—born from melting snow, rainfall, and mountain springs. Their flows change with the seasons, surging with runoff in the spring, slowing to a lazy meander by late summer. They shape their own paths, tumbling over boulders, carving deep pools, and weaving through canyons.

Fishing a freestone river is an adventure. The water is often stained or slightly off-color, meaning trout rely less on sight and more on instinct. These fish hit hard and don't have the luxury of inspecting every meal for imperfections.

One of my best days was on the Gallatin River in Montana after a summer storm. The water had turned a chalky green—perfect conditions for a big terrestrial bite. I tied on a fat foam hopper and chucked it near a deep seam. The take was immediate. A rainbow so aggressive it nearly yanked the rod from my hands.

This is freestone fishing—fast, dynamic, unpredictable.

How Trout Adapt to Their Waters

Trout in different streams don't just live in their waters—they become their waters.

Spring creek trout are cautious, feeding primarily on small insects, moving with precision. Freestone trout are opportunistic, attacking larger prey when available, hiding in turbulent currents.

Tailwater trout? Selective but strong, thriving in food-rich, high-density environments.

High mountain stream trout? Aggressive and fast, with short feeding windows in cold, oxygen-rich waters.

Each river type demands a different approach.

The Influence of Geography

A spring creek in Montana won't fish the same as a freestone river in North Carolina. A tailwater in the Rockies won't behave like one in the Midwest. Geography shapes everything—the current, the insect life, the fish.

And then, there's Canada.

Canadian Trout Streams: A Northern Paradise

Canada's vast wilderness offers some of the most untouched, wild trout waters in the world. Glacial-fed freestones, expansive tailwaters, and remote rivers that see fewer anglers in a season than some U.S. streams see in a day.

The Bow River in Alberta—one of the greatest tailwaters on the planet, home to trophy rainbows and browns.

The Columbia River in British Columbia—a freestone gem, its trout known for their brute strength.

The wild rivers of Labrador, where brook trout grow to legendary sizes, thick-bodied and unpressured, striking streamers in water so pure it barely seems real.

Every stream type presents a different puzzle. Some demand finesse, some require power, and others test your ability to adapt.

The best anglers aren't just the ones who cast well. They're the ones who understand the water.

Reading the River, Understanding the Trout

Next time you step into a stream, don't just fish. Listen.

Watch how the current bends around rocks. Where the foam line drifts. How the trout react to the world around them.

The more you see, the more you'll understand. And the more you understand, the more you'll catch.

Because every great angler knows: fly fishing isn't just about the fish—it's about understanding the water.

The Magic Beneath the Surface

But this goes beyond strategy. Beyond technique.

There's something about trout waters—something that pulls at you.

They aren't just places to fish. They're alive, pulsing with cold, clear currents that shape everything around them. The deep pools. The gravel beds. The oxygen-rich riffles. The undercut banks.

These waters tell a story. A story of movement, survival, and raw beauty.

And if you spend enough time with them, you realize something—it's not just the fish that are shaped by the water.

We are, too.

In the next chapter, we dive beneath the surface, exploring why these rivers hold a magic that other waters don't. Because to truly appreciate fly fishing, you have to appreciate the world beneath the current.

Chapter 16: The Beauty of Trout Waters

There's something about trout water that pulls at you.

It's not just the way it moves—cold and clear, slipping over smooth stones and swirling into deep pools. It's not just the sound—soft and steady, never hurried, never still. It's something deeper, something you feel the moment you step in, when the current wraps around your legs and the river breathes around you.

I've fished enough water to know that no two trout streams are the same. The spring creeks of Montana demand patience and precision, where a single bad drift means rejection. The freestones of the Rockies are wild and unpredictable, their trout aggressive, their hatches erratic. In the Smokies, the streams are intimate, small pockets of clear water where brook trout flicker like fire through the current. And in the far North, in the untamed rivers of Canada, the trout are something else entirely—strong, thick-bodied, shaped by the raw wilderness around them.

Each one teaches you something new. Each one has a different rhythm.

And in all of them, I've learned one unavoidable truth: water will find a way to humble you.

Some anglers wade carefully, calculating every step like they're solving a physics equation. Not me. I seem to have a unique relationship with creeks—I average slipping and getting completely soaked in at least 40% of my trips. I've fallen in spring creeks, tailwaters, freestones, headwaters, and even places so shallow I should have been able to walk through without getting wet at all. But somehow, I always find the one slick rock waiting to send me into the current.

Once, on the Gallatin River in Montana, I had a perfect drift lined up—a hopper-dropper setup rolling through a deep seam. I was watching my dry fly when, out of nowhere, my feet were suddenly in the air. For a brief, weightless moment, I had time to think, Well, this is happening. Then—splash. I went in hard, rod flailing, hat floating downstream like it had somewhere better to be.

A nearby angler gave me the universal nod of every fisherman who's ever taken an unexpected bath—equal parts sympathy and quiet amusement.

The trout, of course, were unfazed.

A World Beneath the Surface

But for all the times I've been dunked by a river, I never mind too much. Because when you're standing in a trout stream—soaked or not—you're standing in a world that's alive.

I remember the first time I really saw what was happening under the water.

It was a spring creek in Pennsylvania, the kind of place where the water runs gin-clear and the trout have a lifetime of watching flies drift overhead. I crouched at the bank, watching a brown trout hover in the current. At first, I thought it was just holding there, waiting. But then I noticed the details—the slight flick of its fins, the way its body shifted with the flow, the tiny adjustments it made with every change in the current.

It wasn't just sitting there. It was working the water. Reading it. Using it.

That's when I realized trout don't live in water the way we think they do. They live with it. They don't fight the current—they use it. The seams, the eddies, the plunge pools—every part of the river is a tool, a shelter, a food source.

The best trout streams aren't just pretty landscapes. They are ecosystems, perfectly balanced, each part feeding into the next. The deep pools offer safety. The riffles bring oxygen. The undercut banks provide ambush points. And beneath it all, insects cling to the rocks, crayfish scuttle through the gravel, and the river itself shapes everything that lives within it.

The Fish That Call These Waters Home

Every trout stream has its own personality, and so do the fish that live in them.

Brook trout are the ghosts of the high-country waters, hidden in cold, untamed headwaters where few anglers venture.

They're the most beautiful trout I've ever seen—blue halos, fiery bellies, their colors shifting in the light. They survive where other fish can't, in tiny streams barely wide enough to cast.

Brown trout are different. Smart, cautious, predatory. They own the deeper pools and the cutbanks, the places where shadows stretch long. They're not impressed by sloppy presentations, and they don't forgive bad drifts. I've spent entire afternoons trying to fool a single brown trout, only to watch it slip back into the depths, untouched.

Rainbows are the acrobats of the river, quick to strike, quick to run, launching themselves skyward when hooked. I still remember the first time I watched a rainbow explode out of the water, my line going slack as it spit the hook mid-air. I stood there, rod in hand, stunned. The fight lasted less than ten seconds, but I replayed it for days.

Trout aren't just fish. They're characters. And the more time you spend in their world, the more you realize—each one has a story.

The River Through the Seasons

A trout stream is never the same river twice. It changes, shifts, transforms with the seasons, taking on a different rhythm with each passing month.

Spring is restless. Snowmelt surges through the valleys, filling the streams with cold, powerful currents. The trout shake off their winter sluggishness, feeding aggressively as the first hatches of the year begin.

Summer slows everything down. The water runs lower and clearer, trout retreating into the deeper pools, seeking shade beneath overhanging branches. Grasshoppers, beetles, and ants tumble from the banks, and every cast feels like a chance for something big.

Autumn sets the river ablaze. The air turns crisp, the water sharper. Leaves drift like tiny sailboats across the surface. Brown trout prepare for the spawn. The mornings are cold, the evenings stretch long, and the river is at its most breathtaking.

Winter silences everything. The creek locks in ice at its

edges, the water slows, the trout move sluggishly, conserving energy, feeding only when they must. I love the river in winter. It's patient. It doesn't rush. It moves the way it always has, with a rhythm all its own.

Reading the Current, Finding the Trout

But understanding the beauty of a trout stream is only the beginning.

If you want to catch fish consistently, you need to see the water the way a trout does. To recognize where they hold, how they feed, and why certain spots are more productive than others.

A river is never static. It's always moving, always reshaping itself around obstacles. And if you know how to read it, you'll know where to cast before the first trout even rises.

In the next chapter, we break down the anatomy of a trout stream—how to find the most productive water, from riffles and eddies to deep pools and undercut banks.

Because once you understand the river's language, you'll never look at moving water the same way again.

Chapter 17: Reading the Water

A trout stream is never still. It shifts, bends, carves itself into the landscape, always moving, always changing. To catch fish consistently, you have to do more than just cast a fly—you have to read the river, understand how it flows, where trout hold, and why certain areas are more productive than others. The river isn't static. It's alive, shaping itself around obstacles, creating the perfect hiding places for fish that know how to use every current to their advantage.

Trout aren't reckless. They don't waste energy chasing food through fast-moving water. Instead, they position themselves where the river does the work for them. They wait in seams, just outside the rushing current, where food naturally drifts into their strike zone. They tuck into eddies, where circular backflows collect insects, giving them a buffet without the effort. They hold under cutbanks, where the eroded earth offers protection from predators above. In deep pools, they rest, conserving energy until the next feeding window. And in riffles, where the water churns and oxygenates, they feed aggressively, taking advantage of the steady supply of drifting nymphs and larvae.

Every spot serves a purpose. Every position is a decision.

The Role of Light and Shadows

Trout don't just rely on the current to survive—they use light to their advantage too.

On bright days, they sink into the depths, retreating to deeper water or shaded cover. Overcast skies give them confidence, making them more willing to feed in open water. Early mornings and late evenings, when the sun sits low on the horizon, create the perfect window for dry fly action.

And then there's your approach.

Trout see almost everything. They have near-panoramic vision, their eyes positioned to detect the slightest movement above them. But they have one weakness—a blind spot directly behind them and under their chin. That's your only advantage. Approach from behind. Stay low. Move slowly. If they see you before you see them, the game is over before it even starts.

I've learned this the hard way. Once, I watched a brown trout feeding lazily in slow water, positioned perfectly for a cast. I took my time, picked the right fly, and stepped forward to make my shot. But before I could even lay out the line, the fish was gone. No splash, no panic—just a flick of the tail and it vanished, as if it had never been there at all.

The biggest trout don't just hide. They disappear.

Where Trout Hold and How to Catch Them

Some water holds fish all day. Some is just a highway, a place trout pass through but don't stay. The best feeding spots—the primary lies—are where the current delivers food with minimal effort. These are seams, submerged rocks, soft pockets just inside the main flow. When you find these spots, cast slightly upstream and let your fly drift naturally into the feeding lane.

But trout aren't always feeding. When they spook, they retreat to secondary lies—the deep pools, the undercut banks, the shaded pockets where they feel safe. These fish aren't aggressive, but they aren't uncatchable. A slow, patient nymph presentation or a well-placed streamer can coax them out.

And then there are transitional lies, the in-between zones. A trout might pause here for a moment or use it as a temporary rest stop before moving on. These spots are unpredictable, but sometimes, that's where the biggest fish make their mistakes. A swung streamer, a drifting dry fly—just enough movement to trigger a reaction.

Where you hook a trout changes the entire fight. A fish in a deep pool will drop into the depths, making you work for every inch. A fish in a riffle will turn the current into its ally, using the rushing water to pull against you. Hook one near an undercut bank, and you'll have about two seconds to steer it out before it buries itself under a root system and breaks you off.

The Ghosts Beneath the Surface

If there's one thing I've learned from years of filming underwater, it's that the real story of the river happens below the surface.

I've filmed more footage underwater than above because that's where the magic is. Watching trout shift in the current, adjusting ever so slightly to feed. Seeing a mayfly struggle to break free from its nymphal shuck, drifting helplessly into the strike zone of a waiting brown. Watching a trout inhale a caddis pupa mid-column before it ever reaches the surface. These are the things we miss when we're standing above the water, rod in hand, only seeing the top layer of a world far more complex than it appears.

The best trout are the hardest to see. They blend with the river, shifting with the current, using every rock and shadow to their advantage. You won't notice them at first. But if you watch long enough—if you train your eyes to see the subtle movements, the tiny flick of a tail, the brief flash of a feeding fish—you'll start spotting them before they spot you.

And that's when everything changes.

In the next chapter, we'll break down how trout use cover and camouflage to stay hidden—where they hold, why they vanish before your eyes, and how to spot them before they spot you. Because finding trout is just as important as knowing how to catch them.

Chapter 18: How Trout Use Cover and Camouflage

Trout are the ghosts of the river. They exist in plain sight, yet they are nearly invisible. They don't just hide—they blend, disappear, and become part of the environment. Survival for a trout is a chess match. Every flick of the tail, every shift in position is calculated to one end: to remain unseen.

The Science of Camouflage: Why You Never See the Big One Until It's Too Late

The best trout are the ones you never notice. They sit motionless in the shadows, perfectly matched to the riverbed, waiting for food to drift by. Their color isn't just beautiful—it's functional. Browns and greens merge with the stones. Speckles mimic the broken light of the stream. Even their bellies are paler, making them harder to see from below.

But their camouflage goes beyond color—it's about movement. A trout that stays still is nearly invisible. The moment it moves, it breaks the illusion, giving away its position.

The Art of Holding in the Current: Why Trout Don't Fight the Flow

Ever notice how trout seem to hover in the current with little effort? They're not fighting the river—they're using it. By positioning themselves behind rocks, logs, or depressions in the streambed, they can rest without wasting energy and let the river bring food directly to them.

A smart angler doesn't cast randomly—they read the river. They look for the "lies," those places where the water slows, and trout can rest while watching for food. Learn to see the stream through the eyes of a trout. Cast into these spots, not just any old stretch of water.

Shadows and Shade: The Unsung Heroes of Trout Survival

Trout understand the value of shadows. In bright sunlight, they seek shade—beneath overhanging branches, next to cutbanks, or in the deep pools where the light barely touches. Shadows keep them hidden from predators and help them see food drifting by.

For anglers, this means fishing in the shadows, not the open runs. That gnarly log jam? It's not just a mess of wood—it's prime trout territory. That undercut bank that looks ready to collapse? It's probably holding the biggest fish in the creek.

The Predator's Perspective: Why Trout Think Everything Wants to Eat Them

Trout live in a constant state of vigilance. It's not paranoia—it's survival. Birds of prey, otters, bigger fish, and even humans are all hunting them. This is why trout vanish at the first sign of danger.

Anglers who rush into the river, casting aggressively, don't catch these fish. The ones who move slowly, use natural cover, and approach carefully—they're the ones who hook the biggest trout.

Log Jams, Boulders, and Undercuts: Trout's Natural Hideouts

Structure isn't a luxury for trout—it's life or death. Log jams provide overhead cover, keeping predators at bay. Boulders break the current, creating pockets of slow water where trout can rest without wasting energy. Undercut banks? They're like secret bunkers—safe, cool, and nearly impossible for predators to reach.

If you're not fishing these spots, you're not fishing where the trout live.

Why Trout Prefer Dirty Water

Ever notice how trout seem more active in slightly stained water? It's not because they like the mud—it's because the murk gives them an edge. Slightly murky water makes it harder for predators to see them, but still allows them to detect movement and vibration.

Some of the best fishing happens after a rain, when the river's slightly colored but not blown out. Trout feel safer in this water. They move into feeding lanes more aggressively. Anglers who understand this don't curse the runoff—they embrace it.

The Art of Being Invisible: How Anglers Give Themselves Away

Think trout don't see you? Think again. They're watching. Your shadow, your movement, the ripple you send through the water—they know you're there before you even cast.

Smart anglers don't just cast—they approach like ghosts. They stay low, use the terrain, and minimize unnecessary movement. The best way to catch a trout is to act like you're not there at all.

Why Trout Face Upstream (And Why That Matters to You)

Trout always face upstream—that's where their food comes from. The river is a conveyor belt, delivering insects and small prey straight into their feeding lane. An angler who approaches from downstream stays out of sight. But an angler approaching from upstream? That's just another predator closing in.

Want to catch more trout? Approach from behind. Stay out of the water when possible. Let the river do the work for you.

The Slow Rise: When Trout Are Testing the Waters

A trout that rises slowly to your fly and then refuses it isn't being picky—it's testing the waters. A sudden, aggressive take is a risk. A slow, cautious rise is a trout's way of inspecting without committing.

When you see this, don't just cast again blindly. Adjust. Change the angle, the drift, or the fly. Recognize that trout aren't just feeding—they're analyzing. The best anglers pass this test.

Why You Never See the Big One First

The biggest trout don't sit in the open. They don't rise carelessly. They don't chase flies recklessly. The best trout—the ones that haunt your dreams—are the ghosts. They sit where most anglers don't look. They feed when most anglers aren't watching.

And when they do show themselves, it's usually just for a split second—long enough to make you doubt if you really saw what you think you saw.

The Trout Are Watching

The best trout don't just hide—they hide behind an angler's bad decisions. The guy who false casts 15 times? The trout sees that. The one who splashes into the water like a Labrador? The trout's already gone.

Every trout in the river knows the game better than you do. They've survived otters, eagles, floods, and droughts. And yet, somehow, they lose to the patient angler who understands their world.

So, the next time you're on the river, remember: The trout see you before you see them. The river knows you're there before you make your first cast. And the biggest fish? They're watching, waiting, deciding if you're worth their attention.

Make it count.

Watching the Water, Watching the Hatch

Trout aren't just watching you—they're watching the water, the current, and, most importantly, the insects.

Mayflies are at the heart of a trout's diet. When the hatch is in full swing, the river transforms. It's not just food—it's an event. To catch trout, you don't just need to see them—you need to see what they see.

In the next chapter, we'll dive into the world of Ephemeroptera—the mayflies that bring rivers to life. You don't have to be an entomologist to understand them, but if you want to fool a trout, you do need to pay attention. When the hatch begins, the rules of the river change.

Chapter 19: The Ephemeroptera

The Mayfly Hatch: When the River Comes Alive

Fly fishing is more than skill, patience, or the perfect cast. It's about paying attention—to the insects trout are feeding on, the rhythm of the river, the way the fish behave when something changes. Mayflies, belonging to the order Ephemeroptera, are some of the most fascinating to observe. They live brief, delicate lives, and when a hatch happens, the river transforms.

I wouldn't call myself an expert. But I've spent enough time standing in the middle of it all—watching, learning, filming more underwater than above—because what happens below the surface has always been more interesting to me than what's happening on top.

Why Mayflies Matter

Mayflies are fragile, but they hold the river together. Their name—Ephemeroptera—comes from the Greek for "short-lived." Once they emerge from the water, they live for mere hours or days. But in that brief window, they become an all-you-can-eat buffet for trout. When a hatch happens, it feels ancient, like stepping into a scene that has played out for thousands of years, long before anyone stood in waders trying to figure out what fly to use.

The Mayfly Lifecycle: What Trout See

Mayflies move through different stages, and trout key in on them at each one. Understanding what's happening in the water column can be the difference between catching fish and watching them ignore everything you throw at them.

They start as nymphs, crawling along the riverbed, clinging to rocks, barely moving. When I flipped stones on the Nantahala River, I found them clustered together, easy pickings for trout waiting just downstream. When they emerge, they rise through the water, struggling toward the surface. Some make it. Some don't. On the Davidson River, I watched trout flashing just beneath the surface, intercepting emergers before they could break free.

Once at the top, they transform into duns, young adult mayflies with upright wings. They float on the surface, waiting for their wings to dry. Some make it. Some don't. I've seen Blue Winged Olives hatch in perfect conditions, but the trout ignored them—still locked onto the stage before, where the insects were helpless in the film.

Then comes the spinner stage—after mating, mayflies return to the water to lay eggs. Their spent bodies drift in the current, helpless. On the Nantahala, I stood in the middle of a spinner fall, the air thick with dying mayflies, their wings shimmering in the last light. Trout fed with precision, sipping them in the slowest pools.

Matching the Hatch: Size and Color

Trout aren't always picky. But when they are, it's usually about two things: size and color.

If they're feeding but refusing your fly, it's probably too big. Drop to a smaller size. A size 16 might work, but sometimes a size 20 or smaller is the only answer.

Color matters too. Most mayflies fall into three main shades—olive, tan, and rusty brown. If you're missing fish, switching from light tan to darker brown can be the difference between getting ignored and getting a strike.

The Most Important Mayfly Hatches in North Carolina

Some hatches are famous for a reason. When they happen, the river shifts. Trout behavior changes. The water feels different.

The Hendricksons mark the beginning of the real season in April and May, a hatch that wakes trout up after the cold months. March Browns follow in May and June, bigger and harder to miss. Pale Morning Duns stretch through the summer, especially in tailwaters where cool water flows keep them active. Blue Winged Olives are the year-round hatch, the reliable answer when nothing else is happening. And then, for those lucky enough to catch it, Hexagenia in late summer—a rare, massive mayfly hatch that brings out the biggest browns.

Watching the Hatch, Not Catching a Thing

One early evening on the Nantahala, I found myself in the middle of something unreal. The sun dipped behind the ridgeline, casting long shadows. The air had that damp, electric feel that signals the evening rise. Then, almost on cue, the river woke up.

Mayflies drifted past me, their wings catching the last of the light. A trout moved just beyond my reach, flashing as it fed. Then another. And another. Soon, the surface was alive with feeding fish, breaking the water in deliberate, rhythmic patterns.

I tried everything. A size 16 Sulphur Dun, then an 18, followed by an emerger. Nothing. Trout were everywhere, taking something, but whatever they were locked onto, I wasn't offering.

By dusk, I was out of ideas. I sat on the bank, watching the quiet frenzy play out in front of me. I didn't land a fish that night, but it didn't feel like a loss. Some days, the river lets you in on its secrets. Other days, it humbles you. And that's okay.

The River Is a Living Thing

Mayflies are more than just trout food. They are the river's health, the pulse of its ecosystem. They live only in clean, oxygen-rich water. Their presence means the stream is alive and thriving.

Fly fishing is never just about the fish. It's about learning to read the water's language, noticing the smallest details, recognizing that every current, every stone, every hatch is part of a cycle older than us. If you learn to listen, the river will tell you everything you need to know.

When the Hatch Is On

Mayflies are just one part of the story. Trout don't eat randomly. They feed with purpose, guided by instincts honed over millions of years. Nothing awakens that instinct like a hatch.

The first time you see a hatch in full swing, it changes you. It's chaos and beauty—an orchestra of insects and rising fish. In that moment, you aren't just fishing. You're witnessing something timeless, something that unfolds whether you're there or not.

In the next chapter, we'll break down hatch cycles and feeding frenzies—how trout react, when to fish, and what patterns to use when the river is alive with rising fish. Because when the hatch is on, it's something else entirely.

Chapter 20: Hatch Cycles and Feeding Frenzies

Trout don't eat randomly. They eat with purpose, with precision, and with an instinct honed over millions of years. Feeding isn't just about hunger—it's survival. And nothing triggers that primal instinct more than a hatch.

The Hatch: When the River Comes Alive

The first time you see a real hatch, it changes you. It's chaos and beauty, all rolled into one—life bursting from the river, insects emerging, trout rising in rhythmic explosions. In that moment, you realize you're witnessing something ancient, something orchestrated by nature on a timeline older than any cast you'll ever make.

A hatch is a feeding window—a brief, intense moment where trout throw caution to the wind and gorge themselves. And when that switch flips, everything you thought you knew about trout fishing gets rewritten.

Understanding the Hatch Cycle

Hatches don't happen by accident. They follow a pattern—dictated by water temperature, time of year, and insect life cycles. Mayflies, caddisflies, stoneflies—they all have their own moment in the sun before becoming a meal.

Each insect has its stages: nymph, emerger, dun, spinner. Each stage offers trout a different opportunity. And each requires the angler to adjust. If you think a mayfly hatch just means tying on a dry fly, you've already lost the game.

The Nymph Stage: The Silent Feast Below the Surface

Before insects hit the surface, they live as nymphs, crawling along rocks, clinging to submerged branches, waiting for the right moment to emerge. Trout feed on nymphs more than 80% of the time. They're consistent, predictable, and easy prey.

Smart anglers know that before the hatch even begins, trout are already feeding. Fishing nymphs—stonefly, mayfly, caddis larvae—before the emergence starts is one of the deadliest strategies in fly fishing. It's like beating the rush before the restaurant fills up.

The Emerger Stage: When Trout Lose Their Minds

The transition from water to air is when insects are most vulnerable. Emerging mayflies struggle to break through the surface tension, trapped between two worlds. This is when trout go into full ambush mode.

An emerger pattern—half submerged, half breaking the surface—is often key during a hatch. If trout are rising but refusing your dry fly, it's because they're not eating adults yet—they're eating the ones still trying to escape.

The Dry Fly Stage: The Classic Rise

When the hatch reaches its peak, adult insects float on the surface, drying their wings before flight. This is the moment most anglers dream about—the perfect head-and-tail rise, the classic image of fly fishing.

But not all dry fly fishing is the same. If trout refuse your dun pattern, try one with a crippled wing, mimicking an insect that won't make it. A struggling fly is always an easier meal than a perfect one.

The Spinner Fall: When the Feast Ends

After mating, mayflies return to the water to die, wings splayed out, drifting lifelessly. This is the spinner fall, triggering one last feeding frenzy before the hatch cycle ends.

Trout that seemed cautious an hour ago now sip fallen spinners without hesitation. They know the difference between a living insect and a dead one. And if you match the moment—fishing a spent-wing spinner when the fall begins—you'll catch fish long after the rest of the river has settled.

The Frenzy: When Trout Throw Caution to the Wind

There's a moment in every hatch where trout stop analyzing, stop hesitating, and start devouring everything in sight. It's the closest thing to recklessness you'll see in these otherwise careful creatures.

During this feeding window, nearly any properly presented fly will work. It's one of the few times where a perfect drift isn't always necessary. But the window doesn't last long. The frenzy will slow. The rise forms dwindle. And just like that, it's over.

Why Some Trout Still Refuse During a Hatch

Here's the paradox: Even in the middle of a hatch, some trout refuse flies. Why? Because they're dialed in on a specific stage. If they're feeding on emergers, they'll ignore fully-formed adults. If they're on spinners, they won't touch a high-riding dry fly.

It's not enough to match the hatch. You have to match the phase of the hatch. That's the difference between hooking fish and watching them rise to everything except your fly.

Why Big Trout Feed Differently During Hatches

The biggest trout are the smartest. While smaller fish rise aggressively, the giants sit back and observe, taking in everything. They don't chase—they wait for the moment that requires the least effort and delivers the most reward.

Big trout focus on cripples, emergers, and spent spinners—the stages where insects are easiest to eat. The biggest mistake an angler can make is assuming the most aggressive rising fish are the best. The true trophy is often sitting just outside the madness, feeding methodically while the rest of the river loses its mind.

The Hatch That Never Ends: Year-Round Feeding Opportunities

Not all hatches are seasonal. Some insects, like midges, hatch year-round. These tiny bugs sustain trout when bigger meals aren't available. The angler who masters midge fishing—tiny flies, light tippet, perfect presentations—will always have fish to catch, even in winter.

The Hatch That Stays With You

Witnessing a hatch sticks with you. It's not just the way the river transforms—it's the way trout, so cautious one moment, become wild the next. It's the feeling that, for just a few minutes, you aren't just fishing—you're part of something bigger.

The best months to witness legendary hatches are from May through September, with peak activity in late spring and early summer when water temperatures stabilize. Hatches happen in the early morning and late evening, when cooler temperatures encourage insect emergence and reduce predator risk. The golden hour just before dusk? That's when the magic happens—the river comes alive, trout rise with abandon, and time slows down.

Every angler remembers their first great hatch. The first time the river boiled with life. The first time they saw trout feeding with reckless abandon. And the first time they realized that, in those moments, everything else disappears. The world narrows to nothing but the river, the rise, and the rhythm of nature at its purest.

And if you haven't had that moment yet? Keep fishing. When it happens, you'll never look at a trout stream the same way again.

Chasing the Hatch: Timing It Right

But for some anglers, just fishing a hatch isn't enough—they want to be in the right place, at the right time.

There's a moment—if you're lucky enough to be on the water when it happens—when everything changes. The river, once still, comes alive. A few dimples appear, then more. The air fills with mayflies, caddis, or midges—a swirling mass of wings and desperation. The trout take notice. You take notice. It's on.

This is the magic of the hatch. And for some anglers, just being there by chance isn't enough. They want to chase the hatch, follow it across rivers and states, and experience nature's greatest trout events as they unfold. Like storm chasers tracking tornadoes—except instead of high-speed winds, it's trout with tunnel vision inhaling bugs.

In the next chapter, we'll break down where and when to find the greatest hatches in the U.S.—the rivers, the timing, and the best strategies for chasing them. Because if you want to experience the river at its most alive, you have to be there when the switch flips.

Chapter 21: Chasing the Hatch

When the River Wakes Up

There's a moment—if you're lucky enough to be on the water at the right time—when everything changes. The river, once quiet and steady, comes alive. A few dimples appear, then more. You look up, and suddenly, the air is filled with mayflies, caddis, or midges—a swirling mass of wings and desperation. The trout take notice. You take notice. It's on.

This is the magic of the hatch. For some anglers, fishing isn't just about catching fish—it's about being there when nature flips the switch. These are the hatch chasers, the ones who don't just fish when they have time but rearrange their schedules to be on the water when the bugs say it's time. They track hatches like storm chasers track tornadoes, following water temps and insect activity instead of weather radars and wind speeds.

The Hatch Chaser's Mindset

A true hatch chaser doesn't just show up and hope—he studies, watches, and predicts. He knows when, where, and how the big hatches happen, like a bookie setting the odds for the Super Bowl. His calendar isn't filled with birthdays or anniversaries—just Hex Hatch, Salmonfly Hatch, and Trico Time, scrawled in Sharpie.

It's an obsession that requires more than luck. Timing, elevation, water temperature—get just one of them wrong, and you'll miss it entirely. But when the bugs arrive, and the fish turn reckless, everything else fades away.

The Greatest Hatches in America

If you're going to chase a hatch, make it a good one. Some hatches are so legendary they've made anglers quit their jobs, drive cross-country, and put everything else in life on hold just to be there when it happens.

The Salmonfly Hatch turns Western rivers into chaos. These prehistoric two-inch bugs crawl out of the river like they survived the dinosaur age. They cling to branches, shake their wings dry, and launch into the air—only to get devoured by trout that lose all self-control. If you've never seen a five-pound brown trout throw itself clear out of the water for a salmonfly, you haven't lived. The Madison River, Henry's Fork, and the Deschutes are the places to be when it happens.

The Hex Hatch is for night owls. The biggest mayflies in North America emerge just after sunset, bringing out huge, lazy trout that suddenly act like starving piranhas. You fish in darkness, relying on feel and sound, setting the hook purely on instinct. The rises are explosive, and you never know if you've hooked a two-pounder or a monster until it runs. The Au Sable in Michigan, the Driftless Area in Wisconsin, and the Mississippi River backwaters all host this madness.

The Green Drake Hatch is a feast no trout can ignore. These mayflies are big, slow, and plentiful—like cheeseburgers floating down the river. Even the pickiest trout lose all hesitation. When they emerge, it's like a five-star buffet being dumped into the current. Henry's Fork in Idaho, Penns Creek in Pennsylvania, and the Gunnison in Colorado are prime waters when the drakes start popping.

The Mother's Day Caddis Hatch is pure insanity. When it's on, you can barely breathe without inhaling a bug. The air, the water, the sky—it's all caddis. The trout feast, the anglers celebrate, and the river turns into a feeding frenzy. If you want to witness it, head to the Yellowstone, Madison, or Arkansas River in May.

The Hatch My Buddy Missed (And Still Regrets)

There's a special kind of pain in missing a perfect hatch. My buddy learned that the hard way. He had one shot at the Green Drake hatch on Henry's Fork. The reports were unreal—trout gorging themselves, bugs covering the river. He packed his gear, set his alarm for 3 AM, and hit the road.

But overnight, a cold front rolled in. The hatch fizzled. The fish sulked. He drove 200 miles to stand in a river and rethinking everything.

This is the risk of chasing the hatch—sometimes, you lose.

But when you win? There's nothing like it.

How to Chase the Hatch Without Losing Your Sanity

Chasing a hatch isn't for the casual angler. It takes commitment, flexibility, and just enough insanity to justify skipping normal responsibilities. The best hatch chasers track historical hatch dates, watch water temperatures like hawks, and rely on real-time reports from fly shops, fishing forums, and social media. They're ready to move at a moment's notice, sometimes driving through the night if a hatch fires off three hours away.

Showing up unprepared is a mistake you only make once. The right flies—dries, nymphs, and emergers—can make or break the trip. If you think you can just pick some up when you get there, think again. By the time the hatch happens, the local fly shop has probably been picked clean.

Is It Worth It?

Absolutely. Chasing a hatch is unpredictable. Sometimes you strike out and drive home in silence, replaying all the things you could've done differently. Other times, you time it perfectly and have the best day of fishing you've ever had.

But when you're standing in the river, the sky filled with bugs, the water breaking with the sound of rising trout—you get why people do it. Why we keep coming back. Why we drop everything at the hint of a hatch.

Because when the river wakes up, you want to be there.

Where Beauty and Wildness Collide

Maybe that's the real reason we fish—not just for the trout, not just for the hatch, but for the places where it all happens. Somewhere, tucked deep in the mountains, a trout flickers beneath the surface of a stream so clear it seems invisible. To the untrained eye, it's just another cold-water fish. But to those who understand the art of fly fishing, this moment is poetry.

The trout's world isn't defined by human standards of beauty—it only knows survival, clarity, and movement. The delicate dance of life beneath the current.

In the next chapter, we'll explore why trout only exist in the wildest, most beautiful places on Earth—and what that says about the world we live in.

Chapter 22: Trout Only Live in Beautiful Places

Somewhere in a hidden fold of the mountains, a trout flickers beneath the surface of a stream so clear it seems almost invisible. To the untrained eye, it's just another cold-water fish weaving through a rocky bed. But to those who understand fly fishing, this moment is poetry. The trout's world isn't dictated by human standards of beauty—it doesn't know ugly. It only knows survival, clarity, movement—the delicate dance of life beneath the current.

The Science of Pristine Waters

For a trout, water quality isn't a preference—it's life or death. These fish demand balance: the right temperature, the right oxygen levels, the right clarity.

Trout thrive in water between 50 and 60 degrees Fahrenheit. Anything above 68 makes them sluggish, more vulnerable to disease. Above 75, they're in real trouble. That's why they call the mountains home. Snowmelt, underground springs, and shaded forests keep the water cold, even in the heat of summer.

Oxygen is just as important. Fast currents and waterfalls inject air into the water, keeping it rich enough for trout to breathe. That's why they're often found in riffles and swift-moving sections. Slow, stagnant water suffocates them. Clarity matters too—trout are visual hunters. They need clean, filtered streams to spot their next meal. Murky water clouds their vision and makes feeding harder.

A perfect trout stream is a living, breathing thing. Gravel beds for spawning. Oxygen-rich riffles for feeding. Deep pools for resting. Every rock, every current, every fallen tree plays a role in keeping the ecosystem alive.

The Sound of Waterfalls and the Allure of Falling Water

Waterfalls draw us in. They stop us mid-hike, make us pull out cameras, and force us to stand in awe. But there's something deeper behind their pull. Falling water is movement, renewal, life. The roar of a waterfall isn't just sound—it's power, it's energy, it's the constant pulse of the river.

Trout know this. Waterfalls act as nature's oxygen stations, supercharging the water with life. Below them, the current churns, creating deep, cool pools where trout gather, waiting for food to wash down. Some waterfalls, too high for fish to pass, create isolated populations above the drop—unique, untouched strains of trout that have adapted to their own small world.

Maybe that's why we're drawn to them too. Maybe it's the same instinct that pulls us toward the sound of rushing water, the same feeling that makes us pause when we stumble upon a perfect hidden stream. Some part of us recognizes the power in it, even if we can't explain why.

Gravel, Rocks, and Camouflage

A trout's world is shaped by the riverbed. Gravel isn't just something beneath their fins—it's their nursery, their hiding place, their foundation. When the time comes to spawn, a female trout searches for loose gravel beds, places where oxygen-rich water can flow through and keep her eggs alive. Without these spawning grounds, the future of the river fades.

Big boulders and submerged logs act as refuge. A trout will sit just behind a rock, barely moving, letting the current bring food straight to it. It's a game of energy conservation—hold steady, wait, strike.

They are masters of disguise. A brook trout's green speckles blend into the dappled light of a forest stream. A brown trout's golden hues mimic the riverbed. Even a rainbow trout, bright as it is, can vanish against the shifting colors of the current. Every pattern, every spot, every shade of their scales is part of an ancient survival code.

The Allure of Pristine Water

I once stood on the bank of a stream so perfect it didn't seem real. A forgotten ribbon of water winding through the Appalachian foothills, untouched by development, hidden from all but those willing to walk far enough to find it. The water was so clear I could count every trout finning beneath the surface.

The property had come up for sale—an opportunity to own a private stretch of wild trout water. The idea was intoxicating. A place where I could fish alone, where I could protect the water, where I could watch trout thrive without interference.

I waded in, feeling the cool gravel shift beneath my boots. A shadow materialized from under a submerged log—a large, wise brown trout, holding in the current like it owned the river. I stood there watching, the idea of ownership still turning in my mind.

And then I understood.

I could never own this place—not really. The trout belong to the water. The water belongs to the land, which has been here long before me and will remain long after. To claim ownership over something so wild felt wrong. I walked away without signing the deed. Some might call it regret, but I call it respect.

Because trout don't know property lines or price tags. They don't know what it means to "own" a river. They only know flow and stone, oxygen and depth, survival and beauty. And if we are lucky, we get to step into their world, even if only for a little while.

Beyond the Trout: The Other Fish in the River

But a trout stream is never just about trout. The water holds more than the fish we chase.

For every brown, rainbow, or brook trout, there's a sculpin darting between the rocks, a dace flashing in the shallows, a smallmouth bass lurking in the deep pools. These fish have outlived ice ages, floods, and human interference. They've carved out their own place in the currents, thriving in the same water that gives trout their home.

A river is more than its trout. It's a world in motion, shaped by the unseen, filled with creatures most anglers never notice. To truly understand a trout stream, you have to look beyond the fish we tie flies for.

In the next chapter, we'll explore the forgotten fish of the trout stream—the prey, the predators, and the unseen life that makes these waters what they are. Because knowing what swims beneath the surface is just as important as knowing how to fish it.

Chapter 23: Who Lives in a Trout Stream?

A trout stream is never just a trout stream. It's an intricate web of life, a symphony of movement, a battlefield, a sanctuary. The fish within have survived ice ages, floods, and human intervention, adapting, evolving, and carving out their place in the rushing currents. To know a trout stream is to know its inhabitants—not just the trout, but the entire cast of characters that fill its deep pools and rocky riffles.

For the angler, understanding these fish is more than knowledge—it's reverence. It's knowing what the trout know. It's understanding what lurks beneath the cutbanks, what hides under moss-covered rocks, what flashes silver in the depths before vanishing into shadow. Each species tells a story. Each one plays a role. And together, they create the drama of the stream.

The Icons of the Current

Brook Trout (Salvelinus fontinalis) – The Ghosts of Cold Water

There's something otherworldly about a brook trout. Maybe it's the way they seem to appear and disappear like ghosts in the tea-stained waters of a mountain stream. Their fiery orange bellies, speckled backs, and white-edged fins flick like brushstrokes in the current. These fish are relics of a time before roads, dams, and logging scars. They thrive in the smallest, coldest waters—streams that feel like secrets when you find them.

Brook trout don't live in easy places. They are sentinels of purity, vanishing as the water warms. A stream that holds brook trout is sacred, a reminder of what once was and what still is, if you know where to look.

Brown Trout (Salmo trutta) – The Survivors

Brown trout are the scrappers, the warriors. They came from Europe, grew larger, meaner, smarter. They hide in undercut banks, moving only when they choose, feeding when they feel like it. Their golden-brown bodies, speckled with halos of red and black, are as deceptive as they are beautiful.

A big brown doesn't play by the same rules. It waits. It calculates. It feeds when it wants to, not when you want it to. It watches your fly drift past a dozen times before deciding whether it's worth the trouble. And when it strikes, it fights like a creature that has spent its entire life learning to survive.

Rainbow Trout (Oncorhynchus mykiss) – The Wild Hearts

Rainbows are the daredevils, never stopping, always on the hunt. Their iridescent pink bands flash like lightning as they tear through the water, aggressive and relentless. Hook one in fast water, and you'll know it. They run, leap, and refuse to surrender. Even when you think you've won, they find a way to spit the hook and disappear back into the depths.

Rainbows remind you that nothing is guaranteed. The best things are always just beyond reach.

Cutthroat Trout (Oncorhynchus clarkii) – The Natives

There's something poetic about a cutthroat trout. Maybe it's the red slashes beneath their gills, glowing like the land itself marked them. These trout belong in a way that no others do. They take dry flies with a quiet confidence, rising lazily, trusting the water to provide. They remind us of a time when rivers were wild, full, and untamed.

The Supporting Cast

Bull Trout (Salvelinus confluentus) – The Giants of the Deep

If brook trout are ghosts, bull trout are monsters. These are the giants, the predators that haunt the darkest pools. To catch a bull trout is to feel raw power at the end of your line.

Mountain Whitefish (Prosopium williamsoni) – The Underestimated

Often dismissed by anglers, mountain whitefish are the quiet residents of the same waters as trout. They glide through the depths, sipping nymphs and feeding efficiently, keeping the river in balance. They may not leap or strike with fury, but they belong just as much as any trout.

Sculpin (Cottidae species) – The Hidden Prey

Sculpin are the secret currency of the river. Small, bottom-dwelling fish, they wait for the moment to dart from cover—only to be ambushed by faster, stronger predators. If you've ever watched a trout charge from the shadows with sudden intent, chances are it was after a sculpin.

Dace, Shiners, and Chubs – The Baitfish of the Current

These minnows are the lifeblood of the stream's food chain, keeping the predators sharp. They play their part in the great theater of the river, feeding those fast enough to catch them.

Lamprey (Ichthyomyzon species) – The Ancient Ones

Lampreys are the forgotten fish. Their presence matters, though—acting as a food source for trout in their juvenile forms. Their survival is another thread in the intricate web of the stream.

The River's Story

A trout stream is not just a place—it's a living, breathing world. Each species has its role, each fish a character in the drama beneath the surface. To know a trout stream is to recognize that every cast is part of something larger.

We fish not just for trout but for the story they tell. The connection they offer to something wild and real. When we step into that cold, rushing water, casting our fly, we are not just anglers—we are part of the river itself.

The Ones That Haunt Us

Some trout leave a bigger mark than others. Every angler dreams of the big one—the kind of trout that makes your hands shake when you finally land it. But the truth is, big trout aren't just bigger—they're different. They play a different game. And unless you understand their rules, you're just another hopeful angler throwing flies into the abyss.

The legendary, scarred-up warriors have learned the hard way what keeps them alive. They're not reckless. They don't make mistakes often. If you want to catch them, you have to think like they do.

In the next chapter, we'll break down what separates a good trout from a great one—how they feed, how they move, and what it takes to fool them. Catching small trout is easy. But landing the old ghosts of the river? That's a different story.

Chapter 24: Big Trout, Big Secrets

The Difference Between a Good Trout and a Great Trout

Every angler dreams of catching the big one—the kind of trout that makes your hands shake when it finally lands in the net. But the truth is, big trout aren't just bigger versions of the small ones. They don't act the same. They don't feed the same. They don't live in the same places.

The big ones—those legendary, scarred-up old warriors—have learned what keeps them alive. They're not reckless. They don't make mistakes often. And if you want to catch them, you have to play by their rules.

That means understanding how they behave, where they live, and why they don't eat the same way their younger cousins do.

The Three Big Trout Personalities

Every trout species has quirks, but when they get big, those quirks become survival strategies. The larger they grow, the smarter they fish.

The Brown Trout: The Apex Predator

If big trout were action movie characters, brown trout would be the lone wolves, the quiet assassins. They don't like company. They don't tolerate competition. And when they decide to eat, they ambush, they strike, they destroy.

A big brown owns its territory. If you pull one out of a deep undercut bank or a slow, shadowed pool, there's a good chance no other big trout will be in that spot. They don't share. They feed less often but when they do, they go for protein—small trout, crayfish, mice. They're not out sipping midges; they're hunting.

If you want to catch a big brown, forget the tiny dry flies. Throw streamers, mouse patterns, and big articulated flies. Skip the midday fishing trips and hit the water when most people aren't—early morning, late evening, or in the dead of night.

The Rainbow Trout: The Bullet Train

Big rainbows are built for speed. They fight harder, jump higher, and seem to have an unlimited supply of energy. If brown trout are assassins, rainbows are the high-speed getaway cars—pure power, zero hesitation.

Unlike browns, they don't sulk in the depths. They move constantly, shifting within the river system to find the best feeding zones. Instead of hiding in deep, slow water, big rainbows stay in the fastest, strongest currents because they're powerful enough to handle it.

They're aggressive but not reckless. A big rainbow will take a dry fly—but only if it's drifting perfectly. Presentation matters. If you want to land one, look for riffles leading into deep pools. They'll hit nymphs, dries, and streamers, but be ready—when a big rainbow takes, it'll test every knot you've ever tied.

The Brook Trout: The King of the Wild

Brook trout don't grow as big as browns or rainbows, but a truly big brookie is something else entirely. They're the ghosts of untouched waters, thriving in seclusion and near-perfect conditions. If you find yourself holding a 20-inch brook trout, you're standing in one of the most pristine places left on Earth.

Unlike browns, brook trout are more social. They'll tolerate others in their territory, but a truly big one will still hold the best water. They love the coldest, cleanest streams—places where oxygen levels are high and human footprints are rare.

If you want to catch a big brook trout, you have to go remote. Drive as far as the road will take you, then hike another ten miles. The biggest brookies live where few people fish. Instead of big streamers, think smaller—terrestrial flies, hoppers, ants, and small leeches. Cover water quickly because brook trout don't always stay put like browns. They move, and so should you.

How Big Trout Think (And How You Should Too)

Big trout don't act like smaller trout because they've survived long enough to know better. They've seen hooks before. They've learned to avoid danger. If you want to catch them, you need to stop thinking like an angler and start thinking like a trout.

A small trout rises eagerly to a well-placed dry fly, competing with others in its school for the first bite. A big trout waits, watching, only eating when it's absolutely certain. A small trout will dart out into the fast water to chase a drifting insect. A big trout stays in the shadows, holding in a deep pool or an undercut bank, waiting for a meal that requires the least amount of effort.

The difference between catching small trout and big trout isn't luck—it's mindset. Stop casting blindly to every fish you see. Think like a predator. Look for the best ambush points. Move quietly. Make every cast count.

The Trophy Trout Myth

Most anglers say they want to catch a giant trout. But are they willing to do what it takes?

Catching big trout means fishing differently. It means staying on the water longer, fishing when others don't, resisting the urge to cast to easy fish when you know the big one is lurking in the depths. It means walking past the obvious pools and putting in time where others won't.

Most of the time? They win.

But every once in a while? You do.

Seeing the River Through a Trout's Eyes

What if you could see trout before they had a reason to fear you? What if you could step into their world—not as an angler, but as an observer?

I learned that the day I put on a wetsuit, slipped into a waterfall pool, and watched trout in a way I never had before. No rod, no flies—just me, the water, and the fish.

What I learned changed how I see every trout stream, every deep pool, and maybe even the fish themselves.

Chapter 25: What I learned About Trout While Snorkeling in a Waterfall Pool

Seeing the River Through a Trout's Eyes

Most fly fishers think they know trout. We spend hours watching the surface, analyzing rises, debating fly choices, and convincing ourselves that we understand these fish. But until you've been in their world, until you've floated silently in their current and watched them exist without the filter of a fishing line, you don't really know them at all.

I found that out the day I put on a wetsuit, slipped into a waterfall pool, and saw trout in a way I never had before. No rod, no flies—just me, the water, and the fish. What I learned changed how I see every trout stream, every deep pool, and maybe even the fish themselves.

Trout Aren't Afraid—They Just Know the Rules

As anglers, we assume trout are always terrified of us. We creep along banks, whisper like we're breaking into a safe, and act like any sudden movement will send them bolting. But what I saw in that waterfall pool? Trout aren't afraid. They just have boundaries.

When I first slipped into the water, I expected an underwater stampede—fish fleeing for cover. Instead, they held their ground. They kept a distance, sure, but they didn't run. They weren't frozen in fear. They just adjusted, shifting slightly but never abandoning their position.

It was like watching a herd of deer in a field—you can walk toward them, and they'll move, but they won't bolt unless you cross some invisible threshold. These trout were doing the same thing. They knew where they needed to be, and they weren't about to give up a prime feeding lane just because some neoprene-clad human had entered the scene.

That changed everything for me. Trout aren't delicate little ghosts that vanish at the first sign of trouble. They're calculated. They'll tolerate you—as long as you respect the space they've decided is safe.

Trout Colors Are a Lie

Every angler has marveled at the colors of a freshly caught trout. The electric blue halos, the fiery orange underbellies, the perfect speckling like divine artwork. But when I saw those same trout underwater? Muted. Almost camouflaged.

The brilliant golds and reds weren't glowing—they were dulled by the water, blending into the riverbed. From above, trout look vibrant. From below, they look like part of the landscape.

It made me think—how much of what we see is real? How often do we mistake the way light plays off wet fish for how they actually look in their natural environment? And more importantly, what do trout see when they look up at us? Are we shimmering monsters, distorted by the refraction of light? Do we glow with weird colors and angles?

Maybe we're the ones who stand out. Maybe the trout are always blending in.

Holding Ground: The Power of Positioning

One of the biggest surprises? How still the trout were. Not frozen, not scared—just anchored. Perfectly balanced in the current. They weren't struggling, weren't fighting to stay in place. They just were.

As an angler, you assume trout are constantly in motion, darting for food, repositioning, always adjusting. But when you see them from below, you realize—they're masters of efficiency. They move only when necessary. No wasted energy. No unnecessary motion. Just precise, calculated shifts.

And here's the kicker—when they did move, it was effortless. A flick of a fin, and they were exactly where they needed to be. They weren't battling the current. They were using it.

That's something every fly angler should remember: trout don't fight the water—they use it. Maybe we should too.

I'll Never See a Pool the Same Way Again

Before that day, a deep pool was just a spot—a place to cast, to drift a nymph, to hope for a strike. Now? It's a world. A kingdom of slow-moving fish, invisible currents, and silent rules. I'll never look at one the same way again.

I think about those trout—how they ignored me until I got too close, how they faded into the rocks, how they moved with such quiet power. I think about the way they positioned themselves, how they weren't afraid, just aware.

That's what fly fishing really is—learning to see the world the way trout do. We spend all this time above the water, guessing, theorizing, making up rules. But down there, in their world? The truth is different. And once you see it, you can't unsee it.

No Rod, No Flies—Just Understanding

I did this alone, with no one else around. Not because I wanted it to be some mystical solo experience, but because I didn't want to bother anyone fishing nearby. The river was quiet, and so was I. No catching, no casting—just watching, learning. And in that stillness, it became one of my most cherished experiences.

Would I do it again? Absolutely. Do I think every fly angler should try it? Without question. Because if you want to truly understand trout, you have to meet them on their terms. Not from a drift boat, not with a rod in hand—but on their level, in their water.

Because the real lessons about fly fishing? They aren't found in books, fly shops, or even at the tying bench. They're down there, in the current, where the trout already know everything you're trying to figure out.

The Dance Between Wild and Tamed

But not every trout in the river was born there.

There's a moment—if you've ever fished hatchery-assisted waters, you know it well. The sound of tires crunching gravel, the hum of an idling engine, and the sharp splash of a thousand disoriented trout hitting unfamiliar currents.

They don't know where they are. They don't know what to do. For the first few hours, they drift in a daze, mouths opening and closing, expecting food to rain down like it did in the tanks they came from.

And then, instinct takes over. Some vanish under cutbanks. Others rush to deep pools, feeling the flow of something older than their hatchery days. The transition begins.

This is the reality of hatchery-assisted fishing. It's not wild versus stocked. It's not pure versus artificial. It's a dance between what nature intended and what man has created.

Some fishermen scoff at these fish, calling them "dumb" or "lesser." Others see them for what they are—a bridge, a doorway, an introduction to something much bigger than a hatchery truck.

Chapter 26: Hatchery Waters: The Pros, Cons, and Reality

The Moment the Truck Arrives

There's a moment—if you've ever fished hatchery-assisted waters, you know it well. The sound of tires crunching gravel, the hum of an idling engine, and the sharp splash of a thousand disoriented trout hitting unfamiliar currents. They don't know where they are. They don't know what to do. For the first few hours, they drift in a daze, mouths opening and closing, expecting food to rain down like it did in the tanks they came from.

And then, instinct takes over. Some vanish under cutbanks. Others rush to deep pools, feeling the flow of something older than their hatchery days. The transition begins.

This is the reality of hatchery-assisted fishing. It's not wild versus stocked. It's not pure versus artificial. It's a dance between what nature intended and what man has created. Some fishermen scoff at these fish, calling them "dumb" or "lesser." Others see them for what they are—a bridge, a doorway, an introduction to something much bigger than a hatchery truck.

Why We Need Hatcheries

The truth? Without hatcheries, a lot of trout waters wouldn't exist. Not in a way that sustains fishing, anyway. Wild populations, fragile as they are, can't support the sheer number of anglers casting a line. These fish are the workhorses of the trout world—poured into rivers to keep the magic alive, to give a first-time angler a chance to feel the electric jolt of a trout at the end of the line.

But let's not pretend it's all the same. A wild brown that's spent years lurking beneath undercut banks, growing wary, learning the water? That fish is something else entirely. It's a ghost, a predator, a survivor. Stocked trout? They have their own story, but it's a shorter one, and it starts with an artificial river made of concrete and controlled flow rates.

Timing the Hatchery Drop: Early Release vs. Late Release

There's strategy to fishing stocked waters, and if you don't understand it, you're missing half the game.

Fishing Right After Release: This is the easy pickings. Trout are confused, disoriented, and hungry. They'll take anything moving—nymphs, dries, even an old gum wrapper if you throw it right. But there's no artistry here. It's shooting fish in a barrel, and most seasoned anglers leave this window to the kids and weekend warriors.

Fishing Days Later: Now it's interesting. The fish have spread out, found shelter, started acting more like trout instead of hatchery escapees. This is when you want to be on the water—when the challenge has returned.

Fishing Weeks Later: If they've survived this long, they've earned their place. Their color deepens. Their wariness kicks in. Their fight becomes something worth writing home about.

Delayed Harvest: The Slow Burn of Patience

Some waters follow Delayed Harvest (DH) regulations, meaning these trout get to live a little longer before harvest season starts. It's like watching someone get a second chance at life—they start off clueless, floating in currents they don't understand, but given enough time, they become part of the river.

Delayed harvest streams create some of the best fishing out there—where stocked fish have enough time to become real fish. They learn to take emergers instead of chasing powerbait. They start hiding instead of swimming out in the open like sitting ducks.

Do Stocked Trout Look and Act Differently?

Yeah, and you can spot them in a second. Right out of the gate, stocked fish are pale, their fins a little ragged, their movements stiff and unnatural. They're hatchery-raised athletes suddenly thrown into a marathon they weren't trained for.

But nature is relentless, and the river doesn't care where you came from. In weeks, their colors change. Their habits shift. They stop reacting like lab-grown fish and start acting like ghosts of the current. The river does what it always does—it makes things wilder, tougher, more real.

The Ethics of Hatchery Fishing

There's always debate. Some say stocked trout cheapen the sport. Others say they save it. Here's the reality—if you've ever handed a fly rod to a kid and watched them light up when they land their first trout, you know exactly why hatcheries matter.

Still, it's worth asking: should you fish for them the same way? Should you hold yourself to the same standards as when you're hunting a wild brown in untouched waters?

Barbless hooks, proper catch-and-release techniques, knowing your local regulations—these things matter whether you're fishing wild or stocked trout. Respect the fish, respect the water, and recognize that these waters wouldn't be what they are without some human intervention.

Personal Story: The Truck Came, But the Fishing Wasn't Easy

One autumn, I found myself on a stretch of river known for its hatchery stockings. The truck had arrived, and the fresh batch of fish was released into the river. I was there—rod in hand, standing knee-deep in the current, expecting the usual. But the fishing wasn't easy.

I cast. Nothing. Switched flies. Nothing. These fish—freshly dumped, confused, supposedly easy—weren't playing along. I watched the water, looking for movement, watching their reaction. They weren't looking up. They weren't chasing. They were spooked—sitting low in the column, ignoring everything.

Then it clicked. No flashy attractors, no big dries. Just a dead-drifted soft hackle nymph through the deeper seams. First drift—nothing. Second drift—nothing. Third drift—a slow, deliberate take. Not a smash-and-grab, but a sip. A thinking fish. A stocked fish that was already learning.

It was pure luck I was there at the right time, but the fishing wasn't what I expected. I landed a handful that day, but they weren't the eager, pellet-raised fish I expected. They had been forced into their instincts faster than usual, and that made every take, every head shake, every release feel different. More earned. More real.

The Reason Hatchery Trout Are So Hungry

I learned something from one of the hatchery biologists: Hatchery trout are famished when they're released. They have to stop feeding them three days before transportation. If they're fed too close to the release date, they'll throw up and get extremely stressed during the journey. This is why, when they hit the water, they're so eager—they're not just hungry; they're desperate to feed.

Does It Matter? The Hatchery vs. Wild Debate

This is where the purists come in. "Only wild fish matter." "Stocked trout aren't real trout." But I've seen stocked fish turn into survivors. I've seen them hold on against floods, predators, and the constant pressure of anglers. Some of them make it. And when they do, they're just as much a part of the river as any wild-born brown or brookie.

Wild trout are special. They always will be. But hatchery fish aren't meaningless. They are an entry point, a lesson, a way to get more people standing in cold water, casting a line, and feeling something primal connect through the rod.

A Dance Between Wild and Tamed

If you've never fished a stocked stream, don't dismiss it outright. If you only fish stocked waters, challenge yourself to seek out the wild ones. The key isn't where the trout came from. It's how you fish for them, how you respect them, and how you let the river change you.

So next time you hear that truck roll up, don't just see it as a delivery service for easy fish. See it as the start of something. The river will shape those trout. And, if you're lucky, it'll shape you too.

Two Rivers, Two Mindsets

But not all rivers shape trout—or anglers—the same way.

If you fish long enough, you'll start to notice that not all trout streams behave the same way. Some flow smooth and glassy, others tumble over rocks in an endless rush of movement. Some require delicate casts and stealthy wading, while others demand aggressive drifts and quick reactions.

These are the two great categories of moving water in a trout fisherman's world: spring creeks and freestone rivers. Knowing the difference between the two—and how to fish them—can turn a good angler into a great one. Because each requires a different mindset, a different rhythm, and a deep respect for the kind of water you're stepping into.

In the next chapter, we'll break down how these two legendary waters shape trout behavior, how they challenge anglers differently, and what it takes to master both. Because understanding the river is just as important as understanding the fish.

Chapter 27: Spring Creeks vs. Freestone Rivers

Understanding the Two Great Trout Waters

If you fish long enough, you'll start to notice that not all trout streams behave the same way. Some flow smooth and glassy, barely rippling unless disturbed by the wind. Others tumble over rocks in an endless rush, their currents powerful and unrelenting. Some demand precision and patience, while others call for aggressive casts and fast-moving flies.

These are the two great categories of moving water in a trout fisherman's world: spring creeks and freestone rivers. Knowing the difference between the two—and how to fish them—can turn a good angler into a great one. Because each requires a different rhythm, a different approach, and a deep respect for the kind of water you're stepping into.

Spring Creeks: The Precision Game

Spring creeks are born from underground sources—cold, mineral-rich water bubbling up from beneath the earth. Unlike freestone rivers, which swell and shrink with rain and snowmelt, spring creeks maintain a steady flow and temperature year-round. This consistency makes them an oasis for trout, a stable environment where fish can grow large, selective, and wary.

The banks of a spring creek are often lush, overgrown with tall grasses bending under the weight of morning dew. The water moves like silk, reflecting the bright blue sky, its surface barely disturbed unless a rising trout breaks through. The clarity is striking—you can see the pebbled bottom, the slow dance of submerged weeds, and sometimes, the unmistakable shadow of a feeding trout shifting just beneath the current.

A spring creek is not a place for sloppy fishing. The water is clear enough to expose the smallest mistake. A bad cast sends ripples across the surface, and a fly that drags even slightly is instantly rejected. Insects hatch in reliable cycles, which means trout in these waters key in on specific food sources and won't take just anything.

Fishing a spring creek is a game of patience. A good cast

isn't enough—you need the perfect cast, with the right drift, at the exact moment trout are ready to feed. These are not fish that make mistakes. And neither can you.

I was knee-deep in a Wyoming spring creek, the kind of water that looks motionless but never stops moving. The morning fog still clung to the willows, the air smelled of damp earth, and the only sound was the occasional splash of a rising trout. There was one fish near an undercut bank, feeding on mayflies in a perfect rhythm. Every twelve seconds, it rose—like a machine, predictable, patient.

I watched it for nearly twenty minutes, tracking its pattern. My first cast? Refused. My second? Ignored. I checked my fly and saw my mistake—it was one size too big. Spring creek trout don't tolerate imperfections. I switched to a size 20 Blue-Winged Olive, adjusted my leader, and made one last cast. Drift. Pause. Rise.

The take was slow, deliberate. But the second I set the hook, the trout erupted, running downstream like it had been waiting for this moment all along. This wasn't just fishing. It was a test.

Freestone Rivers: The Wild Water

Freestone rivers are the opposite of spring creeks—born from melting snow, rainfall, and high mountain runoff. They swell in the spring, slow to a trickle in late summer, and shift constantly with the seasons. Their currents are strong, their paths unpredictable. The riverbed is a mix of smooth, rounded stones and jagged ledges, shifting with every flood.

Standing on the bank of a freestone river, you feel its power. The sound of rushing water drowns out everything else. Boulders the size of trucks sit stubbornly in the middle of the current, splitting the flow into seams and eddies. The air smells of pine and wet rock, and the river moves with an untamed energy that never quite settles.

Trout in freestone rivers don't have the luxury of feeding on one steady hatch. They're opportunistic. They eat when they can, what they can, and that makes them more aggressive—less likely to refuse a well-placed fly. A well-fed brown trout in a spring creek might ignore a fly that's slightly the wrong size. A hungry rainbow in a fast-moving freestone might hammer it without a second thought.

Fishing a freestone river is about movement. The current is stronger, the structure constantly changing. If you're not adjusting, covering water, and reading the flow, you're missing fish. Trout hold where they can find refuge—behind rocks, in seams, in deep pools where they can escape the relentless push of the river.

A spring creek is a game of patience. A freestone river? It's a war.

I was fishing a fast-moving stretch of the Madison River in Montana, high from the snowmelt, running cold and strong. This was big-water fishing—waist-deep wading, casting heavy flies into deep seams, battling both trout and current.

The moment my streamer hit the water, it vanished—something slammed it like a hammer. The brown trout that took my fly didn't just fight. It tried to break me. It ran straight into the whitewater, using every ounce of the river's strength. My reel screamed. My legs burned as I stumbled downstream, boots slipping over slick rocks.

This wasn't just fishing. This was survival.

When I finally pulled the trout into the shallows, my hands were shaking. It was thick, golden, a fish that had survived years of floods and long winters. I let it go, watching it disappear into the rapids, already looking for its next fight.

The Choice: Spring Creeks vs. Freestones

Some anglers thrive on the delicate art of spring creeks. Others need the raw power of freestone rivers. One rewards precision, the other aggression. One requires patience, the other persistence.

If you want a challenge that tests your skill, fish a spring creek. If you want a fight that tests your strength, fish a freestone river. Either way, you'll walk away a better angler.

And if you're lucky, you'll fish both in a single lifetime—learning that trout, like time, move at their own rhythm. It's up to us to adjust.

Where the Air is Thin and the Trout Are Wild

But some waters exist beyond spring creeks and freestones. Higher, wilder, untouched.

There's something about high-altitude waters that changes you. Maybe it's the thin air, the way it forces you to slow down, every breath a little more deliberate. Maybe it's the sheer remoteness—places where the trailhead is just the beginning, where the only way in is to earn it.

Or maybe it's the trout themselves, wilder and more brilliant than anything you'll find down below. The fish that survive here are built differently—tougher, more resourceful. And if you want to catch them, you have to be the same.

In the next chapter, we'll explore the secrets of high-elevation fishing—the alpine lakes that hold cutthroat trout like living jewels, the icy streams that run fast even in August, and what it takes to fish these waters right.

Because in these places, the thin air isn't the only thing that takes your breath away.

Chapter 28: High-Elevation Streams and Lakes

High-Altitude Waters: The Wildest Trout Fishing on Earth

There's something about high-altitude waters that changes you. Maybe it's the thin air, the way it forces you to slow down, every breath a little more deliberate. Maybe it's the sheer remoteness—places where the trailhead is just the beginning, where the only way in is to earn it. Or maybe it's the trout themselves, wilder and more brilliant than anything you'll find down below. The fish that survive here are built differently, tougher, more resourceful. And if you want to catch them, you have to be the same.

This is the world of high-elevation fishing, where the lakes hold cutthroat trout like living jewels, and the streams run fast and icy, even in August. These places aren't just difficult to reach—they demand effort, endurance, and respect. If you get there at the right time, when the ice has finally loosened its grip and the trout are feeding with urgency, you'll experience something that feels almost untouched by time.

The High Country: What Makes These Waters Special

Most trout streams are shaped by time and flow, but high-altitude waters are carved from something older—glaciers, tectonic shifts, the slow violence of mountains rising. These lakes and creeks exist where nothing should, perched on ridgelines or tucked into valleys so high that half the year they're locked under ice.

The water is ice-cold, rarely breaking 50 degrees even in summer, forcing trout to conserve energy and strike only when the opportunity is worth it. Their growing season is short—three, maybe four months at best—so they don't hesitate when food is available. The clarity of these waters is almost unnatural. Looking down, you can see twenty feet to the bottom, the stones sharp and clean, the trout suspended like ghosts in liquid glass.

Food is scarce. These lakes and streams aren't fertile like a lowland river, where caddis and stoneflies hatch in endless cycles. Up here, trout survive on midges, leeches, and whatever unlucky insect the wind carries in. A grasshopper that finds itself on the surface of an alpine lake is doomed, and the trout know it.

Fishing here demands more than skill. It requires endurance, patience, and an understanding that in these places, nature is in control.

Seasons in the High Country: When to Go

There's a window, and if you miss it, you're out of luck. Unlike lower-elevation rivers that fish year-round, high-elevation waters run on a strict seasonal clock.

Spring is a time of waiting. Even in May and June, ice still locks many lakes in place, and the streams that do flow are near-frozen torrents of runoff. If you try to fish them too early, you'll find nothing but silence.

Then, almost overnight, summer takes hold. By July and August, the ice has receded, the trout are awake, and the backcountry is alive. This is when the fishing is at its best—when the high-elevation bite is in full swing, and the fish are feeding aggressively.

Fall is the season most people forget about, but it's when the mountains are at their finest. The tourists are gone. The trout are fattening up for winter, their colors sharpening into deep golds and reds. The aspens are turning, their reflections shifting in the still water. It's the time for big fish, cold mornings, and rivers so empty it feels like you have them to yourself.

By winter, everything locks down again. The lakes disappear beneath snowdrifts taller than your truck, the creeks slow to a whisper under a layer of ice. The trout remain, motionless in the depths, waiting for another year.

The Challenge of High-Elevation Fishing

This isn't drive-up-and-fish country. The best high lakes demand effort. Eight miles, maybe ten, climbing through switchbacks with enough gear on your back to make you question every life decision. The thin air at 10,000 feet makes everything harder—your breath, your movements, even your casting. The water is clear enough that the trout can see you before you see them. Stealth isn't optional; it's survival.

The weather can betray you at any moment. A morning that starts with bright blue skies can turn into a thunderstorm in minutes. One second, you're casting into the calm; the next, you're sprinting for cover as lightning cracks over the ridgeline. Up here, nature doesn't negotiate.

The trout are different, too. They aren't seeing flies every day like a well-trafficked river down below, but that doesn't mean they're easy. They know their water. They won't waste energy chasing something that doesn't look right.

The Lake Above the Clouds

The first time I fished a lake above 11,000 feet, I almost didn't make it. Five miles straight uphill, legs screaming, lungs burning like I was breathing through a straw. The only thing keeping me moving was the promise of what lay ahead.

When I finally crested the last ridge, I saw it—a sapphire bowl cradled in rock and snow, so still it barely seemed real. The water was impossibly clear. From a hundred feet away, I could see the trout cruising, their shadows sliding over the stones below.

The first cast was too easy. A hopper pattern landed, a trout rose, and just like that, I was hooked up. But then the wind shifted, the fish grew wary, and the easy part was over. These weren't dumb stockers—they had survived long winters, short summers, and everything in between. They weren't going to be fooled twice.

I lengthened my leader. Switched to a smaller fly. Moved slower, crouching low, reading every ripple on the surface. It wasn't a battle of strength—it was a test of patience, of knowing when to wait and when to move.

When I finally landed that cutthroat, its gills flared red in the high-altitude sun, I knew the climb had been worth it. That's what high-elevation fishing is. It's not just about catching fish. It's about finding places that make you feel small, and in that smallness, discovering something bigger than yourself.

Tactics for High-Elevation Success

Fishing high-country lakes and streams isn't about gear—it's about approach. The water is clear, the fish are smart, and every move matters. Stealth is everything. Move slow, wear muted colors, and approach from an angle that keeps you hidden. High-altitude trout are used to small, delicate food sources. A size 10 mayfly might be ignored, but a size 18 parachute Adams will get crushed.

Overcasting is a mistake. The best fish are often right near the shore, holding in the shallows where the water warms first. Cast too far, and you'll miss them. In open alpine lakes, the wind is your friend and your enemy. Cast into the breeze, use its drift to your advantage, and adjust accordingly.

Most importantly, stay prepared. Bring extra layers, a rain shell, and enough food. The mountains don't care about your plans.

Final Thoughts

Some of the best trout fishing in the world isn't on a famous river or in a guidebook. It's up in the thin air, waiting for the anglers who are willing to go farther, push harder, and embrace the unknown.

You don't fish high-elevation waters for easy days or big numbers. You fish them because they remind you of something we all forget—that nature is bigger than us, that time moves slower up here, and that the best things in life aren't handed to you. They're earned.

So find a map, lace up your boots, and start climbing. The trout are waiting.

Finding Wildness Where No One Expects It

But not all great trout waters exist in remote, untamed places. Some are hiding in plain sight—tucked between highways and high-rises, winding through the sprawl of human ambition.

Most people don't think of trout when they think of cities. They think of traffic, skyscrapers, the hum of industry. But in some of those rivers, flowing through the shadows of overpasses and beneath neon reflections, there are trout.

Urban trout fishing isn't about escape—it's about adaptation.

In the next chapter, we'll explore the overlooked world of urban trout waters—the rivers that snake through our cities, the fish that call them home, and the anglers who refuse to let concrete define their boundaries. Because wildness isn't just out there in the mountains. Sometimes, it's right in the heart of the city.

Chapter 29: Urban Trout Waters

Trout in the City: Finding Wildness Where You Least Expect It

Urban trout fishing is about adaptation. It's about finding beauty where most people don't even bother looking. It's about standing beneath a freeway overpass, roll casting into a riffle, and watching a wild brown trout rise between reflections of neon billboards. It's about learning that nature doesn't need vast wilderness to survive—it just needs water.

These are the overlooked rivers, the ones that snake through our cities, carrying fish that exist in the margins, thriving in a world that barely notices them. The anglers who chase them aren't just fishing; they're reclaiming something—a sense of wildness hidden in plain sight.

The Urban River: A Different Kind of Trout Water

Urban trout rivers aren't pristine. They don't have the postcard appeal of high-mountain streams or spring-fed creeks. But they have something else—resilience. These rivers have been dammed, diverted, polluted, cleaned up, and reclaimed. And still, against all odds, the trout remain.

Fishing these waters means adapting to an ecosystem that's part wild, part engineered, and entirely unpredictable. The currents don't always follow the logic of a natural river. Many urban waters are controlled by dams and flood channels, their flow dictated by unseen hands rather than the slow rhythms of nature. A perfectly fishable run in the morning can be a roaring torrent by afternoon, depending on what buttons get pushed upstream.

Trout here aren't just feeding on mayflies and caddis—they've learned to take advantage of whatever drifts their way. A grasshopper blown in from a park, a baitfish washed out from a storm drain, even the occasional cigarette butt gets a curious inspection. They're survivors, opportunists, thriving in places that shouldn't hold fish at all.

Water quality is a gamble. One day, the river is clear, running cool and perfect. The next, a hard rain turns it into something resembling chocolate milk, a flood of runoff carrying everything the city has washed down its gutters. The fish adjust. They always do. And the ones that make it through grow smarter, harder to fool.

The Challenge of Urban Trout Fishing

Fishing for trout in a city is a different game. Out in the wilderness, the biggest challenge is reading the water and finding the fish. In an urban setting, the challenges multiply.

There's pressure from more than just other anglers. These fish aren't just dodging fly fishermen—they're avoiding kids skipping rocks, dogs splashing through riffles, and joggers tossing breadcrumbs from bridges. Finding access can feel like a puzzle, navigating public land laws, private property lines, and the occasional underpass that makes you question whether this fishing spot is worth the risk.

Then there's the noise. Instead of the peaceful sounds of a remote stream, you get sirens, honking horns, and the occasional blast of music from a passing car. But if you can tune out the distractions, there's magic to be found.

The Bridge Brown

I was waist-deep in a river that ran straight through a downtown district. On one side, there was a line of parked cars and a row of coffee shops. On the other, an old factory with busted-out windows, its bricks worn from decades of neglect. This wasn't exactly the untouched wilderness I was used to.

Then I saw it—a flash beneath the surface, holding in a seam near a bridge pylon. A trout.

I made the cast, a tight loop beneath the overpass, dodging a half-submerged shopping cart on the backcast. The drift was clean. The take was subtle. And when I set the hook, that brown fought like hell, running straight toward the deepest part of the channel. For a few moments, nothing else existed. Not the city, not the noise—just me, the rod, and the fish.

I landed it, a 16-inch brown, golden and speckled like something pulled straight from the most remote backcountry stream. I released it back into the urban current, watching it disappear beneath the shadows of a world that barely knew it was there.

That's the thing about urban trout waters. They don't need your approval. They survive whether you notice them or not.

Best Tactics for Urban Trout Fishing

Fishing an urban river means adjusting your approach. These trout are wired differently. They've learned to navigate a world of unpredictability, so your tactics have to evolve.

Stealth is key, even in a loud world. You'd think noise wouldn't matter in a city, but these fish are hyper-aware of movement. Approach low, avoid sudden motions, and keep your casts smooth. The best urban trout are often caught by those who know how to disappear into the background.

Flies don't have to follow the traditional rules. Standard patterns work, but don't be afraid to get creative. A sunken ant pattern, a tiny black leech, or even a beadhead worm can outfish traditional dries and nymphs. These trout aren't just eating insects—they're eating what survives in a city.

Timing is everything. Early morning and late evening are the sweet spots. During the day, foot traffic and noise push fish into hiding, making them nearly impossible to catch. But when the city quiets down, the river comes to life.

Some of the best trout hold in places that don't look fishy at all. A neglected stretch of water beneath an abandoned bridge, a deep cut beside a storm drain—these are the places that get overlooked, and that's exactly why the biggest fish hold there.

Adaptability is survival. After rain, urban rivers often blow out with runoff. Fish the edges, look for clearing seams, and wait for the window when trout start feeding again.

The Ethics of Urban Fishing

Just because you're fishing in a city doesn't mean you should treat it any differently. If anything, these waters need more respect. They're fragile, constantly under threat from pollution, development, and overuse. The people fishing them are often the only ones who notice when something goes wrong.

Pack out more than you bring in. If you see trash, pick it up. These rivers already fight an uphill battle, and every little bit helps.

Handle fish with care. These trout already have it rough. Barbless hooks, wet hands, and quick releases make a difference.

Be aware of your surroundings. Know local laws, respect private property, and be mindful of the people around you. The last thing urban fishing needs is more reasons for access to disappear.

Finding Wildness Where You Least Expect It

Some anglers scoff at urban trout waters. They want the

solitude of the mountains, the purity of backcountry streams. But wildness isn't just found in places untouched by man. Sometimes, it fights its way into the spaces we least expect.

The next time you drive over a river on your morning commute, take a second look. Watch the water. Watch for a rise. Because somewhere down there, beneath the reflection of skyscrapers and streetlights, a trout is holding in the current, waiting for the perfect drift.

And if you're lucky enough to meet that fish on its terms, you'll understand: wildness isn't a place. It's a mindset.

The Hidden Blue Lines That Lead to Untouched Waters

But what if you didn't just find trout in places where others overlooked them? What if you went looking for waters no one else even knew existed? The best trout streams aren't always the ones you read about. The rivers with the fly shop reports, the ones with parking lots full of SUVs and drift boats—they have their place, but they aren't the end of the story.

Real trout water is discovered, not given. It's the blue lines on a topo map, the unnamed streams that trickle down from nowhere, the forgotten waters where the fish haven't seen a fly in years.

In the next chapter, we'll break down how to find those places—the art of reading maps, following the signs, and uncovering trout streams that others overlook. Because the best waters—the ones that stay with you—are the ones you earn.

Chapter 30: The Blue Lines on the Map

The Best Waters Are the Ones You Earn

The best trout streams aren't always the ones you read about. The crowded rivers with the fly shop reports, the ones where SUVs and drift boats fill the parking lots—they have their place. But they aren't the real story. The best waters are the hidden ones, the ones you have to discover for yourself. The thin blue lines on a topo map, the unnamed streams that trickle from nowhere, the forgotten waters where fish haven't seen a fly in years.

Finding those places isn't about luck. It's about knowing

how to read the map, follow the clues, and recognize the waters that others overlook. The best streams don't come with signs or brochures. They don't tell you where to park or which run holds the biggest fish. They are places you earn—step by step, mile by mile, cast by cast.

The Search for Hidden Water

Most anglers fish where they're told to fish. They follow reports, head to the well-known access points, wade into water that's been cast over a thousand times before. There's nothing wrong with that. But the best stories—the ones that stay with you—don't happen in places with worn-out footpaths and parking lots full of drift boats. They happen when you push past the obvious, when you go searching for water that doesn't come with a guarantee.

Hidden trout streams aren't always in the middle of nowhere. Some are tucked away just beyond popular rivers, overlooked because they're smaller, harder to access, or require a little extra effort to reach. Sometimes, the best water is just a few bends upstream from where everyone else stops fishing. Sometimes, it's miles deep in a canyon where only the most determined anglers go.

How to Read the Water Before You Ever See It

A good angler doesn't wait until he's on the water to start fishing. He's already been fishing—in his head, on the map, in the details no one else notices.

It starts with maps. Old topo maps, satellite images, and USGS stream data hold more secrets than any guidebook ever could. Thin blue lines that snake through valleys, tucked beneath ridgelines, winding away from roads—those are the streams worth chasing. Elevation is everything. Trout need cold water, and the higher you go, the better your chances of finding a stream that runs cold year-round.

Tributaries hold secrets of their own. That big, famous river might be crowded, but what about the tiny creek feeding into it five miles upstream? If it has enough flow, if the water stays cold, it could be holding wild fish that see more bears than fly rods.

And when in doubt, look for obstacles. A waterfall, a steep canyon, private land that forces a workaround—anything that makes a stretch of water harder to reach makes it more likely to be filled with unpressured trout.

The best way to find fish is to understand what a trout needs. A stream that drops too fast won't hold them; they need pockets, pools, places to rest. Too flat, and the water warms up, losing oxygen. The sweet spot is in between—a series of riffles and deep runs, shaded by thick forest or carved through rock. Trees mean shade, shade means cold water, cold water means trout. And if a stream has a spring feeding into it, mark it down. Springs are nature's air conditioners, keeping temperatures stable even in the heat of summer.

The Stream with No Name

The first time I fished a truly forgotten stream, I found it on a map. A thin blue line, twisting through a canyon—no name, no trails, just a theory that it might hold fish. I had no way of knowing until I got there.

The hike was brutal—no marked trail, just fallen trees and switchbacks steep enough to make my legs burn. But when I finally reached the stream, it was clear as glass, barely more than a trickle weaving through the rocks. I scanned the water, wondering if I'd made the trip for nothing. Then I saw it. A flash in the tailout of a pool, a trout holding in the shadows.

The first cast was off. The second landed where I wanted, a short drift through the seam. And just like that—bam. The fish hit like it had never seen a fly before. Maybe it hadn't. A wild brookie, barely eight inches, but perfect in every way. The kind of fish that makes you feel like the first person to ever step into that water.

That's the magic of finding your own stream. It's not just about the fish—it's about the discovery, the moment when the unknown turns into something real.

The Tools of Exploration

Finding undiscovered trout water takes more than a fly rod. It takes a willingness to put in the miles, to go where others don't, to trade easy access for the kind of fishing that feels like exploration.

Maps and GPS are your best friends. Cell service won't help when you're miles deep in the woods, so downloading offline maps is a must. USGS streamflow data can tell you whether a blue line actually holds water or if it dries up in the summer. And packing light makes a difference. A small rod, a handful of flies, a good pair of boots—you don't need much, just enough to fish hard and cover ground.

But more than anything, you need a sense of adventure. The best trout streams don't come easy. You'll climb over logs, wade through thick brush, hike farther than you planned. But at the end of the trail, when you step into water that no one else has touched, it'll all be worth it.

Why It Matters

There's a difference between catching trout and discovering them. One is easy, the other is an art. Anyone can fish a famous river, follow a guide, stand in a well-known run where countless anglers have hooked trout before. But finding your own water? That's different. That's exploration. That's stepping into a story no one else has told.

That's why we do it. Because out there, beyond the highways and the crowded rivers, there's a thin blue line on a map—waiting for someone willing to put in the effort to find it.

The Rivers That Have Already Been Found

But what about the rivers that have already been discovered? The legendary waters—the blue ribbon streams—where anglers have fished for generations?

Some would say those rivers have been fished out, that their magic is gone. But the truth is, every river holds its own mystery, its own lessons. A river doesn't stop being great just because people know about it. What matters is how you approach it, how you fish it, and whether you can make it feel like your own, even if you're not the first to stand in its current.

In the next chapter, we'll explore what makes a river "blue ribbon"—and why, at its core, the best stream is always the one that calls to you.

Chapter 31: 50 Blue Ribbon Streams

The best trout streams aren't always the ones you read about. The rivers with the fly shop reports, the ones with parking lots full of SUVs and drift boats—they have their place, but they aren't the end of the story. Real trout water is discovered, not given. It's the blue lines on a topo map, the unnamed streams that trickle down from nowhere, the forgotten waters where the fish haven't seen a fly in years.

This is about how to find those places. The art of reading maps, following the signs, and uncovering trout streams that others overlook. Because the best waters—the ones that stay with you—are the ones you earn.

What Makes a Stream "Blue Ribbon"?

A blue ribbon trout stream isn't just about great fishing—it's about conditions that meet the highest standards for water quality, habitat, and trout populations. These streams are home to wild trout, thriving naturally, and often come with the best opportunities in the country. What makes a stream blue ribbon?

High water quality – Cold, oxygen-rich water keeps trout populations healthy.

Strong natural reproduction – These streams sustain wild trout without needing stocking.

Diverse aquatic life – A robust ecosystem, from insects to forage fish.

Public access and conservation efforts – Many are protected and sustainably managed.

50 Legendary Blue Ribbon Streams

While there are countless great trout streams in the U.S. and beyond, here are 50 of the most revered blue ribbon waters and included those with year-round fishing.

Western U.S.

Madison River (MT) – Year-round

Henry's Fork of the Snake (ID) – Year-round

Green River (UT) – Year-round
Yellowstone River (MT)
Big Hole River (MT)
Gallatin River (MT) – Year-round
Missouri River (MT) – Year-round
Deschutes River (OR) – Year-round
Metolius River (OR) – Year-round
Truckee River (CA/NV) – Year-round
San Juan River (NM) – Year-round
South Platte River (CO) – Year-round
Fryingpan River (CO) – Year-round
Arkansas River (CO)
North Platte River (WY) – Year-round
Bighorn River (MT/WY) – Year-round
Beaverhead River (MT) – Year-round
Silver Creek (ID)
Big Wood River (ID)
Yakima River (WA) – Year-round
Snake River (WY/ID/OR/WA)
Midwest & Great Lakes
Au Sable River (MI)
Pere Marquette River (MI)
Brule River (WI) – Year-round
Bois Brule River (WI)
Driftless Area Spring Creeks (WI/MN/IA) – Year-round
White River (AR) – Year-round
Little Red River (AR) – Year-round
Northeast U.S.
Delaware River (NY/PA) – Year-round

Beaverkill River (NY)

Esopus Creek (NY)

West Branch of the Ausable (NY)

Housatonic River (CT/MA) – Year-round

Battenkill River (NY/VT)

Androscoggin River (NH/ME)

Rapid River (ME)

Kennebec River (ME)

Farmington River (CT) – Year-round

Southeast & Appalachians

South Holston River (TN) – Year-round

Watauga River (TN) – Year-round

Davidson River (NC) – Year-round

Nantahala River (NC) – Year-round

Toccoa River (GA)

Chattooga River (SC/GA)

Gunpowder Falls (MD)

Jackson River (VA)

Rockies & Southwest

Rio Grande River (CO/NM/TX)

Animas River (CO)

Cimarron River (NM)

Eagle River (CO) – Year-round

San Miguel River (CO)

Why Every Stream Is Special

It's easy to get caught up in the idea of chasing fish on legendary waters. But the truth is that every stream has its story to tell. A small, hidden creek teeming with wild brook trout can be just as rewarding as the most famous blue ribbon river.

A trout doesn't know whether it's swimming in the Madison or a nameless trickle deep in the woods. It only knows cold, clean water and the rhythms of the current. The beauty of fly fishing is found in more than the destination. It's about the experience, the solitude, and the connection to nature.

Your Own "Blue Ribbon" Stream

Some of the best fishing experiences happen not on famous rivers, but in the waters you discover on your own. Whether it's a backyard creek, a remote mountain stream, or a small tailwater that's never been written about, your blue ribbon stream is the one where you make memories.

So, while this list may inspire travel plans, don't overlook the waters closest to you. The real magic of trout fishing isn't just in where you go—it's in the moments you create along the way.

A Change in Plans That Became One of the Best Days

I remember reading about an angler who had a long-anticipated guide trip booked on the Madison River in Montana. The forecast had called for rain, but what he got was a full-blown storm, making the river unfishable. Instead of canceling, his guide suggested heading to a smaller, lesser-known creek nearby—Odell Creek, a spring-fed stream that doesn't get nearly as much attention but holds its own treasure trove of wild trout.

What followed was an unforgettable day. The drive to Odell Creek was rugged—an unmarked gravel road leading deep into a valley surrounded by tall pines. The stream was crystal-clear, with boulders the size of small cars creating deep pockets of slow-moving pools. An eagle watched their every move from a dead tree along the bank, and the fast-moving water created a constant, soothing hum.

The stream was tight, casting tricky, but the trout—oh, the trout—were everywhere. They caught and released over 20 wild fish, each as beautiful and aggressive as the last. It was a reminder that while blue ribbon waters get all the fame, the lesser-known creeks can hold just as much magic. Sometimes, the best fishing happens when you embrace the unexpected.

Beyond the Famous Waters—Discovering Hidden Gems

But what about the streams that never make the lists? The ones that don't have famous reputations but hold just as much magic?

The best trout waters aren't always the ones you read about in magazines or see splashed across social media. While places like the Madison River, the Henry's Fork, or the Green River have rightfully earned their reputations, there exists a different category of streams—ones that offer solitude, untouched beauty, and trout that have rarely seen a fly.

These underrated trout streams provide some of the most rewarding fishing experiences an angler can have. If you're willing to go off the beaten path, embrace a little adventure, and trade crowds for quiet water, these hidden gems might just become your favorite places to fish.

Chapter 32: The Underrated Trout Streams

The big-name rivers may hold trophy trout, but they also hold something else—crowds, pressure, and often fish so educated they inspect every drift like a food critic. While those rivers still have value, the underrated streams offer something different. They hold trout that haven't seen every fly in existence, stretches of water where you won't see another angler all day, and the sense of true exploration that defines the best fishing memories.

Less fishing pressure means the trout are more willing to take a well-presented fly. They aren't dodging dozens of casts an hour, so they react instinctively rather than with suspicion. The landscapes around these waters remain wild, untouched by heavy foot traffic, offering a sense of peace that's hard to find on a well-known tailwater. These streams don't always hold record-breaking fish, but they make up for it in their natural beauty and the way they connect you to the rhythm of moving water.

The Best Water Isn't Always in the Guidebooks

I learned this the hard way. A few years ago, I made a pilgrimage to a legendary river out West, the kind of place that gets written about in poetic essays, where even the gas station attendants talk about hatch cycles. I arrived with high expectations and a head full of stories about 22-inch browns rising to size 18 dry flies.

What I found instead was a parking lot packed tighter than a Walmart on Black Friday, and a river that felt more like a theme park. Drift boats lined up in parade formation, guides barking at clients to mend, and trout that rose only to inspect flies like a sommelier sniffing a questionable bottle of wine. I caught fish, but it felt more like winning a raffle than an earned success.

A few days later, on a whim, I pulled off a dirt road and found myself standing beside a nameless creek that barely warranted a blue line on the map. It was small, tight, full of overhanging brush, and not a soul in sight. My first cast hooked a wild brown that fought harder than any fish I'd caught all week. I spent the afternoon crawling through underbrush, casting under low-hanging branches, and catching trout that had likely never seen a fly before.

It was, in every way, a better experience than the famous river. That's when it clicked—the best water isn't always the most talked about.

What Makes a Trout Stream Underrated?

Some streams remain underrated because they lack hype, others because they require work. The best ones usually fall into both categories.

Streams that require effort—whether it's a hike, a bushwhack, or a boat ride—often see fewer anglers. If a stream doesn't have an easy pull-off and a well-worn trail leading straight to the best runs, chances are it doesn't get fished much. Lack of name recognition also plays a role. Some rivers just don't have the marketing behind them, and because they don't make the cover of fly fishing magazines, they slip under the radar.

The fish in these waters are different too. They're wild, but not overly educated. While big-name rivers create big-brained trout—fish that have PhDs in artificial fly rejection—lesser-known streams hold trout that simply eat when something looks right. It's not that they're dumb; it's that they haven't spent their lives dodging bad drifts and split-shot splashes.

The Best Stream I Almost Drove Past

A few years back, I was headed to a well-known river in the Appalachians. The plan was simple: get there early, stake out a prime run, and spend the day fishing classic dry-dropper setups. Along the way, I crossed a tiny creek barely wider than a sidewalk. It wasn't in my plan. It wasn't in any of the books I'd read. Hell, I wasn't even sure if it held trout.

I kept driving.

But something nagged at me. After seeing more anglers than trout on the "big-name" river, I turned around.

I pulled over at the creek, rigged up a three-weight, and stepped into water so clear it felt like fishing in a pane of glass. The first cast produced a hit. The second, another. In the next two hours, I caught three beauties between seven and ten inches, all aggressive and stunningly colored. And best of all, I had the place to myself.

That little creek taught me a lesson. Just because a river isn't famous doesn't mean it isn't worth fishing.

Why You Should Seek Out Underrated Waters

The beauty of fly fishing isn't just in the fish—it's in the pursuit, the exploration. The idea that somewhere, beyond the crowds and the well-worn paths, there's a piece of water that's been waiting for you all along.

Underrated trout streams offer something no blue-ribbon tailwater ever will: the chance to feel like you've discovered something. The next time you're scrolling through fishing reports or planning a trip, don't just follow the crowds. Pull up a map, look for the blue lines nobody talks about, and take a risk.

Because the best trout water isn't always the most famous. Sometimes, it's just the water that nobody else thought to fish.

The Joy of the Undiscovered

There's something primal about finding your own secret stretch of water. The solitude, the untouched pools, the chance to connect with nature on your own terms—it's the antidote to crowded tailwaters and overfished rivers. While famous rivers will always draw crowds, it's the hidden streams, whispered about among dedicated anglers, that often hold the greatest memories.

So go explore. Find that thin blue line on the map. Hike in, wade through, and cast into the unknown. You might just find your new favorite trout stream in the most unexpected place.

The Source of It All

What makes these streams special? Why do some waters hold trout year-round while others dry up in the summer heat?

The answer lies beneath the surface. Beyond what the eye can see, a hidden world of underground springs fuels the greatest trout waters on earth. These unseen arteries of cold, oxygen-rich water are the lifelines of wild trout streams. Without them, even the most picturesque rivers would be mere seasonal trickles—

incapable of sustaining the fish we chase.

In the next chapter, we'll explore the underground springs that breathe life into trout water, shaping the rivers we love and the fish that call them home.

Chapter 33: The Hidden Power of Underground Springs

Beneath the surface, beyond what the eye can see, a secret world of underground springs fuels the greatest trout waters on earth. These unseen arteries pump cold, oxygen-rich water into rivers, feeding them with life. Without them, even the most picturesque streams would be mere seasonal trickles, incapable of sustaining the wild trout we chase.

The Hidden Origins of Great Trout Streams

Many of the best trout rivers in the world do not begin as snowmelt or surface runoff but as something far older, deeper—born from limestone aquifers and underground reservoirs. These subterranean rivers snake through the earth, carving passageways through rock over thousands of years before emerging in clear, steady flows that shape the waterways above.

Some of the most legendary trout streams owe their existence to these unseen forces. The Missouri River in Montana is fed by countless underground springs, keeping its water cold and stable year-round. Silver Creek in Idaho is another famous spring-fed stream, known for its crystal-clear water and large, wary brown trout. Then there's Penns Creek in Pennsylvania, a limestone stream that stays cool even in the heat of summer, thanks to hidden springs along its course.

How Springs Shape a River

The presence of underground springs transforms an ordinary creek into a world-class fishery. Unlike rivers that rely on rainfall or snowmelt, spring-fed streams are far more stable. They do not flood as violently, nor do they dry up in the heat of summer. They maintain an almost perfect balance—cool in summer, unfrozen in winter, oxygen-rich, and full of insect life.

The water that bubbles up from underground is often filtered through layers of rock and sediment, making it exceptionally clear. This is why so many spring-fed streams have remarkable water clarity, allowing anglers to spot fish and observe their movements in ways not possible in murkier, runoff-driven waters.

The Coldwater Advantage

Trout are coldwater fish, requiring temperatures between 45°F and 65°F to thrive. Warmer water holds less oxygen, and once temperatures creep past 70°F, trout begin to stress. Past 75°F, they struggle to survive. This is where springs become essential.

Even in the peak of summer, a healthy spring-fed stream remains cold and inviting to trout. A single large spring can release millions of gallons of 50°F water per day, creating a thermal refuge for fish. These cold pockets act like hidden sanctuaries, allowing trout to survive in otherwise inhospitable conditions.

Famous Springs That Feed Trout Waters

The Great Smoky Mountains are home to numerous hidden springs that feed some of the finest trout waters in the Southeast. These underground flows provide a lifeline to legendary rivers such as:

Little River – A classic Smokies trout stream, kept cold year-round by a network of underground springs flowing through its upper reaches.

Abrams Creek – Known for its steady flow and excellent trout population, fed by a mix of seeps and limestone springs.

Deep Creek – One of the clearest and most productive streams in the park, thanks to the cold, mineral-rich water emerging from subterranean sources.

Beyond the Smokies, some of the greatest trout streams in the U.S. are fed by remarkable springs, each with its own story:

Some of the greatest trout streams in the U.S. are fed by remarkable springs, each with its own story:

Big Spring, Missouri – One of the largest in the world, pumping out 286 million gallons of water per day. Its icy flow feeds the Current River, an incredible trout fishery.

Silver Creek, Idaho – A pristine, spring-fed stream known for its glass-clear water and massive brown trout.

Oquaga Creek, New York – Feeds the legendary Delaware River, keeping its East Branch cold and rich with insect life.

Penns Creek, Pennsylvania – A limestone spring system that creates one of the most fertile trout streams in the East.

How Long Does Water Stay Underground?

Spring water does not appear overnight. The water emerging today fell as rain decades, sometimes centuries, ago. Depending on the geology of the region, water may spend anywhere from 10 to 10,000 years beneath the surface, slowly traveling through porous limestone, basalt, or sandstone before reemerging.

This long filtration process removes impurities and stabilizes mineral content, making the water exceptionally clean and chemically balanced—perfect for sustaining aquatic life.

The Impact on Aquatic Life

Beyond trout, underground springs provide stable conditions for entire ecosystems. Mayflies, caddisflies, stoneflies—all essential food sources for trout—thrive in the constant temperatures of spring-fed streams. The cold, mineral-rich water fosters healthy aquatic vegetation, creating oxygen and providing shelter for juvenile fish.

Spring-Fed Streams: A Refuge in a Changing Climate

As climate changes from dry to wet to dry back to wet it threatens many coldwater fisheries, spring-fed streams are becoming more vital than ever. Rivers that rely solely on snowmelt are experiencing shorter runoff periods, increased droughts, and dangerously high summer temperatures. But spring-fed streams? They remain stable, offering a future for wild trout in an uncertain world.

Finding the Hidden Springs

While some springs are obvious, bubbling up in large pools or forming natural seeps along a riverbank, many remain hidden. Experienced anglers know to look for key signs:

Sudden temperature changes – If you step into noticeably colder water in the middle of a stream, you've likely found an underground spring.

Increased vegetation – The constant temperature of spring-fed areas often fosters lush aquatic plant life.

Fog or mist in winter – The relatively warm water of a spring can create visible mist above the surface.

Unfrozen pockets in winter – If a section of a river stays ice-free while the rest freezes, a spring is likely feeding it.

Why Anglers Should Care

Understanding the role of springs is more than just trivia—it's a key to finding the best fishing spots. Trout are drawn to these areas, not just for the cold water but for the abundance of food and protection they provide. The next time you're on the water, take a moment to appreciate the unseen forces shaping the river. The springs may be hidden, but their impact is everywhere.

Final Thought: The Lifeblood of the River

Trout anglers love to talk about hatches, fly selection, and perfect drifts. But the truth is, none of it would matter without the springs. These silent, unseen forces shape the rivers, sustain the fish, and give us the waters we hold dear. They are the lifeblood of the trout stream—the force beneath the surface that keeps it all alive.

The Influence of Current and Flow on Trout Behavior

Trout are creatures of moving water. Unlike stillwater species, they rely on the river's flow not just for oxygen and sustenance but for their entire way of life. Understanding how current affects trout behavior, feeding patterns, and holding positions is key to becoming a better fly angler. Water isn't just a place where they live—it's a force they interact with constantly, adjusting to its speed, depth, and rhythm.

The Current's Influence

Current dictates everything in a trout's world. It determines where they hold, how they feed, and when they move. A fast-moving river creates different challenges and opportunities than a slow meandering stream. A trout in a tailwater behaves differently from one in a freestone river. The more you understand these dynamics, the better your ability to find and catch fish.

Holding Water: Where Trout Rest and Feed

Trout don't waste energy fighting unnecessary currents. They position themselves where they can maximize food intake while minimizing effort. These prime holding spots include:

Eddy Lines – Areas where the current slows down behind a rock or bend, creating a swirling effect. Trout love these spots because they offer a break from the current while funneling food directly to them.

Seams – The meeting point of fast and slow water. These are prime feeding lanes, where trout can sit in the slack water while watching for food drifting by in the faster current.

Pools and Deep Runs – Deeper areas offer security and consistent food. Big trout, especially, tend to settle here when they're not actively feeding.

Undercut Banks – A perfect refuge from fast water and predators. Trout tucked under banks often ambush food drifting by.

Fast Water vs. Slow Water

Not all current is created equal. Trout behave differently depending on water speed and structure.

Fast Water (Riffles, Rapids, and Pocket Water)

High oxygenation means trout can be active and aggressive.

They hold in pockets behind rocks or in seams where the current breaks.

Dry flies and emergers are more effective here, as insects struggle on the surface.

Slow Water (Glides, Pools, and Tailouts)

More cautious, selective trout live here, especially in clear water.

They often inspect flies more thoroughly before taking them.

Nymphing and subtle dry fly presentations work best.

How Flow Affects Feeding

Trout are opportunistic feeders, but they won't burn more energy than they consume. The speed of the current dictates how they eat:

Slow current = Trout rise slowly, inspect food longer, and are more selective.

Moderate current = The sweet spot—trout see a natural drift but must make quicker decisions.

Fast current = Quick reaction feeding—if it looks remotely like food, they take it.

Understanding this lets you match your presentation. If you're in slow water, a perfect drift is crucial. In fast water, a slightly imperfect drift is more forgivable because trout have to react quickly.

Depth and Its Role in Current Strength

Current strength changes at different depths:

Surface water moves faster than bottom currents due to air friction.

Trout hold lower in the water column to avoid fighting unnecessary current.

Weighted nymphs and streamers that get down to trout level increase success rates in deep or fast-moving rivers.

The Impact of Seasonal Flow Changes

Current isn't static. It changes with the seasons, and trout adjust accordingly:

Spring Runoff – High, fast water pushes trout to the edges where current is weaker.

Summer Low Water – Trout move to deeper pools and undercut banks for cooler, oxygen-rich water.

Fall Transitions – Trout move to prime feeding lanes to bulk up before winter.

Winter Holding – Cold water slows trout metabolism; they seek deep, slow-moving pools to conserve energy.

How to Read Current Like a Pro

Every angler should develop an instinct for reading water. Here's how:

Watch the surface movement – Ripples indicate rocks underneath, while calm water signals deeper pools.

Look for seams – If you see two different speeds of water meeting, that's a prime feeding lane.

Identify slow-water refuges – Find the spots where trout can rest while food still drifts by.

Watch for rises – A trout rising in slow water is behaving differently from one rising in fast current. Adjust your approach accordingly.

Using Indicators in Fast-Moving Water

Fishing in fast water comes with its own set of challenges, especially when drifting nymphs or other subsurface flies. The speed of the current makes it difficult to see subtle takes, and if you wait until you feel the fish, you're already too late. This is where strike indicators come in.

Brightly colored indicators (such as foam, yarn, or air-lock styles) help track your drift and give you a visual cue when a trout takes your fly.

Subtle twitches, slight hesitations, or unnatural movements in the indicator signal a bite. If your indicator suddenly stops, moves sideways, or dips under—set the hook.

Adjust your indicator depth based on water conditions. In faster water, setting it higher allows your fly to get down quickly. In slower water, adjusting it lower keeps your presentation natural.

Use small micro-movements. Instead of waiting for a dramatic pull, set the hook at the first sign of hesitation. Many trout take and eject nymphs in less than a second—if you hesitate, you lose the fish.

Using an indicator effectively in fast water requires practice, but once mastered, it significantly improves your catch rate. Watching your indicator with the same intensity as a dry fly can make all the difference.

Adjusting Your Approach Based on Current

For fast water, use heavier flies, weighted nymphs, or

streamers to cut through the current.

For slow water, use delicate presentations—long leaders, lighter tippet, and careful drifts.

For seams and eddies, fish the transition zone, where trout are waiting for food but conserving energy.

The River Never Stays the Same

A river is a living, breathing thing. Its currents shift, its flows change, and the trout within it constantly adjust. As anglers, our job isn't just to cast a fly—it's to read the water, understand the movement, and adapt.

Mastering the influence of current on trout behavior is what separates those who hope for luck from those who consistently catch fish.

(And if you ever get frustrated with tricky currents, just remember—trout have spent their whole lives in this water. You? You've been here for an afternoon.)

But What About the Bigger Picture?

Trout don't just respond to the current of the moment—they respond to the seasons, the temperature shifts, and the ever-changing moods of the river itself.

In the next chapter, we'll break down how each season shapes trout behavior—so you can stop guessing and start fishing with the river, not against it.

Chapter 34: Trout, Seasons, and the Unpredictable Mood Swings of the River

Reading the Water Through the Seasons

If you fish long enough, you start to realize something: trout don't live by your schedule—they live by nature's. What works one day won't work the next, and if you don't learn to read the river in all its moods, you'll spend a lot of time wondering why the fish aren't biting.

Trout fishing demands more than choosing the right fly or making the perfect cast; it's about understanding how the seasons change the game. A trout in July isn't the same as a trout in October. The water changes, the hatches change, and the fish respond in ways that can either make you look like a genius or leave you talking to yourself on the walk back to the truck.

Spring: The Wake-Up Call

Spring is when the river comes back to life. Snowmelt surges down from the mountains, swelling streams and making them run high and fast. Trout, sluggish from winter, start feeding aggressively, eager to make up for lost time. The big hatches begin—blue-winged olives, hendricksons, caddis—and the fish know it.

The Challenge? High water and unpredictable conditions. Wading can go from "pleasantly refreshing" to "why am I suddenly floating downstream?" in seconds. The key to spring fishing is finding the edges—seams where trout can hold without fighting the full force of the current.

One spring, I found myself on a river that looked more like a flooded freeway than a trout stream. But I was stubborn. I picked a promising-looking seam near the bank, tied on a big stonefly nymph, and within minutes, I hooked into a monster. This was the kind of fish that makes your heart jump—strong, heavy, running like it had somewhere important to be.

And then the river took it.

One second I had control, the next I was watching my line rip through the current like a runaway freight train. I never saw that trout. Never even got close. But I learned something: in spring, the river always has the final say.

Summer: The Heat Brings the Hunt

Summer changes everything. Water levels drop, currents slow, and trout get selective. It's no longer about aggression—it's about efficiency. They seek out deeper pools, undercut banks, and oxygen-rich riffles where they don't have to waste energy.

Dry fly season peaks here—hoppers, ants, beetles, PMDs—but timing is everything. Midday heat slows everything down, so the best fishing happens early in the morning or just before dark.

One July afternoon, I made the mistake of fishing under a blazing sun. I threw dry flies at lingering trout, confident in my ability to outsmart them. They didn't even flinch.

Then I noticed something. Every fish in the pool was sitting motionless. It was like they were taking a midday siesta. I waited. And waited. As the sun dipped, I threw the same fly again—and just like that, they all disappeared.

Lesson learned: Summer trout are like good barbecue—low in the water, slow in their movements.

Fall: When Trout Get Greedy

If summer is about patience, fall is about opportunity. The air cools, the water refreshes, and trout sense that winter is coming. Browns start gearing up for the spawn, getting territorial and aggressive. This is when you throw big streamers and expect big takes.

Mayflies still hatch, but terrestrials fade. The fishing is technical, but the payoff is huge—fall produces some of the biggest trout of the year.

Winter: The Slow Game

Winter is when the river goes quiet. The hatches slow, the fish slow, and if you're willing to brave the cold, you'll find solitude like no other time of year. Trout move into deeper pools, feeding on small nymphs and midges, conserving energy until spring returns.

The challenge? Cold hands, frozen guides, and the fact that most people consider you insane for even being out there.

One winter, I decided to test my patience. Armed with a tiny midge nymph, I fished a deep, slow pool. It took me over an hour to hook my first fish—a small rainbow that fought harder than its size should have allowed.

By the time I landed it, my fingers were so numb I could barely unhook it. But I'll tell you what—it was one of the most satisfying fish I've ever caught.

The Key to Year-Round Success

Every season has its own rhythm, and if you want to be a great angler, you have to adapt. Trout aren't affected by the dates on your calendar—they're driven by water temperature, food availability, and conditions.

The best advice? Fish when you can, adjust when you need to, and never assume that what worked last season will work today.

Because in the end, the river doesn't care about your plans. It only rewards those who learn to read its ever-changing moods.

Beyond the Seasons—How We Fish, When We Fish, and Why It All Matters

But adapting to trout behavior requires understanding more than just the seasons—it's also about how we approach each fishing trip. Some days, we have the luxury of wading in for hours, following the bends of the river from sunrise to sunset. Other times, we steal just a few minutes on a local creek before heading back to the real world. Each type of trip has its own beauty, challenges, and rewards.

In the next chapter, we'll explore the difference between short trips and all-day adventures—how each style shapes the way we experience the water, and why, sometimes, the best trip is simply the one you have time for.

Part 4: The Fly Fisher's Journey

Chapter 35: Short Trips vs. All-Day Adventures

The Beauty of a Short Trip

Short trips can be surprisingly fulfilling. They force you to focus, making every cast count. When you only have an hour or two, you become hyper-aware of your surroundings—watching the water for rises, feeling the air temperature shift as the sun climbs or falls, and reading the stream with precision. There's no room for wasted motion. Every decision—where to cast, how to drift, what fly to use—carries weight because time is limited.

A quick outing after work or a pre-dawn escape before the world wakes up can deliver just as much satisfaction as a full-day adventure. The key is embracing the moment and adapting to the limited time you have. There's an urgency to short trips that sharpens your instincts. You don't have time to overanalyze; you fish with purpose, and sometimes, that's when you fish best.

The Rewards of an All-Day Fishing Trip

An all-day trip, on the other hand, is a journey. It starts with preparation—checking the forecast, packing lunch, making sure your gear is ready. You don't just fish the river; you settle into it, learning its rhythms as the hours pass. There's no rush, no pressure. You have time to experiment, to wade deeper, to sit back and watch the way the light changes on the water.

These are the days that stretch from the first morning light to the golden hour before dusk. You work your way through different stretches of the river, hiking into untouched waters, adjusting to shifting conditions. Day trips teach patience. They show you what's necessary and what isn't. Carry too much, and you'll learn the hard way. Carry too little, and you'll feel it when the wind changes or hunger sets in.

There's a quiet thrill in knowing you have time to figure things out. The anticipation builds with every pool, every cast, every pause to watch the water. Make no mistake—if you don't see trout, it doesn't mean they aren't there. They are. They always are. More than once, I've mistaken submerged twigs, grasses, or rocks for trout, only to have the water shift and reveal the outline of a fish perfectly camouflaged against the riverbed. That's the beauty of trout fishing—these fish are the ghosts of the creek, appearing only when they want to be seen.

Lost in the Current: A Full-Day Immersion

One spring morning, I set out for a full-day adventure on the Tuckasegee River in western North Carolina. The river was alive with the energy of early-season runoff—fast-moving, cold, and brimming with promise. Along the banks, three white-tailed deer stepped cautiously into the shallows for a drink, their reflections shifting on the rippling surface. The twitch of their ears signaled their alertness, and with a flicker of their tails, they were gone. Overhead, an osprey circled, waiting for the perfect moment to dive for its breakfast.

The morning bite was slow, but patience paid off. As the sun reached its peak, trout began rising steadily to an early hatch. I moved carefully, casting to feeding lanes, landing a strong brown trout in the shadow of a boulder. The day continued in rhythm—hike, wade, cast, land, release, repeat.

By late afternoon, I found myself deep in a canyon stretch, miles from the nearest road. The wind had picked up slightly, rustling through the pines, and the scent of sagebrush filled the air. A final cast into a slow, deep pool brought the biggest trout of the day—a heavy, golden-bellied brown that fought with every ounce of strength before slipping back into the depths.

As the sun set behind the mountains, I sat on a flat rock, soaking in the moment. These were the days I lived for—the ones where time didn't exist, where the world beyond the riverbank faded away, and where the only thing that mattered was the rhythm of the water and the steady, practiced motion of the cast.

Finding Your Balance

Short trips sharpen your ability to read water quickly. With limited time, you learn to analyze currents, spot trout lies, and make calculated casts with precision. It's a crash course in adaptability—one that trains you to trust your instincts and make every moment on the water count.

On the other hand, long days on the water allow for experimentation. With time on your side, you can change flies, adjust your approach, and observe how trout behavior shifts throughout the day. These trips provide the space to refine your technique, test new waters, and settle into the meditative rhythm of casting and retrieving. They offer a deeper connection to the landscape, revealing the hidden patterns of the river and the creatures that depend on it.

Time slows down when you're on the river. Whether it's a 30-minute trip or a dawn-to-dusk outing, something about moving water resets your internal clock. Minutes stretch, and worries fade. An all-day trip forces you to travel light and carry only what you truly need. A quick trip demands precision—you can't waste time fumbling through your fly box. Some of my best fish have come when I had the least time to catch them.

Weather is always the great equalizer. A bluebird morning can turn into an afternoon downpour. On a short trip, you may be forced off the water. On a long trip, you learn to adapt, to read the clouds, to keep moving.

Solitude feels different depending on how long you stay. A solo hour on the water is meditative. A full-day solo trip is something deeper—by the end, you feel like you belong to the river itself. Energy conservation is key on a long trip. Move too fast, and you'll burn out before the best fishing even starts.

Some rivers demand more time. Spring creeks and tailwaters can take hours to figure out. A long trip gives you the luxury of making mistakes and adjusting. If you're hunting for a trophy trout, patience is your best ally. Some fish don't come easy. They take time.

No trip is wasted. Whether you get skunked or land a personal best, every outing adds to your experience. Each cast is another lesson.

The Balance Between Time and Water

Both short trips and all-day adventures have their place in a fly fisherman's life. Some days, a brief visit to a nearby stream is all it takes to refresh the mind and reconnect with the wild. Other times, you need to lose yourself in the flow of the river for hours on end, letting the water guide you into a deeper state of presence and appreciation.

The beauty of trout fishing is that it meets you where you are. Whether you have twenty minutes or twenty hours, the stream is always there, waiting.

Fueling the Journey—Because Fishing Is Defined by More Than the Fish

Whether you're fishing for a few casts before work or chasing trout from dawn to dusk, one thing remains constant: you need to keep yourself fueled for the adventure ahead.

In the next chapter, we'll dive into the best snacks, drinks, and trail food to keep you hydrated, energized, and focused—without weighing down your pack. Because the last thing you want is to hook the trout of a lifetime while running on an empty stomach.

Chapter 36: Snacks, Drinks, and Trail Food

Fishing Fuel: Because You Can't Catch Trout on an Empty Stomach

Alright, let's talk food. You didn't think we were just here to talk about fishing, did you? Whether you're trekking out for an hour or making it an all-day adventure, having the right snacks and drinks is essential for keeping the energy levels up. It's not just about catching trout—it's about catching them while you're not starving, dehydrated, or hallucinating from low blood sugar.

Now, I'll be honest. Writing this chapter wasn't my idea. This was one of those "publisher-mandated" moments where they told me to include a section on food for the stream, as if that's going to make anyone a better angler. But here we are, and I'm doing my best to convince you that what you eat is just as important as what you fish with. So, let's get into it—without turning this into a boring survival guide.

Hydration is Key (Because You Can't Fish If You're Dehydrated)

First things first: water. Not just the kind flowing through the stream, but the kind you actually drink. Hydration is like the oil in your car engine—without it, you break down. And don't try to convince yourself that a bottle of Diet Coke counts. I've made that argument before. My wife insists I need real water. I tell her, "Diet Coke is 99% water. The other 1% is basically life-giving caffeine and bubbles!" She sighs and hands me a real water bottle, as if I'm not an expert in hydration or something.

How much water should you bring? If it's a short two-hour trip, a liter should do. For a four-hour trip, two liters is safer, and for an all-day trip, plan on three liters or more—depending on the heat, your energy output, and your tolerance for inconvenient bathroom breaks.

Snacks: When You're Too Busy Fishing to Eat Like a Normal Person

Fishing isn't exactly a sit-down dining experience. You need snacks that you can grab between casts, ones that won't leave your hands coated in something questionable when it's time to tie on another fly.

Trail mix is the ultimate snack of chaos and reward. Sometimes you get a peanut. Sometimes you get chocolate. Sometimes you get the disappointment of a raisin. But it has protein, fat, sugar, and enough variety to keep things interesting. Granola or protein bars are another no-fuss option—easy to shove in your pocket and break out when the moment calls for it. Beef jerky works when you need something to chew on between casts and want to feel like a true rugged outdoorsman.

If you're feeling fancy, cheese and crackers give you the illusion of a real meal without the effort. And for something slightly healthier, dried fruit like apricots, figs, or banana chips can do the trick. It might not be the most exciting snack, but at least you'll feel like a responsible adult.

A Lunch Worth Stopping For (Or Just Pretending You're Having One)

If you're lucky enough to have a full-day trip, you'll need more than just snacks. That's when you break out the simple but effective classics. Peanut butter and jelly is my go-to. It's easy, packs an energy punch, and doesn't leave you regretting sticky fingers. A wrap with turkey, cheese, and greens is a slightly fancier option—basically a sandwich disguised as something more sophisticated. Hard-boiled eggs are the surprise protein bomb that will either power you through the day or make your backpack smell like bad decisions if you forget about them.

For something even easier, a tuna packet with crackers takes zero prep. Just tear it open, eat, and get back to fishing. It's the ultimate efficiency meal, and efficiency means more time with a fly in the water.

The Comforts of the Creek (A.K.A. Treat Yourself)

Fishing is hard work, and you deserve a little comfort along the way. A thermos of coffee or tea can change your entire mindset, especially on a crisp morning when the mist is still hanging over the water. There's something about sipping something warm while watching the river that makes the whole experience feel even more complete.

Dark chocolate is another underrated fishing luxury. Just a small piece gives you a quick boost, and let's be honest—you deserve it. And fresh fruit like apples, oranges, or pears not only provides a refreshing bite but also makes you look slightly more responsible than the guy who packed nothing but beef jerky and gas station energy drinks.

Fueling the Experience (So Your Stomach Doesn't Ruin the Mood)

Some foods are just a bad idea on the water. Anything messy will have you wrestling with a fork while trying not to get sauce all over your reel. Overly sugary snacks might seem like a great idea—until you crash hard halfway through the afternoon. And glass bottles? Just don't. The last thing you want is to spend your trip fishing for your own water bottle instead of trout.

Packing the right snacks ensures you stay focused, energized, and present. Because let's face it—the last thing you want is to be on the river, ready to land the fish of a lifetime, only to realize you're too weak from hunger to hold your rod properly.

Some Moments Are Worth Keeping Forever (But Not the Fish)

The best moments on the water aren't always about the fish. Sometimes, they're about the quiet—the way the river slows your thoughts, the way the morning mist drifts just above the surface, the way the sunlight filters through the trees at just the right angle.

Some anglers keep journals, logging every trip with notes on water conditions, fly choices, and the fish they caught. Others film their time on the water, capturing the cast, the fight, the release. Some just tell stories, the kind that get better with every retelling. However you choose to keep track of your time on the water, one thing is clear: memories fade, but a good fishing trip stays with you forever—whether you land the fish or not.

Beyond the Snacks: The Rituals That Make the Trip

For some, the ritual is the pre-trip stop at the gas station for a questionable breakfast sandwich. For others, it's the first sip of coffee as they lace up their wading boots, the smell of damp earth rising with the sun. Maybe it's the feeling of cracking open a cold drink at the end of the day, watching the last light fade from the riverbank.

Fishing is never just about the fish. It's about the entire experience—what you eat, what you drink, how you prepare, and the moments in between the casts.

Now that we've covered the importance of keeping yourself fueled, let's talk about keeping the experience alive. Some anglers write detailed logs. Others film everything. Some just take a mental snapshot and move on. But no matter how you do it, recording your fishing trips—whether through words, images, or video—can change the way you experience the water.

In the next chapter, we'll explore how to document your time on the river without turning into one of those people who spends more time setting up a shot than actually fishing. Because when done right, keeping a record isn't about showing off—it's about remembering why you fish in the first place.

Chapter 37: Capturing the Story: How to Document & Share Your Journey

Capturing the Catch: Preserving the Moments That Matter

There's a moment in every angler's life when you realize that some fishing trips are too good to forget. You're standing midstream, rod tip high, watching the drift of your nymph through a slow, deep run. Then—the slightest hesitation of your indicator. A flick of the wrist, a firm hook set, and suddenly the line goes tight. The fish dives, using the current to its advantage, shaking its head, trying to throw the hook. For a few perfect moments, it's just you, the fish, and the river.

And once it's over—once the trout slips back into the depths—you realize something. This moment is gone forever unless you find a way to capture it.

Some anglers keep a journal, writing down every cast, every strike, every bit of water they fished. Others take pictures or film every trip, hoping to relive it later. Some just tell stories, and those stories get a little better every time they're told. However you choose to document your time on the water, one thing is certain: memories fade, but a well-captured fishing experience lasts forever.

The Notebook Disaster: My Attempt at Classic Record Keeping

I used to be a purist. If Hemingway wrote about fishing in his notebook, I figured I should too. So one day, I packed a journal, a nice pen, and a plan—I was going to document everything. Every cast, every drift, every subtle take. This was going to be literary gold.

For a while, it worked. That afternoon, after a solid few hours of tight-line nymphing through medium-depth riffles, I found a dry rock in the sun, opened my notebook, and started scribbling. I wrote about how the fish had taken a size 16 Pheasant Tail just as it drifted into the seam, the way the indicator hesitated for half a second before I set the hook, the way the trout fought hard but steady, staying deep. It felt good to capture the moment.

Then I got cocky. I decided to find a better vantage point, somewhere I could see more of the river while I wrote. I stepped off the rock, misjudged the slickness of the boulders, and before I knew it, I was sliding straight into the current.

Backpack, notebook, everything—soaked. My pen floated away downstream. My perfectly written notes? Nothing but smeared ink and regret.

That's when I realized—there had to be a better way.

Filming vs. Writing: Which One Captures the Moment Best?

After that notebook disaster, I started rethinking how I document my fishing. Maybe filming was the way to go. Both have their advantages.

Writing forces you to process the experience more deliberately. You reflect on what worked, what didn't, and how to improve. A well-kept fishing journal can last decades, becoming something you look back on years later, each entry a window into past adventures.

Filming, on the other hand, ensures no moment is lost. The footage doesn't fade, and you don't have to struggle to recall details later. It captures natural reactions—the tension in the rod, the way the indicator suddenly dips, the excitement of the fight. It tells a story visually, without needing paragraphs of description.

After losing a full day's worth of notes, I started filming more. Not to make fancy YouTube videos—just to preserve the experience in a way that wouldn't get washed away.

The Best Way to Document a Day on the Water

If you want to preserve your fishing experiences without ruining your gear or wasting too much time, here's how to do it right.

Film It—But Keep It Simple

A GoPro or DJI Action Camera is ideal. Small, waterproof, and perfect for wading, they capture the action without being intrusive. Chest or hat mounts work best, keeping your hands free to fish while still getting great footage. Long recordings aren't necessary—just short clips of key moments.

Keep a Memory Log Instead of a Full Journal

I still like writing things down, but I've simplified the process. Instead of a detailed journal, I keep quick bullet points after each trip:

Date & Time – Helps track seasonal changes and patterns.

Weather & Water Conditions – Clarity, flow rate, temperature—details that matter.

Where the Trout Were Holding – Shallow riffles, medium-depth runs, deep pools.

Best Catch of the Day – Fly, depth, location, drift style.

Biggest Lesson Learned – What worked, what didn't, what I'll do differently next time.

That's it. Later, if I want to expand on a great trip, I can. But I don't have to worry about soggy notebooks ever again.

Capture the Right Moments on Video

Filming everything is unnecessary. Focus on the key moments. The first hookup of the day, when the rod bends and the fish runs. The net job, when the trout is finally landed, its colors flashing in the sun. A close-up of the fly in the trout's mouth, proof that your choice of pattern was the right one.

Sharing Your Journey (Without Looking Like a Social Media Addict)

There's an art to sharing your fishing experiences without coming across as the guy who can't fish without an audience. Post selectively—one killer shot or clip from the day is better than a dozen mediocre ones. Tell a story, don't just say, "Look at me." Share something helpful—a technique, an observation, a lesson. And please, don't geotag every spot. Some waters are special because they're not widely known.

Why It's Worth Documenting

Years from now, you'll look back on your time on the water and realize that some of your best moments happened knee-deep in a trout stream. Whether you write them down, film them, or just take a few photos, the goal is the same—to preserve the experiences that matter.

But if you take one lesson from me, just make sure your notebook doesn't end up in the creek.

Beyond the Notebook—Bringing Fishing Memories to Life

Writing down stories is one thing, but sometimes, a picture—or a video—captures what words can't.

Fishing trips aren't just about the catch. They're about the quiet moments, the unexpected encounters, the beauty of the surroundings. Capturing these experiences on film preserves memories, shares your passion, and even helps refine your technique. But, as with all things in fishing, filming is an art in itself.

In the next chapter, we'll dive into how to film and record your fishing experience the right way—without missing the moment in front of you.

Chapter 38: Filming and Recording Your Experience

Filming the Fishing Experience: Capturing the River

Fishing trips are about more than just the catch. They're about the quiet moments, the unexpected encounters, and the beauty of the surroundings. Capturing these experiences on film can preserve memories, share your passion with others, and even help refine your technique. But, as with all things in fishing, filming is an art in itself.

Why Record Your Fishing Adventures?

Recording your fishing experiences isn't just about showing off a big catch. It's about storytelling. Some moments on the water are so special they deserve to be shared—the dance of a rising trout, the way morning mist rolls over the river, the struggle of a hard-fighting fish that finally slips away. A well-shot video or a series of photos can bring these moments to life in ways words alone cannot.

But beyond storytelling, filming is also a learning tool. Watching your own footage can reveal subtle details you might miss in the moment—how trout react to your casts, how your presentation looks from a different angle, or what adjustments could have made the difference between a take and a refusal. Seeing yourself fish from the outside allows you to analyze and improve in ways that memory alone never could.

The Best Gear for Filming on the Stream

While a full-blown camera rig might sound appealing, most anglers prefer lightweight, durable options that won't interfere with fishing. Action cameras like GoPros or DJI Osmo Action cameras are perfect for hands-free filming, easily mounted on a chest strap, head mount, or even a rod. A waterproof smartphone case makes modern phones an excellent option for quick captures, offering high-quality footage without extra bulk.

For those wanting to go beyond personal perspective shots, a small drone can add cinematic quality, capturing aerial views of rivers winding through valleys or the vastness of a high-mountain lake. But simplicity is key—the best fishing footage is often the most natural, and cumbersome setups only take away from the experience.

Capturing the Best Shots Without Overcomplicating It

Filming a fishing trip is about balance. A chest-mounted camera captures the intensity of a cast and hookset from a first-person view, giving the audience a true angler's perspective. A tripod or riverbank setup provides wide, steady shots, perfect for filming casting form or the entire flow of the stream. Underwater shots, captured with a waterproof camera or housing, can turn a simple release into a mesmerizing moment, showing a trout as it slips back into the depths, fins flashing in the current.

Rod-mounted cameras may seem like a fun idea, but in reality, they often shake too much to be useful. The best footage happens when you think like a filmmaker—choosing angles that highlight the moment rather than just recording for the sake of it.

When My Battery Died at the Worst Possible Time

I had the perfect setup—GoPro strapped to my chest, memory card cleared, conditions perfect. The morning mist rolled off the water, and I had already filmed a few stunning clips of casts landing precisely in feeding lanes. It was shaping up to be a great day, the kind that would make for a perfect highlight reel.

Then it happened.

Trout were flashing beneath the surface, feeding aggressively. My heart pounded as I knew I was in the right spot. I made the cast, my fly drifted into a deep pocket, and my line went tight. This wasn't just another fish. This was the fish of the trip—a massive brown trout, the kind that haunts you if you lose it. The fight was everything I could hope for, with blistering runs, jumps, and a final, heart-stopping moment where it barely fit into my net.

I was already picturing how the footage would look—the perfect cast, the battle, the moment of triumph. But as I reached to stop the recording, my stomach dropped. The red light wasn't on.

The battery had died ten minutes into the trip.

All I had recorded was me wading into the river, setting up my gear, and muttering something about how "today feels like a good day." That fish—the fight, the moment, everything—was gone, existing only in my memory. It stung for about five minutes, but then I laughed. Some moments aren't meant to be filmed. Some moments are meant to be lived.

Still… charge your batteries before every trip.

The Best Footage Happens When You Least Expect It

The most beautiful shots are rarely planned. A deer drinking at the river's edge, the ripple of a rising trout, the way the sunlight filters through the trees—these moments happen when you least expect them. The best approach is to be ready but not obsessed. Let the river tell the story. Stay flexible enough to capture the unexpected without turning the trip into a production.

Why Sound Matters More Than You Think

A fishing video isn't just about the visuals. The sound of rushing water, the hum of insects, the distant call of a bird—all of these elements add depth to a film. But wind noise, muffled voices, or a shaky microphone can ruin an otherwise perfect shot. If you're serious about quality, a small external microphone or wind-reduction settings on an action camera can make all the difference. A reel screaming as a fish runs downstream or the splash of a trout breaking the surface is just as powerful as the image itself.

Film the Journey, Not Just the Catch

Too many fishing videos focus only on the fish. The hookset, the fight, the release—it's all important, but the real magic of fly fishing is in the journey. The early morning drive, the fog lifting over the river, the first cast, the moment of stillness between takes. These details make a fishing trip what it is. Capturing them on film brings back the full experience, not just a highlight reel of fish landed.

You'll Watch These Videos More Than You Think

A day will come when you're stuck at home, staring out the window, wishing you were on the water. When that happens, watching back your own fishing footage isn't just nostalgia—it's a portal back to those moments. It's the next best thing to standing in the current. And for those days when you can't fish, sometimes that's enough.

The Balance Between Filming and Being Present

Filming your fishing trips is a great way to preserve memories, but don't let it take away from the experience itself. Some moments—like watching a fish rise in the golden light of evening—are best appreciated without a screen between you and nature. Be mindful of when to record and when to simply be there, fully immersed in the moment. The river doesn't care if you got the shot. But you? You'll remember it either way.

The Evolution of Fly Fishing—From Riverbank Wisdom to YouTube Highlights

A generation ago, fly fishing knowledge was passed down like a family heirloom—whispered riverbank wisdom, stained with tobacco smoke and black coffee. Now, it's slow-motion, high-production drone footage, beamed into your phone in 4K resolution. The old-timers grumble about the new-school approach. The YouTubers see the past as a sepia-toned mystery. Both sides claim superiority.

The truth? They're both right—and they're both ridiculous in their own way.

In the next chapter, we'll explore how technology has changed fly fishing, for better or worse, and what that means for the future of the sport. Because whether it's learned from an old guide in a drift boat or from a YouTube tutorial at midnight, the love for fly fishing remains the same.

Chapter 39: Then vs. Now

There was a time when fly fishing was passed down like a family heirloom—through whispered riverbank wisdom, stained with tobacco smoke and black coffee. Now? It's a high-production, slow-motion, drone-footage, "Fish on, bro!" spectacle, beamed into your phone in 4K resolution. The old-timers grumble about the new-school approach, and the YouTubers look at the past like a sepia-toned mystery. Both sides claim superiority. The truth? They're both right—and they're both ridiculous in their own way.

Let's break it down.

The Philosophy

Old-Timers: "It's about the process." They believed in quiet mornings, slow wading, and letting the river teach you. There was no rush. Every mistake was a lesson, every tangle an opportunity to learn patience. If you caught a fish, great. If not, you still had a good day because you were part of the water. They didn't need an audience, just the river.

YouTubers: "It's about the content." Every trip is a mission. The GoPros are rolling, the drone is in the air, and there's a "shot list" to get through. If you didn't get the hookset in slow motion, did the fish even count? The biggest sin isn't getting skunked—it's not having footage of the fish you caught.

Winner?

If you enjoy being in the moment, old-timers win.

If you want to make sure everyone on the internet knows you caught a fish, YouTubers take it.

The Way They Talk

Old-Timers: "Keep your rod tip up. Mend your line. Don't spook 'em." The old-timers speak in practical advice, often in short, clipped sentences. They don't yell "Fish on!" because why would they? The guy standing next to them can see it. And if they lose a fish, they don't blame the rod, the reel, or the leader. They just mutter, shake their head, and keep fishing.

YouTubers: "Let's goooo! Fish on, fish on! Absolute tanker! That's a big ol' brownie or a chunky brookie! Hit that like and subscribe, dude! Bow bow bow! That's a mondo, dude!" You can hear them before you see them. They narrate everything out loud, not because their buddy doesn't know what's happening, but because their audience does. Every fish is a "unit." Every cast is "textbook." Losing a fish means dropping a slow-motion black-and-white replay with dramatic music and an overlaid "Nooooo!"

Winner?

If you prefer stealth and dignity, the old-timers win.

If you like energy and entertainment, YouTubers take it.

The Fashion

Old-Timers: "Wool and canvas. That's all you need." Filson, old Patagonia, and whatever vest they've had since Reagan was in office. Their waders are patched and stained. Their hats aren't new; they've got sweat rings and fly hooks in the brim. Their fishing shirts? Just shirts. No brand logos the size of billboards.

YouTubers: "High-performance everything." Full-sleeve sun shirts with sponsor logos bigger than a NASCAR hood. Buffs pulled up to their eyes, making them look like fly-fishing commandos. Polarized sunglasses that cost more than their first car. And waders? Brand new, spotless, with a "review video" coming soon.

Winner?

If you like functional and timeless, old-timers win.

If you want high-tech and social media-ready, YouTubers take it.

The Approach to Fishing

Old-Timers: "Find a good spot and settle in." They move slow, study the water, and take their time. They know when to fish, when to wait, and when to just sit on a rock and appreciate the morning. They don't care about covering miles of river. They care about learning one stretch so well that they can predict where the trout will be.

YouTubers: "Cover water, get footage, move on." They fish fast, hit a spot, film the action, and move to the next "fire hole." Drone shots, slow-mo releases, action-packed hooksets—it's about creating a highlight reel, not settling in for a quiet morning.

Winner?

If you want to become part of the river, old-timers win.

If you want to get the most action in the least time, YouTubers take it.

The Battle with Snags

Old-Timers: "It happens." They don't panic. They don't make a scene. They wade over, untangle the mess, maybe sacrifice a fly, and get back to fishing. They accept that trees and branches own more flies than trout do.

YouTubers: "Unbelievable! Are you kidding me? That's brutal, dude!" They get snagged and instantly look around—because this is wasted fishing time and wasted filming time. If they lose a fly, expect a dramatic zoom-in, a sarcastic comment, and maybe even an on-screen counter keeping track of how many flies they've lost that day.

Winner?

If you believe in accepting fate, old-timers win.

If you want drama and viral moments, YouTubers take it.

Which Is Better?

Neither. And both.

Old-timers understand the soul of fly fishing. They know that it's about time, patience, and experience, not how many followers you have or how cinematic your hookset looks.

But YouTubers bring energy, accessibility, and excitement—they've inspired a new generation to pick up a fly rod, and that's not a bad thing.

The best anglers? They take a little from both. They fish slow when they need to and cover water when they need to. They appreciate a good fight but don't need to announce it to the world. They can wear a buff without looking like they're about to rob a bank.

Maybe the real lesson here is: Don't be too much of either one.

And if you ever find yourself yelling "Fish on! Let's gooo!" while an old guy nearby just gives you a quiet nod, congratulations.

You're both part of the river now.

A Different Kind of Silence—Fishing in the Dead of Winter

But what happens when the river isn't buzzing with energy? When there are no crowds, no slow-motion hero shots, and no easy hatches?

There's something about a trout stream in winter that feels completely different. The silence is heavier, the air sharper, and the landscape stripped down to its bare bones.

Snow and ice replace the vibrant greens of summer, and even the water seems to move more deliberately, slowed by the grip of the cold.

In the next chapter, we'll explore the quiet beauty, challenges, and rewards of winter trout fishing—for those willing to brave the elements in search of a fish that moves as slow as the season itself.

Chapter 40: Trout Fishing in the Dead of Winter

I wanted to go to the creek and see the icicles hanging from overhanging branches, to witness the frozen pools forming along the edges of the current. But mostly, I wanted to test out my new waders and boots. The fly rod came along more as a prop—just in case. And of course, I packed my camera, because if there's one thing better than winter fly fishing, it's having proof that you were crazy enough to attempt it.

My wife looked at me with suspicion. She knew. She always knew. She gave me that sideways glance that said, "You're not fooling anyone. I know exactly what this is." And she was right. I had never landed a trout in the dead of winter before. But that didn't stop me from trying.

The Winter Fishing Reality Check

Winter fly fishing is not for the casual angler. The cold turns every small inconvenience into a real problem. Your fingers go numb, making knots almost impossible to tie. Your guides freeze over, turning your line into a stiff, ice-coated mess. The air burns your lungs, and standing still in frigid water feels like slowly turning into stone.

But it's also magical. The crowds are gone, and the river is yours. The crunch of snow under your boots and the steam rising from the water make it feel like you've stepped into another world—one where time slows and every cast matters.

I waded in carefully, expecting the worst. The first few minutes were spent just adjusting to the cold, flexing my fingers, pulling my collar up against the wind. The water was lower than usual, clear as glass, and painfully cold. I watched my breath drift away in white plumes, laughing at the absurdity of it all.

Finding the Winter Holding Spots

Trout don't just disappear in winter. They adjust. When the water is this cold, they slow down, conserve energy, and move to deep, slow pools where they don't have to fight the current. This means you won't find them in the same places you did in the summer.

They won't chase a poorly presented fly. They won't rise for a flashy streamer ripping through the current. And they definitely won't waste energy on anything that looks off. Precision is key. Small, natural flies. Dead-drifted. No wasted motion.

I knew all this. I had read the books, watched the videos, talked to the guys at the fly shop. But knowing and executing are two very different things. Winter trout demand perfection.

The First Cast and the Reality of Winter Fishing

I tied on a small midge pattern—size 20, practically microscopic. The first cast was a disaster. Ice on the guides, frozen fingertips, a stiff leader—it all combined into the most embarrassing, pathetic roll cast imaginable. The line barely made it out past my boots.

I cleared the ice, stretched out my fingers, and tried again. The drift was slow, the tiny fly nearly invisible in the water. I watched the leader like a hawk, waiting for the smallest hesitation. And then—it happened. Or at least, I thought it did. A tiny pause, almost imperceptible.

I lifted the rod, expecting nothing.

And I got exactly that.

No tug, no resistance, just the silent realization that my fly had likely drifted past indifferent fish, or worse, nothing at all. Still, I kept at it, moving between deep pools and slow eddies, convinced that sooner or later, a trout would make a mistake.

It never did.

Back to the Fire

After that, I called it a day. My fingers were useless, my boots felt like lead, and my camera battery had died in the cold. But none of that mattered.

When I got back home, my wife saw the look on my face. She didn't even have to ask. She just shook her head and said, "So, when are you going back?"

I just smiled. Because we both knew the answer.

Choosing Fly vs. Spinning—Why Pick a Side When You Can Have Both?

Fishing, much like winter trout fishing, often brings out strong opinions. Some debates in fishing never end. Dry flies vs. nymphs. Waders that smell like a swamp vs. ones that smell like an industrial chemical plant. But few rival the great Spinning Rod vs. Fly Fishing debate.

The spinning rod crowd says fly fishing is impractical, a fancy way to complicate catching a fish. The fly fishing purists scoff at spinners, calling them "bait chuckers" who lack soul.

But here's the thing—both have their place. And any angler who tells you otherwise? They're missing the point.

Chapter 41: Fly Fishing vs. Spinning Rod

Why Pick a Side When You Can Have Both?

Fly anglers and spinning rod enthusiasts love to argue. It's right up there with debating dry flies versus nymphs or whether to wear waders or tough it out with a solid pair of boots. Both get the job done, depending on the approach, but for some reason, the debate never ends.

Here's the thing: both methods work. And—dare I say it—you can enjoy both.

I know because I do. More importantly, I let my kids use spinning rods. Yes, you read that right. My own flesh and blood, carrying my name and outdoor legacy, throw spinners while I cast dry flies. And I'm fine with it. Because sometimes, you just want to catch a fish, not overanalyze the metaphysical nature of a trout's selective feeding habits.

The Spinning Rod: Reliable, Efficient, and Easy to Love

If fishing were just about efficiency, the spinning rod would win every time. It's easy to use, requires minimal technique, and lets you cover a ton of water quickly. There's no need for a perfect cast, no stress over drag-free drifts, and no painstaking selection of the right fly—only for it to be ignored by every trout in the stream.

When I take my kids fishing, I hand them a spinning rod. Why? Because kids want action. They don't care about the purity of presentation or the history of fly fishing's origins in England. They just want to feel that tug and bring in a fish. And if I'm being completely honest, sometimes I do too.

There's a beauty in simplicity. Cast, retrieve, repeat. Spinning gear allows you to focus on fishing without worrying about mending line, perfect loops, or whether your backcast is tangled in a tree.

Also, let's be real—spinning rod guys don't take themselves as seriously. They aren't out there with $800 rods whispering about the art of the drift. No, they're in cargo shorts, cracking a beer, and saying things like, "I'm not putting on a vest to go fishing." Meanwhile, the fly guy is adjusting his leader like he's defusing a bomb.

Fly Fishing: A Love Story with a Learning Curve

Now, let's be clear—I love fly fishing. There's nothing like the thrill of watching a trout slowly rise and commit to your fly like it's making a life decision. It's intimate, artistic, and makes you feel like you've outsmarted nature itself. But let's also be real—fly fishing takes effort.

It took me years to get decent. My first attempts at casting looked like I was trying to swat a wasp with a car antenna. My leader constantly ended up in knots, my flies spent more time in trees than on the water, and I probably scared more fish than I ever caught.

And then there's the gear. Fly rods are delicate. Too delicate. A spinning rod gets tossed in the back of a truck and still works fine. But a fly rod? Look at it wrong, and the tip snaps. Leave it propped against the tailgate for one second, and congratulations—you just turned your $900 rod into a very fancy, very useless stick.

But when it finally clicks, when you land that first fish on a perfectly placed dry fly, it's like a secret door to the universe has opened. You don't just catch fish—you enter a different world.

The Unnecessary Debate: Why Not Both?

For some reason, there's an unspoken rule that you have to choose sides. Fly anglers look down on spinners. Spinners think fly guys are pretentious. Meanwhile, the trout sit in the river, completely indifferent to the gear drama happening above the surface.

The truth? They're both fun. They both catch fish. And you don't have to pick one over the other.

A spinning rod is a tool for covering water and catching fish quickly. It's great for big rivers, lakes, and when you're introducing someone new to fishing. A fly rod, on the other hand, is an experience. It's about slowing down, getting in rhythm with the water, and feeling like you're part of something timeless.

There's a time for both, and if you're smart, you'll use whatever works best for the conditions.

But Be Warned: Fly Fishing Might Steal Your Heart

If you're new to fly fishing and still clutching your spinning rod with pride, be careful. Because once you start—once you feel that first dry fly take—you might just become one of those people.

The kind who talks about "hatches" like they're religious events. The kind who suddenly owns a $900 fly rod but still drives a 15-year-old truck. The kind who plans vacations around rivers instead of resorts.

I've seen it happen. I've lived it. And while I still let my kids use spinning rods, I know that one day, they'll make the switch. They'll feel the magic. They'll stop asking for a spinner and start asking, "Dad, what flies are hatching?"

And when that day comes, I'll just smile. Because I know they've crossed over.

To the dark side.

And they're never going back.

When the River Fights Back

But just because you've mastered the art of the fly doesn't mean you've mastered the water around it.

Fly fishing isn't just about casting into water—it's about navigating everything around it. The trees that swallow backcasts, the grasses that snag leaders, the thorny bushes that leave you questioning your life choices.

Some rivers are wide and forgiving. Others feel like jungle gyms built to punish optimism. Vegetation determines everything—where trout hold, how you cast, and how many flies you'll donate to the wilderness.

In the next chapter, we'll take a deep dive into the green walls that frame our favorite streams—and the never-ending battle between angler and nature.

Chapter 42: Brush, Branches, and Broken Leaders

This is a deep dive into the green walls that frame our favorite streams—and the battle between angler and nature.

Smoky Mountains & WNC: Where Rhododendron and Mountain Laurel Steal Your Flies

The first time I fished deep in the Smokies, I thought I had discovered fly fishing paradise. The water was crystal-clear, the pools untouched, and the brook trout darting through the current. Everything felt perfect. Then I tried to cast.

Western North Carolina streams come with a truth most anglers learn the hard way: the trees own this place. Rhododendron and mountain laurel aren't just growing near the stream; they consume it, forming tight, suffocating tunnels that make backcasting an impossible dream. Mixed in are flame azaleas, beautiful in the spring but just another thing to dodge when threading a cast through a two-foot window.

You're not casting in the Smokies—you're negotiating with nature. Roll casts? Required. Bow-and-arrow casts? Necessary. Overhead casts? Forget it. The hike in alone is a test of patience—roots, fallen logs, and spiderwebs every five feet.

But the trout? Wild and perfect. If you're willing to fight the vegetation, dodge the branches, and leave with fewer flies than you started with, the reward is worth it.

Spring Creeks: The Tall Grass Trap

Spring creeks lull you into a false sense of security—smooth currents, no overhanging trees, just open banks lined with wildflowers and reeds. But these waters play a different game. If you're used to freestone rivers with casting lanes, spring creeks will humble you fast.

The grass is the enemy here. Tall, thick, and waiting. It doesn't care if your backcast was perfect—it will take your fly and refuse to give it back. Every movement sends ripples through the crystal-clear water, and every trout is watching. There's no room for error.

Stealth is everything—slow, low, and deliberate. Every cast needs to be precise, every mend gentle, every drift perfect. And even then? You might still get skunked.

Rocky Mountains: Wide Open... Until the Wind Arrives

The first time you step onto a Rocky Mountain river, it feels like fly fishing heaven. Big water. Open space. No trees to steal your flies. You can finally cast without fear of snags. And then? The wind shows up.

Casting here is a test of endurance. A flawless loop can be ripped sideways mid-air, sending your fly straight into a sagebrush 10 feet off target. You learn fast that sidearm casting is your friend and that your hat will eventually end up in the river.

But the beauty of the West is that trout love structure—fallen logs, undercut banks, deep seams. Unlike in tight Smoky Mountain streams, here, you can actually spot fish holding in the current. If you can fight the wind and get your drift right, the takes are aggressive and unforgettable.

Southwest Desert Creeks: The Tamarisk Nightmare

The Southwest offers trout fishing like nowhere else. The creeks are thin ribbons of cold water cutting through red rock canyons, and the trout are survivors. But the real problem isn't the heat, or even the rattlesnakes—it's tamarisk.

Tamarisk is the Southwest's cruel joke—hoarding water, choking the banks, and treating your fly line like a chew toy. You don't just wade here—you climb, crawl, and duck. And when you do hook a trout? It immediately wraps your leader around the nearest submerged branch.

Fishing these waters requires adaptation—short rods, roll casts, and a willingness to let nature win sometimes. It's rough, wild, and frustrating—but when you land a fish in these conditions, you've earned it.

The Vegetation Lesson—The Challenge of the Wild

The forest doesn't flinch at your perfect loop. It was here before your first cast and will be here long after your last. The wind twists and turns, rewriting the rules of your cast mid-air.

The grass stands silent, poised to snatch your fly the moment you falter.

But that's what makes fly fishing great.

Every lost fly, every tangle, every hike through dense brush is part of the deal. Mastering these waters involves more than reading currents—it's learning to fight through the green barriers that stand between you and the perfect drift.

And when you finally pull that trout from the same snags that tried to steal your fly?

It's worth every broken leader.

Fishing Alone vs. Fishing with a Partner—Two Very Different Experiences

Fly fishing is often painted as a serene, meditative experience—a lone angler, knee-deep in a river, lost in the rhythm of cast and drift. And most of the time, that's exactly what it is.

But then there's the other kind of fishing—the "buddy trip"—where you decide to introduce someone new to the sport.

You envision laughter, shared triumphs, and a lifelong fishing partner hooked on fly fishing just like you.

Instead, you spend the entire day untangling knots, retying flies, cutting line, worrying about them falling in the river, and questioning every life decision that led you to this moment.

Chapter 43: Solo Fishing vs. Fishing with a Buddy

Fly fishing is often painted as a serene, meditative experience—a lone angler, knee-deep in a river, lost in the rhythm of cast and drift. And most of the time, that's exactly what it is.

The Worst Fishing Day Ever

A few years ago, I was convinced I had the perfect plan: Take my friend—an avid outdoorsman but a total fly-fishing rookie—on a trip to one of my favorite rivers.

I imagined him getting that first perfect drift, watching a trout rise to sip his dry fly, and then grinning like a kid on Christmas morning. I would be the wise mentor, nodding in approval, sharing in the success of his first fish on a fly rod. This was going to be incredible.

Except…it wasn't.

From the moment we arrived, everything went wrong.

The Equipment Disaster

My buddy, let's call him Dave, showed up with a beginner fly-fishing combo rig—not bad, but he had no idea what to do next. To make matters worse, he was wearing hiking boots and jeans, completely unprepared for what was ahead.

I blinked.

"Where's your waders?" I asked, already dreading the answer.

"Oh, I figured I'd just wade wet. Feels more natural."

This was a mountain river in early spring. The water temperature was somewhere between hypothermia and full cardiac arrest. But sure, "natural."

I handed him an extra pair of waders and boots, but he struggled to get them on. Forty-five minutes later, we were finally in the water.

The Art of Untangling Knots

The first cast went about six feet before wrapping around his head.

The second cast landed directly in the trees.

By the third cast, his leader resembled a bowl of spaghetti.

I spent the next two hours doing nothing but fixing line, untangling knots, cutting tippet, and explaining why "whipping the rod like Indiana Jones" was not the correct casting technique.

Meanwhile, my rod sat untouched. I wasn't fishing—I was running a full-time fly-fishing daycare.

The Wading Crisis

About an hour in, I realized I wasn't just his guide—I was his lifeguard.

Dave had the balance of a newborn deer. Every time he stepped into the current, his arms shot out like he was on an invisible balance beam.

At one point, he took one step too far and went down like a sack of potatoes—waders full, hat floating, rod somehow still in his hands.

I waded over, helped him up, and heard him gasp, "I think my soul just left my body."

The First (and Only) Fish

After several hours of this, some divine force took pity on us, and Dave actually hooked a fish.

A small brown trout, maybe 10 inches, but to him, it was the Loch Ness Monster.

He screamed like he'd just landed a tarpon.

"Okay, easy," I said, trying to keep him calm. "Just keep the rod up, don't—"

Before I could finish, he set the hook like he was trying to launch the fish into orbit.

The trout flew out of the water, over his head, and landed in the bushes behind us.

Silence.

Then Dave turned to me, eyes wide with horror. "Did I just kill it?"

I retrieved the fish, gently released it, and tried to remember why I thought this was going to be fun.

The Harsh Truth About Fishing with Friends

Here's what I learned that day:

Fly fishing is NOT like hiking, camping, or even spin fishing. You can't just "pick it up."

Teaching someone to fly fish while trying to fish yourself is impossible. You will do one or the other, but not both.

Fishing with a beginner is like a scratch golfer playing with a 30-handicapper. It is not going to be fun. It will be work.

The Joy of Solo Fishing

When you fish alone, none of this happens.

No one to untangle.

No one to rescue from drowning.

No one to apologize to when you realize you're going to spend the next five hours in complete silence.

Solo fishing means total control over the day. You pick the spot. You move at your own pace. You lose yourself in the rhythm of casting, mending, and reading the water. No distractions. No explanations. Just fishing.

The Freedom of Fishing Alone

Fishing alone also forces you to become a better angler. Without a buddy there to break the silence, you find yourself observing more, making better decisions, and truly sinking into the environment. You get lost in the river.

You also don't have to pretend you're thrilled that your buddy just caught the biggest fish of the day.

Final Thought: Lessons Learned

Would I take Dave fishing again? Sure. But only after I get my own fishing in first.

Because, as I learned that day, fly fishing is best when you're the one actually fishing.

(And if anyone asks if I want to "introduce them to the sport," I just hand them a book and tell them to call me in a year.)

Fishing with an Experienced Angler Partner

If fishing with a beginner can be an exercise in patience, fishing with an experienced angler is like finally speaking the same language. There's an unspoken rhythm to the day, a shared understanding that doesn't require words. It's a different experience entirely—one that makes you a better angler without even trying.

The Dance of Two Skilled Anglers

Fishing with someone who knows what they're doing is like two musicians playing in harmony. You don't step on each other's notes, you move instinctively, and you both know how to read the river and adjust without a discussion.

An experienced angler doesn't need coaching, doesn't need constant help untangling knots, and doesn't require a personal safety officer wading next to them. Instead, you both just fish.

No Need for Babysitting

When you fish with another skilled angler, there's no, "Wait, what do I do now?"

There's no "Uh-oh, my line's wrapped around my boot again."

And most importantly, there's no "Hey, can you retie this fly for me?"

Instead, the two of you move through the water like a team. One might fish the head of a run while the other covers the tailout. No wasted space. No stepping on each other's opportunities.

A Silent Understanding

A good fishing partner doesn't need to narrate every moment. There's an awareness that comes with experience—a subtle nod when the fish are rising, a quiet glance to signal "this pool looks good, you take it."

The conversation is easy and effortless, with long stretches of silence that aren't awkward but welcomed.

When Two Experienced Anglers Fish Together

The biggest difference? Less talking, more fishing.

There's no need to explain basic casts or techniques.

No one is babysitting the other's wading skills.

If one of you hooks into a fish, the other isn't watching in confusion—they're right there, net in hand, ready to assist.

Sharing Success Instead of Struggling

Fishing with another skilled angler makes you better. You see their approach, their fly selection, their casting decisions, and their ability to read the water. Without even realizing it, you pick up habits, small adjustments, and a sharper instinct for what works.

And if they catch a monster trout right in front of you? There's no bitterness—only motivation.

Final Thought: Choosing the Right Fishing Partner

Fishing solo is great. But if you're going to fish with someone, make sure they're either as skilled as you—or better. A good partner pushes you, makes you better, and adds to the experience rather than taking away from it.

Because nothing is worse than a trip where you spend more time tying someone else's knots than casting your own flies.

The Psychology of the Big One—Why It Captivates Us

For years, I told everyone that I loved small trout. "The little ones are just as fun," I'd say, nodding confidently while unhooking a spirited 8-inch brookie. "Big trout? Overrated."

I leaned into it hard. If someone posted a photo of a 24-inch brown, I'd casually comment, "Yeah, but I bet a 10-incher would've fought harder." If my fishing buddies grumbled about only catching dinks, I'd shake my head and tell them, "Size isn't everything."

And it wasn't.

Not for me.

Because I had never caught a trout over 15 inches, so I truly had no idea what I was talking about.

Chapter 44: Why Catching a Big Trout is More Mental Than Physical

Denial: Convincing Yourself That Small Fish Are Better

Here's the thing about convincing yourself that small trout are just as fun—it works right up until you hook into something big. I spent years believing my own nonsense. Big trout? Too much hassle. Small ones? More action, more fun, less heartbreak.

The people who bragged about giant browns were missing the point. Trout fishing was about presentation, movement, the feel of the water, the art of the cast. The size of the fish? An afterthought. Or so I told myself.

Then, one day, the river had other plans for me.

The Moment Everything Changed

It happened on a quiet morning—one of those days where you have no expectations, just a fly rod, an open schedule, and a good stretch of river. I was fishing a small caddis dry, the kind of fly that gets eaten by trout no bigger than your hand. Perfect. Just the way I liked it.

Then I saw the rise.

It wasn't a little sip. It wasn't the casual plop of a curious juvenile fish. It was a slow, deliberate swirl, the kind that only comes from something that's been in the river longer than I've been alive.

I hesitated. I don't fish for big trout. I don't need to. But my instincts took over, and before I even realized what I was doing, my fly was floating toward the exact spot where the water had just boiled.

The Hookset That Almost Didn't Happen

When you spend a lifetime catching small trout, you develop a certain kind of muscle memory. The quick set, the easy control, the immediate pull back toward you. It works when the fish weighs about as much as your car keys.

It does not work when the fish on the other end is a fully

grown aquatic predator with zero interest in coming to the net.

The second I lifted my rod, the world shifted. Instead of feeling the familiar light tug, my entire arm nearly got ripped into the river. My fly rod bent so hard I was convinced I'd hooked a submerged log—until the log started moving.

Negotiating with a Fish

Here's a little-known fact: the moment you hook a big trout, you become a bargaining maniac.

"Okay, okay, stay on. Just let me see you. That's all. I won't even net you."

"Please don't run downstream, I have terrible footwork."

"I take it back. Big trout are good. You're good. We're good."

Reality Check: Fighting a Big Trout Is Not Like the Movies

You picture it a certain way. A dramatic fight, a heroic stance, the perfect control. The truth? Chaos.

I stumbled. I tripped. At one point, I had my line wrapped around my boot.

The fish ran downstream. I scrambled after it like a man chasing a winning lottery ticket caught in the wind. My net was nowhere near where I needed it. My reel screamed. My pride disintegrated.

Somewhere in the madness, I realized something important: I had no idea what I was doing.

The Netting Debacle

Eventually, somehow, the fish tired. Not because of my skill, but because it got bored with my incompetence.

I reached for my net. My hands were shaking. This was it—the moment.

And I missed.

The trout, which had spent the last five minutes proving that it was the superior being, bolted one last time. I gasped. The hook held.

I tried again. This time, somehow, miraculously, I got its head in the net. Victory.

The Aftermath: Coming to Terms with My Lies

I knelt in the water, staring at the biggest trout I'd ever caught. It was over 20 inches—twice the size of anything I'd ever hooked.

And that's when I knew.

I had been lying to myself for years.

The Emotional Spiral of a Big Fish

Here's what happens when you land a big trout for the first time:

Denial – This can't be real. I don't catch fish like this. I must be dreaming.

Shock – Did that just happen? Did anyone see that?

Panic – Quick, take a picture before it escapes!

Existential Crisis – I have to rethink everything I've ever believed about fishing.

Addiction – I need to do that again. Right now.

Big Trout Change You

There's no going back. Once you've felt the weight of a truly big fish, once you've seen the way they move, the way they fight, the way they refuse to be fooled twice, you understand something deep in your soul.

Size does matter.

Final Thought: The Lies We Tell Ourselves

These days, when someone brags about small trout, I just nod and smile. "Yep, they fight hard," I say.

But deep down, I know the truth.

I still love small trout. I do. But there's nothing in the world like hooking into a fish that makes your hands shake, your heart race, and your reel scream.

And how does the song go? If loving big trout is wrong, I

don't want to be right.

Knowing When to Walk Away—Or Keep Casting

But what happens when the big ones aren't biting? When you've been casting for hours, the wind has turned against you, and your last good drift happened before lunch?

There's a point in every fly fishing trip when you have to ask yourself:

Am I fishing, or am I just standing in water, flailing like an idiot?

We don't like to admit it, but sometimes the river wins. Sometimes, the fish don't care about your pride. The river doesn't owe you anything. And yet, we stay. Cast after cast. Hoping.

Because walking away feels like defeat.

But is it?

Or is it wisdom?

Because knowing when to pack it in isn't giving up—it's understanding the game.

Chapter 45: The Hardest Skill: Knowing When to Walk Away

The 5 Stages of Fishing Denial

Every angler goes through these stages before finally calling it a day:

Optimism: Today's the day. It's going to be epic.

Confusion: Huh, no bites yet. Must be the wrong fly.

Determination: I just need to switch spots. The fish are here.

Delusion: If I leave now, a giant trout will rise the moment I step away.

Resignation: Fine, I'll leave. But I'll be thinking about this river for weeks.

And then, of course, we make the classic mistake—"One more cast." We all know how that goes.

One More Cast Syndrome: The Trap That Gets Us All

I've lost hours of my life to the phrase, "One more cast." It's never one. It's ten. Then twenty. Then suddenly, it's dark, you can't feel your fingers, and you realize you left your truck headlights on five hours ago.

One time, I told myself I'd leave after catching one last fish. That was at noon. By sunset, I was still standing there, shivering, while my fly drifted uselessly through fishless water. At that point, I wasn't even fishing—I was just being stubborn. The trout had outlasted me.

And that's the lesson: the river doesn't care about your timeline. The fish don't operate on your schedule. Knowing when to leave is about understanding that the best days are earned, not forced.

Signs That It's Time to Leave

Here's how you know it's time to leave:

You've changed flies more times than you've made good casts.

Your feet are numb, but you convince yourself it's "just a little cold."

You've been fishing the same hole for an hour, convinced the trout are "just waiting."

You've said "last cast" at least five times.

You haven't seen a single rise, but you're still throwing dries.

You can't feel your fingers well enough to tie a new fly.

You're hungry, but tell yourself, "I'll eat after I catch one more."

You're talking to yourself.

At some point, you have to recognize the river is done with you for the day. And that's okay.

The Art of Leaving on a High Note

Most of us don't know how to quit when we're ahead. We land a great fish and think, just one more. But there's something to be said for leaving when things are still good—while the magic is still there.

The best days I've ever had? I left while I was still smiling. I didn't wait for frustration to set in. I didn't let the fish beat me down. I walked away still loving the river, not cursing it.

It takes discipline. But when you leave while you're still in love with the day, you remember it better. You hold onto it longer. And the next time you come back, it's not with desperation—it's with anticipation.

The Day I Didn't Walk Away (And Should Have)

I once fished through a storm because I refused to admit defeat. Wind whipping sideways, rain soaking my waders, lightning cracking over the hills—I was still casting.

At some point, a gust of wind sent my fly straight into the side of my head. That was the river's way of saying, Go home, idiot.

I didn't listen.

I kept casting. Because I had driven too far to quit now.

Because I knew a fish was out there. Because if I left, it meant the river won.

The river did win. I caught nothing. I walked back to my truck, drenched, exhausted, and questioning all my life choices.

I should have left hours earlier. But my ego wouldn't let me.

Why Walking Away Isn't Quitting

We equate leaving with failure. We think staying longer makes us tougher, more dedicated. But the best anglers I know? They know when to call it. They aren't stubborn. They aren't ruled by their egos. They read the water, listen to the conditions, and make the smart call.

They also don't get caught in lightning storms while waving around a graphite rod.

How to Walk Away Without Regret

If you struggle with knowing when to leave, try this:

Set a time limit before you start. If you say, "I'm leaving at 4 PM no matter what," you avoid the spiral of denial.

End on a good note. Don't wait until you're miserable—leave while you're still enjoying yourself.

Listen to the river. If it's dead, it's dead. Forcing it won't change that.

Ask yourself: Am I fishing or just being stubborn?

If you follow these, you'll walk away without regret. And more importantly—you'll want to come back.

Walking away from the river means knowing when to quit—it's also about training yourself to be okay with not knowing.

What if you left, and the biggest trout of your life rose five minutes later? What if one more cast really was the one?

You'll never know.

And that's part of the deal.

The best anglers learn to live with unanswered questions.

They don't let what could have happened haunt them. They trust that there will always be another day, another river, another chance.

The Fish Will Still Be There

It's hard to leave because we think we're missing out.

That one last cast could be the one. That next bend in the river could hold a trophy.

But the truth is?

The fish will still be there. The river isn't going anywhere.

Walking away isn't losing.

It's just saving something for next time.

Understanding the Trout's World—How They See, Hear, and Survive

But while we spend our time wondering what we might have missed, trout are living in a world that's completely different from our own—one where light bends, sounds travel differently, and survival depends on sensing the smallest disturbances in the water.

Trout don't experience the world as we do. They live in a different dimension—one of constant motion, filtered light, and unseen vibrations.

To fish for them successfully, you must step into their world, understand their instincts, and see the river as they do.

Part 5: Trout Behavior & Underwater Truth

Chapter 46: The World Through a Tout's Senses

Vision: The Window to a Trout's World

Imagine standing on the bank of a river, peering into the water. To you, the surface is reflective, sometimes clear, sometimes murky. To a trout, the world is an ever-changing mosaic of light and movement. Their eyes are positioned on the sides of their head, giving them nearly 360-degree vision, yet they lack depth perception directly in front of them. This means a well-presented fly that drifts into their feeding lane must look natural—no sudden movements, no drag.

Trout perceive colors differently than humans. In clear water, they can detect subtle variations in hue, which is why fly selection matters so much. Browns, greens, and blacks blend into the environment, while unnatural colors like bright red or fluorescent pink can trigger suspicion. Under low light, they rely more on contrast than color, which is why black flies tend to outperform others at dawn and dusk.

Trout also have a polarized vision, allowing them to see through the glare on the water's surface far better than we can. This is why a rising insect on the film of the water is so obvious to them while remaining nearly invisible to the angler above. A drifting mayfly, a crippled caddis, or an emerging nymph—they see it all. The challenge is making your artificial fly indistinguishable from the real thing.

Hearing and the Power of Vibration

Trout don't have ears in the way we do, but they "hear" in ways we can barely comprehend. Their inner ear, combined with their lateral line, allows them to sense vibrations and pressure changes in the water. The lateral line—a series of sensory receptors running along the sides of their body—detects movement up to several feet away. A struggling baitfish, a wading angler, even a rock dislodged upstream—it all sends signals through the water.

This is why stealth is everything. Heavy footsteps on the bank, careless casts that slap the water, or wading too aggressively can send trout darting for cover before you even make a presentation. The best anglers move like ghosts—slow, deliberate, and quiet.

Even fly choice can be influenced by vibration. A beadhead nymph rolling along the bottom, a weighted streamer pulsating with each strip of the line, or a popper slapping the surface—all create unique vibrations that a trout will key in on long before they see the actual fly.

Smell: The Sense We Ignore

Trout do not just see and hear the river; they smell it. Their olfactory system is highly developed, capable of detecting scent molecules in concentrations as low as one part per billion. This ability allows them to navigate back to their home waters during spawning season, recognize food sources, and even detect predators through subtle chemical changes in the water.

For anglers, understanding trout's sense of smell means recognizing the importance of keeping foreign scents off your flies and gear. Sunscreen, insect repellent, even the oils from your hands—these can send warning signals to a wary fish. Some seasoned fly fishers rub their hands with river mud before tying on a fly to mask unnatural odors.

Trout also use their sense of smell to detect what's safe and what's dangerous. A fly that has been in the mouths of multiple fish can sometimes trigger more strikes because it carries the scent of previous trout. Conversely, if a trout is caught and released in an area, other fish may pick up on the stress signals it released into the water and shut down feeding temporarily.

The Sixth Sense: How Trout Predict Danger

Trout have survived for millions of years because they have evolved an almost supernatural ability to detect threats. Their reaction time is faster than a blink, allowing them to escape predators before most threats even register. They process movement differently than we do—recognizing patterns rather than focusing on objects. A heron stalking in slow motion appears harmless, but a quick-moving shadow from above means imminent danger.

This is why approaching trout requires careful positioning. If you're silhouetted against the sky or standing in direct sunlight, they'll see you. If you wade directly into their line of sight, they'll vanish before your fly even touches the water. The best approach? Stay low, use natural cover, and present your fly from a position that keeps you hidden.

Even the movement of your fly line can be enough to put them on high alert. A shadow that suddenly flickers across the water, a splash too close to where they are holding—trout react instantly. The angler who understands this moves deliberately, casts strategically, and presents a fly with precision rather than force.

How Trout Feed Based on Their Senses

A trout's entire world revolves around opportunity and efficiency. Their senses dictate when and how they feed. On bright, clear days, they rely heavily on vision to target insects on the surface. On cloudy days or in murky water, they switch to their lateral line and hearing, honing in on movement and vibration.

This is why streamers work so well in off-color water—big, moving targets create strong signals that a trout can detect even when visibility is poor. Meanwhile, in crystal-clear spring creeks, where trout rely primarily on sight, a dead-drifted dry fly presented perfectly can mean the difference between a take and a refusal.

Trout also learn from experience. Older, more experienced fish have seen countless insects drift past and can detect the tiniest inconsistencies in movement. They have been hooked before and remember the unnatural drag of a fly tied to a tippet. The best anglers know that fooling a wise trout requires more than just the right fly—it demands the right drift, the right speed, and the right presentation.

The Key Takeaway—Thinking Like a Trout

Fly fishing is a game of adaptation. The angler who understands how trout see, hear, smell, and sense their world will always have an advantage.

Use stealth to avoid triggering their lateral line.

Match your fly's movement to the natural drift of insects.

Consider light conditions when choosing fly color.

Avoid foreign scents on your flies and gear.

Approach from angles that keep you hidden.

Learn to cast with precision to avoid unnecessary movement that could alert trout.

Once you start seeing the river as a trout does, everything changes.

The water becomes clearer. The currents make sense.

And suddenly, catching trout requires more than luck; it calls for understanding.

The Science of the Rise—Why Trout Feed the Way They Do

But understanding how trout sense the world is only half the battle. To catch them, you need to know why they feed, when they rise, and what makes them commit.

Trout are opportunists. They don't waste energy chasing food they can't catch, nor do they rise indiscriminately to anything that drifts by.

Every rise is calculated. Every take is deliberate.

If you want to catch more trout, you have to understand the science behind why—and how—they feed.

Chapter 47: The Science of the Rise

The Perfect Drift: Why Presentation Matters More Than the Fly

Picture a mayfly caught in the surface film, struggling against the current. It doesn't move erratically; it drifts, surrendered to the water's flow. Below, a trout watches, studying how the insect moves, how the current carries it. The moment something looks unnatural—a slight drag, a strange angle, a tiny ripple caused by an angler's tippet—the trout refuses.

This is why presentation often outweighs fly selection. Anglers obsess over choosing the right pattern, but how a fly moves is often more important than what it looks like. A perfectly matched fly with the wrong drift is ignored. A slightly off-pattern fly with a flawless drift? That's the one that gets taken.

Trout rise when they feel safe, when the flow is predictable, when the food source is consistent. If the drift is broken—by an unnatural current, a careless cast, or an angler's movement—the rise never happens.

The Different Types of Rises and What They Mean

Not all rises are the same. A subtle dimple on the surface is different from a full-bodied explosion, and both tell you something about what the trout is feeding on.

A classic head-and-tail rise is the sign of a cautious trout sipping delicate mayflies or midges. The trout breaks the surface with its nose, takes the insect, and disappears smoothly. A splashy rise, on the other hand, is aggressive and explosive, often seen during caddis hatches when trout chase down erratic-moving insects.

Some rises never break the surface at all. A subsurface swirl means a trout is feeding just below, keying in on emergers, nymphs, or drowned insects. A sipping rise, barely noticeable dimples in the water, means trout are locked in on midges or tiny flies that require precision to match. Then there's the false rise—a trout moving to inspect an insect but not committing. Either the fly was wrong, or something in the presentation seemed off.

A skilled angler watches for these cues and adjusts. If trout are sipping midges, tying on a giant stonefly won't work. If they're swirling on emergers, switching from a dry fly to a wet fly or soft hackle might turn refusals into takes.

Why Trout Feed at Certain Times (And Ignore You at Others)

Trout don't feed all the time. Their metabolism, water temperature, oxygen levels, and available food sources dictate when they eat and when they shut down.

Morning and evening are prime times because insects are most active then. The cooler water holds more oxygen, making fish more comfortable. Midday in summer, the water warms, oxygen drops, and feeding slows. After a cold front, trout get sluggish and hesitant. After a rain, they turn on as increased flow dislodges nymphs and brings a buffet of food drifting downstream.

Knowing when trout are most active allows an angler to be efficient. Fishing at noon on a blazing summer day is often a waste of time. But waiting for that last hour of daylight, when the sun drops and insects return, brings the river alive.

Selective Feeding: Why Some Trout Ignore Everything But One Fly

Ever watch a trout rise over and over, eating everything but your fly? It's not personal—it's science. Trout can become hyper-selective, focusing only on a specific stage of an insect's life cycle.

During a mayfly hatch, they might ignore fully-formed duns but gorge on emergers trapped just below the surface. During a spinner fall, they might take only spent mayflies with wings splayed out flat. Anglers who don't adjust get ignored.

The best approach is to observe first, cast second. If you see trout rising but refusing your fly, look closely. What exactly are they eating? Are insects trapped in the film? Are they floating high? Are they struggling? The answers to these questions dictate your fly selection.

The Science of Surface Tension and the Rise

A trout's mouth is designed to take advantage of surface tension. When an insect gets caught in the meniscus, it creates a disturbance that trout can sense from below. The film of the water acts almost like a magnifying glass, exaggerating movement.

This is why a struggling insect triggers strikes, while a poorly presented fly that sits unnaturally is ignored. Anglers who understand this fish with low-riding flies, soft hackles, or emergers that break the surface tension just enough to mimic the real thing. If a dry fly sits too high on the water, it can look unnatural. A slight adjustment—dressing only the hackle or using a pattern that rides lower—can make all the difference.

Water Currents, Foam Lines, and Feeding Lanes

Trout don't just eat anywhere. They position themselves where food comes naturally. Foam lines, current seams, and back eddies act as buffet lines, concentrating insects and allowing trout to sit in slow water while feeding in faster water.

Smart anglers don't just cast randomly. They identify feeding lanes and place their flies where food is naturally being delivered. This not only increases strikes but allows for more efficient fishing—spending time in the right places rather than hoping for a miracle cast.

The Energy Equation: Why Big Trout Feed Differently

A 20-inch trout doesn't rise the same way as a 10-inch trout. Larger fish have spent years refining their energy calculations. They don't waste effort chasing tiny mayflies when a single struggling grasshopper delivers more calories with less effort.

This is why targeting big trout requires different tactics. Instead of focusing on the delicate dry fly game, anglers hunting trophy fish often use big streamers, drowned terrestrials, and high-protein meals that demand attention. A large brown trout lurking under a cutbank won't rise for a size 20 midge, but a fat stonefly struggling in the current? That's worth the energy.

Why Some Trout Become Nocturnal Feeders

As trout grow older, some become primarily nocturnal feeders. The largest, most cautious fish recognize that feeding at night reduces their risk of predation while allowing them to ambush food more effectively.

Anglers looking for trophy trout often turn to night fishing with large, slow-moving streamers or mice patterns that create a silhouette trout can detect even in near darkness.

How Water Clarity Affects a Trout's Decision to Rise

In clear water, trout rely heavily on sight, scrutinizing flies with a level of precision that forces anglers to use finer tippets and perfect drifts. In stained or murky water, trout depend more on vibration and silhouette, making larger flies or exaggerated movements more effective.

This is why the same fly might work perfectly one day and fail miserably the next—the fish are responding to changes in visibility and sensory priority.

The Final Truth—Rise Form Is a Language

Every rise is a message. Every refusal is an answer.

Trout aren't random in their behavior. They are methodical, calculating, and deeply in tune with their environment. The angler who learns to read the rise, interpret feeding patterns, and adjust presentation accordingly is the angler who consistently catches more fish.

Most importantly, trout don't play by our rules. The rise happens on their terms, dictated by their senses, instincts, and the invisible science that governs life beneath the surface.

To master the rise, you don't just need the right fly—you need to understand why trout eat and how they decide what's worth taking.

Water Temperature—The Silent Force That Controls Everything

But feeding behavior is shaped by more than insects and instincts. It's also about temperature. Trout are prisoners of their environment. Unlike humans, they don't regulate their body temperature internally.

Their world is dictated by the temperature of the water they swim in, and everything—how they move, when they feed, and even whether they survive—depends on it.

If you understand water temperature, you understand trout. And the key to knowing when the river comes alive starts with knowing the magic range: between 50 and 65 degrees.

Chapter 48: How Water Temperature Shapes Trout Behavior

Trout are prisoners of their environment. Unlike humans, they don't regulate their body temperature internally. Their world is dictated by the temperature of the water they swim in, and everything—how they move, when they feed, and even whether they survive—depends on it. If you understand water temperature, you understand trout.

The Magic Range: 50-65 Degrees

There is a reason why seasoned anglers carry thermometers. 50-65°F (10-18°C) is the sweet spot—the range where trout are most active, aggressive, and willing to eat. This is the golden zone, where metabolism is high enough to keep them feeding, but not so high that they burn through their energy too quickly.

In this range, trout are opportunistic. They position themselves in feeding lanes, actively rise to insects, and chase down streamers with the kind of aggression that makes anglers come back for more. A day on the river in this temperature zone means action. Fish are alert, responsive, and playing their part in the predator-prey dance that makes fly fishing so addictive.

Cold Water: When Everything Slows Down

Below 45°F (7°C), trout begin to change. Their metabolism drops, their feeding slows, and they become sluggish. In the dead of winter, when the water hovers just above freezing, trout are barely moving. They are conservationists, using as little energy as possible to survive.

At these temperatures, food isn't burned through quickly, so trout don't need to eat as often. They won't chase down a fly; they won't expend unnecessary energy. If you're fishing in water below 40°F, you need small, slow, and precise presentations. Nymphs, dead-drifted with pinpoint accuracy, are your best bet. If you think you're moving the fly too slow—slow it down even more.

The 40-50 Degree Zone: The Transition Period

Water in the 40-50°F (4-10°C) range can be a tricky zone. Trout aren't completely lethargic, but they're not in high gear either. Feeding is inconsistent. One hour, they might be aggressively taking streamers, the next they're glued to the bottom, refusing everything.

This is where the time of day matters. Early mornings in this temperature range are often dead—fish are too cold to care. But by midday, as the sun has warmed the water a few degrees, the river can come alive. Understanding this transition means the difference between wasting time in the morning versus timing your approach for the window when trout actually turn on.

The Heat Problem: When Water Gets Too Warm

Above 65°F (18°C), things start to go wrong. A trout's metabolism speeds up, but the water's oxygen levels drop. They burn energy faster but have less oxygen available to sustain them. In the high 60s, trout become stressed. They might still feed, but each fight drains them more.

Above 70°F (21°C), catch-and-release fishing can kill trout even if they swim away. They become so oxygen-deprived that even a short fight pushes them past recovery. This is where ethical angling comes into play. If the water is above 70°F, smart anglers pack up their rods or move to colder water—spring-fed creeks, tailwaters, or shaded high-elevation streams where temperatures are still safe.

Oxygen and the Lethal Zone

At 75°F (24°C) and above, trout are in survival mode. They stop feeding. They seek the deepest, shadiest, most oxygen-rich pockets of water available. If they can't find refuge, they die. Period. The high 70s are lethal. No amount of skill, presentation, or fly selection can change that.

This is where anglers have a responsibility. Fishing in these conditions is not just ineffective—it's unethical. The best move? Know your river, carry a thermometer, and respect the limits of the fish you love to pursue.

How Trout Adapt to Temperature Changes

Trout are survivors. They don't just sit there and take what nature throws at them—they adapt. In warming water, they move. They seek shade, deep pools, and oxygenated riffles. In cold water, they settle into slow-moving wintering holes, where energy conservation is key.

This is why knowing where trout go at different temperatures is just as important as knowing when they feed. A river that was productive in the spring might be lifeless by summer if the water gets too warm. But a feeder creek, a shaded canyon, or a bottom-release tailwater might still hold fish.

How Temperature Affects Fly Choice

The right fly depends on more than matching the hatch—it's about matching the trout's behavior. In cold water, slow and small presentations work best. Midges, tiny nymphs, and egg patterns dominate. In the 50-65°F range, everything is on the table—streamers, dries, nymphs, big terrestrials. Once the water starts to warm into the high 60s, efficiency matters. Bigger meals like grasshoppers, stoneflies, and large nymphs get better returns because trout want the most energy for the least effort.

In summer, when water gets dangerously warm, wet flies and nymphs in oxygen-rich areas become key. Finding cooler tributaries or deeper holes where trout can feed without excessive stress makes all the difference.

Seasonal Shifts: Understanding Temperature Patterns

Trout aren't reacting to today's temperature alone—they're responding to seasonal shifts. The gradual warming of spring wakes them up after months of sluggish metabolism. Summer brings peak activity, but also the risk of heat stress. Fall triggers aggressive feeding before winter slows them down again.

The best anglers think ahead—they anticipate how trout will behave weeks in advance, not just based on what's happening today. They watch long-term weather trends, study how their local rivers warm and cool, and know when to move upstream or downstream to stay in the ideal temperature zone.

The Thermocline: The Hidden Barrier in Lakes

In lakes, trout respond to water temperature differently than in rivers. Instead of moving laterally to find better water, they move vertically. The thermocline—a distinct temperature boundary in deeper water—becomes critical. Above it, the water is too warm. Below it, there's not enough oxygen. The perfect zone? Right along the thermocline, where food and comfort meet.

Anglers fishing lakes need to adjust depth accordingly. In summer, trout are rarely near the surface unless it's dawn or dusk. Deepwater trolling, sinking lines, and vertical jigging become essential techniques.

Reading the River—The Skill Every Angler Needs

The best fly fishers don't just fish where the fish should be—they fish where the conditions dictate the fish will be.

They understand how temperature shifts trout behavior, how seasonal patterns dictate feeding, and how a few degrees in water temperature can mean the difference between an empty net and the best day of the season.

The Angler's Responsibility

We aren't just fishermen—we are stewards of the water. Trout can't control the conditions they live in, but we can control how we fish for them. Knowing when to fish, when to switch tactics, and when to walk away is part of becoming a complete angler.

Trout are remarkable survivors, but they aren't invincible. If you love the sport, you respect the fish. That means learning the rules of the river, watching the thermometer, and making decisions that ensure the next generation of anglers gets to experience what we do.

Because that's the real game—understanding the world beneath the surface, respecting its limits, and fishing in a way that keeps the magic alive.

Why Coweeta's Work Matters

But protecting trout involves more than what happens on the river—it's about understanding the water itself. Some places deserve more recognition than they get. You hear about the big conservation efforts—the national parks, the protected trout streams, the flashy restoration projects—but you rarely hear about the quiet laboratories deep in the mountains, working day after day to keep our waters flowing.

That's where Coweeta Hydrologic Laboratory comes in. It isn't just a research facility—it's a watchtower for the health of our rivers. Nestled in the southern Appalachian Mountains of North Carolina, Coweeta has been studying forest watersheds since 1934, making it one of the longest-running hydrologic research sites in the world.

Chapter 49: Coweeta: Guardian of the Flowing Waters

Some places deserve more recognition than they get. You hear about the big conservation efforts—the national parks, the protected trout streams, the flashy restoration projects—but you rarely hear about the quiet laboratories deep in the mountains, working day after day to keep our waters flowing.

Tucked away in the misty folds of the North Carolina Appalachians is the Coweeta Hydrologic Laboratory part of the US Forest Service. It is more than a research station—it's living experiment. Rain falls, streams rise, and the forest breathes, all under the watchful eyes of scientists who track every drop, every shift in the southern Appalachian Mountains. Working here isn't about sitting in a lab—it's about wading into mountain creeks, hiking dense ridges, and decoding the hidden patterns of water, soil, and trees.

But Coweeta's impact doesn't stop at these mountains. This outpost of the Southern Research Station has been studying forest watersheds and has shaped national water and forest policies, influenced global ecological studies, and connected with projects across the Rockies, the Pacific Northwest, and even tropical and arid regions. As part of the Long-Term Ecological Research (LTER) Network, its work ripples across the world, influencing how we understand and manage ecosystems. (There will be a quiz at the end—hope you were paying attention.)

This isn't abstract science—it's real, boots-on-the-ground research sites in the world., tracking how water moves, how forests survive, and how landscapes adapt in a changing world

It doesn't have the allure of a wild trout stream or the mystique of a legendary fishing spot, but without places like Coweeta, many of those streams wouldn't even exist as we know them.

A Personal Connection

I tell everyone about the work being done at Coweeta. Most of the time, I get polite nods and blank stares—the kind people give when they appreciate your enthusiasm but have no idea what you're talking about. That's fine.

But every now and then, I find someone who gets it. Someone who understands that Conservation involves more than protecting fish—it's preserving the water that gives them life. And when you protect the water, you protect everything that depends on it.

I once met an older gentleman on a trout stream, a lifelong angler who had fished more days than most of us could dream of. He saw my curiosity about the river, about its flow, its rhythm. He grinned and said, "If you really want to know a river, don't just fish it. Watch it. Listen to it. Learn where it comes from."

That advice stuck with me. And the more I learned, the more I realized that the people at Coweeta were watching and listening to our rivers better than anyone.

The Fight to Keep Creeks and Rivers Flowing

Conservation stands for more than slapping a "protected" sign on a stream and hoping for the best. It's about understanding what makes a river healthy and fighting like hell to keep it that way.

Coweeta's research has shown us how logging, farming, and even urban development upstream can cripple a fishery downstream. They've proven that trout need cold, oxygen-rich water to thrive—and that shade from trees along the banks is more than just a nice aesthetic; it's a survival mechanism.

Every year, policies affecting our waters are debated. Some favor short-term gain over long-term health. But places like Coweeta keep providing hard data—the kind that policymakers can't ignore.

What Can Anglers Do?

As fly fishers, we're already stewards of the water, whether we realize it or not. But knowing what's at stake means we have an even greater responsibility.

Support organizations that protect watersheds – Groups like Trout Unlimited, the U.S. Forest Service, and local watershed alliances rely on angler advocacy.

Think beyond the fish – A thriving trout population starts long before the fly ever hits the water. Pay attention to policies affecting forests, agriculture, and water management.

Educate others – Most people have no idea how fragile our trout streams really are. The more anglers talk about it, the more people care.

Paying Attention to the Source

If there's one thing Coweeta teaches us, it's this:

A river is only as healthy as its source.

So next time you wade into your favorite creek, take a moment.

Look upstream.

Think about where that water is coming from. Think about the decades of research, the laws, the people who fought to keep it clean and flowing.

Because the best trout streams aren't just lucky.

They're protected, watched over, and fought for.

And if we want them to be here for future generations, that fight never stops.

The Value of a Single Trout

But protecting trout isn't limited to the water they live in—but also how we treat them when we catch them.

There's a certain reverence that comes with catch-and-release fishing.

The idea that a single fish can bring joy to multiple anglers over its lifetime is something truly special.

For those who have spent enough time on the water, the understanding develops naturally—

Trout are too valuable to catch just once.

Chapter 50: Why a Trout is Too Valuable to Catch Just Once

The Moment That Changed My Perspective

I'll never forget the day my four-year-old daughter unknowingly taught me the most profound lesson in fishing. I had just landed a beautiful rainbow trout, its colors shimmering in the sunlight as it rested in my net, submerged in the water. Wanting to capture the moment, I set my rod down and turned to fetch my camera. When I turned back, the fish was gone.

I looked at my daughter, who stood there with an innocent smile.

"Sweetheart, what happened to my trout?" I asked.

She simply looked up at me and said, "Daddy, I felt bad for him. He really wanted to go back to his family."

That was it. No long-winded explanations, no debate about conservation, no deep philosophical reasoning. Just a simple truth.

Without needing to be taught, she understood. She knew the fish belonged to the river, that it had a life beyond the moment I held it in my hands.

At that moment, I realized something—this new generation gets it. Without needing to be taught, she understood the importance of returning the fish to where it belongs, ensuring it would live on to swim another day.

Catch-and-Release: Preserving the Future of Fishing

The philosophy behind catch-and-release is simple: sustain the fishery so future generations can experience the same joy of fishing. Every time we release a fish, we're giving it another chance—to grow, to spawn, and to be part of the intricate balance of the ecosystem.

Many trout waters are limited in their ability to reproduce fish naturally. Some streams rely heavily on stocking programs to maintain their populations, while others hold self-sustaining wild trout that require careful management. By practicing catch-and-release, we help keep these fisheries thriving.

That doesn't mean keeping a fish for the table is wrong—there's a place for selective harvesting. But the balance matters. Letting the big, healthy fish go ensures a strong population, one that will provide future anglers with the same thrill we chase every time we step into the water.

And beyond the science, there's something deeper—the spirit of the sport itself. Fly fishing isn't just about catching fish. It's about the connection to nature, the challenge of the pursuit, and the respect that comes with understanding that we are just visitors in the trout's world.

Best Practices for Catch-and-Release

If you're going to release a fish, do it right. Keep the fish wet, minimizing air exposure as much as possible. Use barbless hooks to make for an easier, less damaging release. Handle the fish gently, wetting your hands before touching it to protect its delicate slime coating. And when it's time to let it go, hold the fish in the current, allowing it to regain its strength before it slips back into the depths.

Trout are survivors. But how well they survive after an encounter with an angler depends on how we handle them.

A Lasting Impression

To this day, I think about that moment with my daughter every time I release a fish.

The look on her face. The wisdom in her words. The way she saw the world in a way so many of us forget.

Maybe that's the ultimate goal—not just to catch fish, but to pass down the respect and responsibility that comes with being an angler.

Because in the end, it's not just about the fish.

It's about what the fish represents—wildness, adventure, and the endless cycle of life in the rivers we cherish.

I think that's why this was my favorite chapter to write. Some fishing memories fade, but this one remains as vivid as the day it happened. And maybe that's the point—some moments on the water aren't meant to be forgotten.

Part 6: The Heart of the Stream: Fly Fishing's Deeper Meaning

Chapter 51: The Essence of Trout Fishing

Somewhere deep in the mist-veiled hollows of the Appalachians, a brook trout rises. The ripple spreads, barely disturbing the stillness of a backwoods pool hidden from time. That moment—the rise, the take, the tension on the line—is something more than a simple act of nature. It's a conversation, a lesson, a communion between angler and stream, predator and prey, man and the wild. If you've stood knee-deep in a freestone creek, rod in hand, you know this feeling. And if you haven't, well, this chapter is for you.

The Pull of the Stream

Trout fishing is not just about the catch—it never has been. It's about the pull. Not just the tug on the line, but something deeper. The way a stream seems to call to you, pulling you away from the world of concrete and deadlines, leading you back to something raw and untamed. The river bends and twists, shaping the land as it moves, just as it shapes the angler who wades into it. You enter as one person and emerge, whether successful or skunked, as someone changed.

The philosophy of trout fishing is the philosophy of the patient hunter. The one who knows that some days, the fish will rise, and other days, the water will flow smooth and silent, offering nothing but its own mystery. It's about accepting the rhythm of the world without needing to control it. The best fly fishermen don't fight the current—they move with it.

A Lesson from a Hidden Pool

I remember one morning deep in the Smoky Mountains, fog hanging thick as wet cotton over the water. I had hiked for miles into a stretch of water I'd been told was untouched, a stream that only showed itself to those willing to work for it. I stood at the edge of a pool so still it reflected the trees above with near-perfect clarity.

The first cast was perfect. A tight loop, an easy laydown of the line, the dry fly kissing the surface like a whispered promise. Nothing. Second cast, a little closer to the submerged log where I thought an old brown might be lurking. Still nothing.

Then, a third cast, right against the bank. The fly sat for half a second before it disappeared in a swirl. The fight wasn't a battle, not a show of power—just a dance between a wild creature and an angler trying to earn his place in the woods. When I brought him to hand, a speckled marvel of gold, green, and crimson, I felt something deeper than excitement. I had done something right, something old and sacred. And then, just as quickly, I let him slip back into the current.

The Appalachian Masters

The Appalachian Mountains have bred some of the finest fly fishermen in history, men who understood that this pursuit was more than sport—it was an art, a discipline, a way of being. Among them was Theodore Gordon, often called the father of American dry fly fishing. Though he was more tied to the Catskills, his influence stretched southward, where Appalachian anglers began refining their own techniques, making adjustments to meet the unique challenges of mountain streams.

Then there was Lee Wulff, a man who believed that trout fishing wasn't just about catching fish but about preserving wild places. His philosophy was simple: a trout is too valuable to be caught only once. Catch and release, an idea many of us take for granted today, was radical in his time.

And of course, there's Jim Gasque, who wrote Hunting and Fishing in the Great Smokies, capturing the spirit of Appalachian fly fishing like few others. His words, much like the streams he fished, had a rhythm, a patience, and an understanding that trout fishing is a lesson in humility and wonder.

The Stream as a Teacher

If you listen, the water will teach you everything you need to know. How to be still when needed, how to move when required. How to blend in, how to anticipate, how to wait.

A river never hurries, yet it carves mountains. The best fly fishermen understand this. There's no need to force the cast, no need to muscle the rod. Let the fly land where it should, let the water take it where it will. The fish will decide.

The first time I fished with an old-timer from North Carolina, he barely spoke. He just watched. I fumbled my casts, spooked fish, cursed under my breath. He said nothing. Only when we sat on the bank for lunch did he finally offer a single piece of advice: "Don't fish against the river. Fish with it."

I didn't understand then, not fully. But years later, when I found myself standing in another quiet mountain stream, letting my line drift with the current, I finally got it. It wasn't about the fish. It was about learning to trust the water, to be a part of the world instead of trying to control it.

The Drunken Angler's Night by the Creek

Then there was the time a friend of mine had a little too much to drink by the fire after a long day of fishing. The whiskey had been smooth, the trout plentiful, and before he knew it, he had drifted off into a deep sleep against a fallen log. When he woke, the fire had burned out, and the stars hung overhead like distant embers. But the real problem? It was pitch black, and the trail back to his truck was nowhere to be found.

With nothing but his fishing gear and the sound of water rushing nearby, he did what any half-sober angler would do—he made himself at home. He curled up in his waders, used his fishing bag as a pillow, and let the symphony of the stream lull him back to sleep. By morning, the rising sun cut through the trees, leading him back to the trail like a guiding hand. He never admitted to being scared that night, but I saw the way he looked at that creek afterward—with reverence, respect, and maybe just a hint of wariness.

The Romance of the Rise

There's a romance in trout fishing that's hard to explain to those who've never felt it. It's not just the solitude, or the beauty of the backcountry, or even the challenge of fooling a wild fish with a bit of feather and thread. It's the moment when, against all odds, a trout rises. That perfect, fleeting instant when instinct and artistry collide. It's a feeling that lingers, that calls you back to the water time and time again.

And in the end, that's the philosophy of trout fishing. It's not a sport. It's not a pastime. It's a calling. A way of life. A reminder that somewhere, right now, a trout is rising. And maybe, just maybe, it's waiting for you to answer.

The Flow State of Fly Fishing

There's a moment in every angler's life when the world fades away—the only thing that exists is the line, the water, and the fish. This is the flow state of fly fishing, a deep immersion in the act, where time slows down, and everything outside the river disappears. The rhythm of casting, the anticipation of a strike, the gentle mend of the line—it all becomes second nature, a movement as instinctual as breathing.

Psychologists call it "flow", the state of being fully present and engaged in an activity. Anglers just call it "a good day on the water." It's why hours can pass unnoticed, why we return from the stream feeling lighter, more centered. Fly fishing is one of those rare pursuits where success isn't measured by the number of fish caught but by the depth of the experience itself.

Trout Fishing as a Form of Storytelling

Every angler is a storyteller, whether they realize it or not. A day on the river is never just a day on the river—it's a collection of moments strung together like beads on a line. The fish landed, the ones that got away, the near-miss with a hidden log, the hawk that circled overhead as you stripped in your fly—these details become the stories we tell over and over.

The best fishing stories aren't always about the biggest fish. Sometimes, they're about the absurdity of human error—the time you hooked your own hat, the misstep that sent you sprawling into the current. Other times, they're about the unexpected beauty of the day—the rise of a trout just before dusk, the reflection of the sky in the water, the laughter shared with a friend. We don't just fish for the catch. We fish for the stories.

The Ritual of the Cast

There's a rhythm to fly fishing that borders on ritual. The gentle pull of line from the reel, the measured back-and-forth of the cast, the delicate laydown of the fly on the water. Done well, it is seamless, effortless—a ballet between angler and river.

For many, the cast itself is as satisfying as the catch. There is an artistry in getting it just right, in finding that perfect arc, in letting the fly land with the lightest touch. And when you do, it feels like an act of precision, of patience, of complete control.

But fly casting is also humbling. The wind will take your perfect loop and turn it into a tangled mess. A hidden branch will grab your fly mid-air. Your line will collapse in a heap at your feet for no apparent reason. And so, the ritual repeats. Cast, mend, drift, retrieve. Over and over until the motion becomes second nature, until the river rewards you for your patience.

The Language of Water

A seasoned angler doesn't just look at a stream—they read it. The river speaks in ripples, seams, and eddies, and those who listen closely will hear what it has to say.

A riffle whispers of oxygen-rich water where trout wait for drifting insects.

A deep pool murmurs of sanctuary, a hiding place for the wise old fish that have seen too many hooks.

A bubble line hints at a natural conveyor belt of food, where a drifting fly is more likely to be met with a rise.

Every bend in the river has a story. Every rock and fallen tree changes the way water moves, creates new feeding lanes, offers new challenges. The more you study a stream, the more it reveals. Fly fishing is not just about casting a line—it's about listening to the water and learning to speak its language.

Lessons in Patience and Precision

Trout fishing teaches patience. It demands that you slow down, observe, and adjust.

The perfect cast is worthless without the right drift.

The right fly is meaningless if it doesn't land naturally on the water.

You can't force a trout to take your fly—you have to convince it.

The best anglers aren't just skilled casters; they're patient observers. They don't rush. They don't force the moment.

They wait, watching the water, noting the rise forms, adjusting their presentation.

And when they do cast, it's deliberate, precise, intentional.

Fly fishing isn't about control—it's about partnership with nature.

The river sets the tempo.

The fish decides the game.

The angler, if he is wise, simply learns to play along.

Time moves differently on a trout stream.

If you're paying attention, you feel it shift.

One moment, you're watching the slow, deliberate rise of a feeding brown, the next, you realize the sun has drifted past the canyon wall, shadows stretching across the water.

Hours vanish between casts.

And in those moments, you understand something that the modern world never lets you see—time isn't a clock, it's a current.

Chapter 52: What Trout Teach Us About Time

A Trout's Time vs. A Human's Time

Trout don't check watches. They don't schedule meetings. They hold in the current, waiting, watching, responding only when the moment is right. A hatch begins—they rise. A predator moves—they disappear. Everything they do is dictated by the now, not by some artificial deadline.

Fish for them long enough, and you start to slip into their rhythm.

We, on the other hand, live in constant distraction. We fill our days with alerts, obligations, endless movement. Fly fishing forces a reset. It anchors you in the moment, because if your mind drifts, the trout wins.

The Drift and the Moment

In fly fishing, success happens in seconds. The perfect drift. The subtle sip. The heartbeat pause before the set. If you aren't present for it, it's gone.

And just like in life, the best moments aren't the ones you planned. They're the ones you were paying attention to.

The Fish That Changed Time

The stream was a series of small plunge pools, each one clearer than the last, reflecting the golden afternoon light like liquid glass. The scent of wet pine and earth lingered in the air, mingling with the distant hum of insects.

I waded in, the icy water tightening around my legs, making each step deliberate, calculated.

I saw the trout before I cast—a wild cutthroat, suspended mid-current, perfectly still except for the faintest flick of its tail. The water was so clear I could see every spot along its golden flank, the sharp black outline of its fins against the rocky bottom.

I don't know how long I stood there watching it. Minutes? An hour? Time didn't work the same way anymore.

I knelt, cast upstream, watched my dry fly drift perfectly into its lane. The fish rose, took the fly so gently it looked like it was sipping air. I lifted the rod, felt the weight, and for a few seconds, there was nothing else in the world but me, the fish, and the river that carried us both forward.

The River Never Stops, and Neither Do We

A trout stream is always moving, never the same twice. The water today is different from the water yesterday. And in the same way, so are we.

We spend our lives trying to hold onto things—moments, places, people—but like a trout stream, time doesn't stop for us. It moves, whether we chase it or not.

The same bend in the river might look familiar next season, but the water flowing through it will be entirely different.

And so will you.

Maybe we aren't meant to control time.

Maybe we're meant to move with it.

The Day That Slipped Away

There was a time I fished a familiar river with an old friend. The air was thick with late-summer warmth, cicadas buzzing in the distance. We waded carefully, feeling the smooth stones beneath our boots, eyes scanning the water for the telltale flash of feeding trout.

The fish weren't rising.

We fished anyway. Not for numbers. Not for the perfect cast. Just for the sake of being there.

Cast after cast, hour after hour, we talked less and listened more. The river spoke in trickles and surges, in wind through the pines, in the occasional splash of a feeding trout.

Before we knew it, the light had shifted, the sun dipping low. We had let time slip away without ever checking a watch.

I don't remember how many fish we caught that day.

But I remember how it felt.

Like time didn't own us.

Like we had stepped outside of it, if only for a few hours.

Let the Current Take You

Trout don't fight the river.

They ride it.

They use the current, not fight against it.

Maybe that's how we should live too—not trying to stop time, but flowing with it, embracing each moment as it comes.

Because in the end, we don't control time.

We only decide how we spend it.

Chapter 53: The Unwritten Code of the River

The Unspoken Rules of the River

Fly fishing is more than just a sport—it's a tradition, a discipline, and in many ways, a form of silent respect between anglers and nature. While fishing regulations are printed on pamphlets and websites, the real rules of the river aren't written down. They're passed from angler to angler, generation to generation.

I've talked about this before in other chapters, and I'll say it again here—because it's worth repeating. If you've read other fly fishing books, you'll notice this subject doesn't get much attention. That's a mistake. These rules matter. They shape how we fish, how we treat the river, and how we interact with other anglers. Ignore them, and you'll ruin more than just your own experience. Follow them, and the entire river becomes a better place to fish. So if I'm repeating myself, excuse me—but I'd rather hammer this home than let it go unsaid.

A trout stream isn't a crowded subway. If you see another angler on the water, give them room. A good rule of thumb? Stay at least a couple of casting distances away—more if possible. If the stream is small, consider waiting your turn rather than squeezing in. Elbowing into someone's drift is one of the fastest ways to make an enemy on the water. If someone is fishing upstream, don't move in above them. If they're fishing downstream, don't move in below them. Follow the flow.

Splashing through the river like an excited Labrador ruins fishing for everyone—including yourself. Trout feel vibrations in the water and will scatter if you stomp through their world. Approach slowly, step lightly, and avoid unnecessary movement. If you see another angler stalking a fish, stop and observe. You might learn something—or at least not ruin their shot.

Arriving at a stream before sunrise has its perks—you get to choose your spot. But with that privilege comes responsibility. If you're first in a section, set the tone for how the day should go. If you're working methodically upstream, others will follow suit. If you're hopping from hole to hole, expect the same. And if you arrive later, watch the rhythm of the anglers before you and adjust accordingly.

Every angler has a secret fly pattern or technique, but there's a difference between keeping a few tricks to yourself and being a closed book. If someone asks what's working, share a little. Maybe you don't give away the exact fly, but a general tip can go a long way. A simple, "They seem to be hitting small caddis dries today," builds goodwill. A cold shoulder does the opposite.

The phrase "A trout is too valuable to be caught only once" exists for a reason. If you practice catch and release, do it right. Wet your hands before handling fish, keep them in the water as much as possible, and never squeeze. If you want a picture, make it fast—a fish out of water for too long is a fish that might not recover. And if you see another angler mishandling a fish, educate kindly, not condescendingly. We all start somewhere.

Trash on the riverbank doesn't just ruin the scenery—it disrespects the very thing that gives us this experience. Pack out everything you pack in. If you see a tangle of fishing line, pick it up. If you find an old beer can, carry it out. The river doesn't belong to us—it belongs to itself. We are just visitors. Leave it better than you found it. Future anglers—including your future self—will thank you.

A simple nod, a quiet "good morning," or a lifted hand from across the stream can go a long way. Fly fishing is often a solitary pursuit, but it's also a community. Respect is the currency of the river, and the smallest gestures carry weight. And if an angler hooks up near you, root for them. A shared victory on the river is better than a solo one.

If a prime fishing spot is producing, it's tempting to stay there all day. But if others are waiting, consider moving on after you've had your fill. Rotating spots keeps the experience fair for everyone. Fish it, enjoy it, and pass it on.

Did you get skunked? Say so. Catch a monster? Enjoy it without boasting. Fly fishing isn't a competition—it's a lifelong pursuit of small victories. The best anglers aren't the ones who catch the most fish—they're the ones who respect the experience, the river, and those who share it. Fish stories are fine, but credibility is worth more than exaggeration.

The river has its own set of rules—some written, most unspoken. Follow them, and you become part of something larger than yourself, something timeless. Ignore them, and you'll feel it. Maybe not right away, but sooner or later, the water reminds you.

Because fly fishing isn't just about what you do on the river—it's about how you approach it. The way you step into the current, the way you handle your gear, the way you prepare before that first cast.

Every angler, whether they realize it or not, follows a ritual.

And that ritual? That's where the real magic begins.

Chapter 54: The Ritual of Fly Fishing

More Than Just a Cast

Fly fishing isn't just about catching fish. It's a ritual—a sequence of moments, repeated, refined, and woven into the rhythm of an angler's life. The early morning drives, the scent of wet earth, the feel of cold river stones beneath wading boots—it's all part of something deeper. Something sacred.

The ritual starts long before you step into the water. It begins with the preparation—the careful selection of gear, the laying out of flies, the rhythmic spooling of tippet onto a reel. It's the act of standing at the water's edge, taking a deep breath, and letting the sound of the river reset you. It's the quiet reverence before the first cast.

And in these rituals, we don't just find fish. We find ourselves.

The Forgotten Gear & The Lessons It Teaches

One early October morning, my fishing buddy and I packed up and drove deep into the mountains, heading for the Upper Nantahala—a stretch of river known for its wild browns, deep pools, and deceptively tricky water.

The weather was perfect. High blue skies, a slight bite in the air. The kind of day that makes you believe you were born to stand in a river and cast a fly.

We parked at the trailhead, loaded up our packs, and began the hike in. We talked about everything and nothing—trout myths, bad coffee, our best casts, and worst misses. The kind of rambling conversation you only have with someone who's waded into enough rivers alongside you to know your stories before you tell them.

Then we reached the water, and I realized something was wrong.

I opened my pack, reached inside, and felt... nothing. No reel. Just an empty space where my most essential piece of gear should have been.

I turned to my buddy, eyes wide.

"You're not gonna believe this."

He looked at my open bag, then at me. There was a pause. Then a grin.

"Again?"

I had done this before. Left something crucial behind. Waders. A net. Once, an entire fly box. And now, here I was, deep in the woods, without a reel.

He shook his head, reached into his pack, and pulled out an old, dented spare.

"Lucky for you," he said, "I know you."

And just like that, the trip was saved. The drift was what mattered. And I learned—again—that part of the ritual of fly fishing is rolling with the punches, laughing at your own mistakes, and always having a backup plan.

The Technical Side: The Dry-Dropper Setup

That morning, I decided to rig up a dry-dropper—a Parachute Adams up top with a small Pheasant Tail nymph trailing below. The Upper Nantahala can be tricky, and trout here often feed just beneath the surface. A dry-dropper setup lets you cover both zones—if they weren't rising, they'd take the nymph drifting naturally below.

It's a delicate balance—too much weight on the dropper, and the dry fly sinks. Too light, and the nymph never reaches the strike zone. Adjusting the leader length and weight is key, reading the water as much as the fish. The setup gives you an edge—one fly acting as a strike indicator, the other increasing your odds.

I made my first few casts, watching my Adams ride high along the current. The take was subtle, just a slight hesitation of the dry fly, barely noticeable if you weren't paying attention. I lifted the rod and felt the pull—a beautiful, buttery brown had inhaled the nymph.

Moments like this, when technique and instinct align, remind you that fly fishing is both science and art.

The Perfect Morning & A Story That Stuck

Some fishing trips stick in your mind forever, even if nothing particularly extraordinary happens.

One morning, not long ago, everything just felt right.

It was late spring. The world was waking up. The air smelled of pine and damp earth, with that cool, crisp scent that comes only when morning sun hits freshly melted snow. The river was running clear, cold, alive.

We arrived just as the first golden rays slipped over the ridgeline, painting the water in streaks of orange and blue. There were risers—tiny rings breaking the glassy surface, trout feeding lazily, unhurried. The kind of scene that makes an angler slow down, take a deep breath, and know today is going to be a good day.

We fished without pressure. Without expectation. Just two guys, waist-deep in the current, watching our casts unfold against a backdrop of endless mountains.

Then, the moment.

I made a cast—not a perfect one, but good enough. My Adams drifted along a slow seam, and a brown trout rose, took it so gently it barely made a sound. The fight wasn't long or dramatic, but it was honest.

When I brought the fish to hand, it was like holding a piece of the river itself—gold and green, speckled and wild.

I turned to my buddy, held it up, and said, "Now that's a trout."

He laughed. "You ever notice how you say that every time?"

And I realized—I do.

Every fish, no matter the size, the species, or the circumstances, is always a trout worth catching.

That's the ritual. Appreciating each moment. Each cast. Each fish.

Why We Keep Coming Back

Fly fishing is a series of rituals—some deliberate, some accidental.

The morning coffee.

The drive.

The slow ritual of tying on a fly.

The first cast. The first fish.

The moment the sun hits the water just right and turns the river into liquid gold.

The stories told on the walk back to the truck.

The gear packed up, ready for another day.

We don't just fish to catch trout.

We fish to repeat these moments, over and over, refining them, perfecting them, letting them shape us as much as we shape the experience itself.

The ritual stays, no matter the conditions, no matter the fish count. It's what calls us back.

Every single time.

Passing It On

But there comes a moment in every angler's life when the greatest joy isn't found in the fight of a wild trout or the perfection of a cast—

It's found in watching a child's eyes light up as they feel the first tug of a fish on the line.

Fishing is more than a pastime—it's a tradition, a rite of passage, a way to connect generations.

Passing on the love of fishing to children is about more than teaching them to cast—

It's about teaching patience, appreciation for nature, and the quiet joy of time spent outdoors.

Chapter 55: Fishing with Kids and Passing It On

Passing It On: Fishing with the Next Generation

There comes a moment in every angler's life when the greatest joy isn't found in the fight of a wild trout or the perfection of a cast, but in watching a child's eyes light up as they feel the first tug of a fish on the line. Fishing is more than a pastime—it's a tradition, a rite of passage, and a way to connect generations.

In a world full of digital distractions and packed schedules, taking a child fishing offers something rare: a chance to unplug, slow down, and be present. It's an opportunity to teach patience, problem-solving, and respect for the natural world. A child who spends time on the water learns more than how to catch a fish. They begin to understand ecosystems, water conditions, and fish behavior, fostering a natural respect for conservation. They develop patience, learning that rewards come with effort and time. They gain confidence, mastering the simple yet powerful skills of baiting a hook, casting a line, and landing a fish. Most importantly, they build memories that last a lifetime—moments of laughter, excitement, and awe beside the water, stories they'll carry long after childhood fades.

Fishing with kids is different from fishing alone. Success depends on finding the right water, a place where they can actually catch fish and where the experience is fun, not frustrating. Ponds and small lakes stocked with panfish and bass are ideal, offering easy access and higher catch rates. Slow-moving streams provide a chance to wade and observe fish in their habitat. Family-friendly fishing areas, sometimes stocked with trout specifically for children, can guarantee action and excitement. Deep, fast-moving rivers aren't the place to start. The goal is enjoyment, not frustration.

The right gear can make or break the experience. Simple is best. A light spinning rod, four to five feet in length, is easy for small hands to manage. A bobber and worm setup maximizes action, giving kids the instant feedback of a dipping float.

Barbless hooks make it easier to release fish safely—and prevent painful accidents. A small, tangle-free tackle box keeps things organized and frustration low. If introducing a child to fly fishing, a shorter rod with a floating line and a few forgiving flies—Woolly Buggers, Parachute Adams, or Foam Beetles—keeps it approachable. Short roll casts and simple drifts are the way to go.

Techniques need to match a child's attention span. Bobber fishing keeps them engaged, as every movement on the water signals potential excitement. Casting and retrieving lures like small Panther Martins or Mepps spinners gives immediate feedback. In small streams, handlining or dapping—simply dangling a fly or bait over the water—works wonders. Letting them scoop minnows or turn over rocks teaches them about fish habitats in ways they'll remember far longer than a lecture.

Fishing has become an incredible way for me to connect with my children, and I love watching them develop their own approaches to the sport. My daughter loves releasing the fish, making sure each one swims away safely. She sees it as her way of giving back to nature, ensuring that the fish continue their journey. My son, on the other hand, loves the thrill of the catch—the tug on the line, the fight, the moment of success. Two different practices, both equally important, and it's fascinating to watch each child grow with their own inclinations.

But no matter their differences, one thing remains constant—our morning prayers. Every school day, on the way to drop them off, my son and daughter make sure to thank God for the fish. Whether it's the excitement of the catch or the reverence of the release, they both recognize fishing as something bigger than just a pastime. It's a gift, a blessing, and a lesson in gratitude.

A child's first fish is a milestone. Whether it's a three-inch sunfish or a ten-inch trout, it's cause for celebration. The best thing an adult can do is step back and let the child do it themselves. Resist the urge to cast for them, to set the hook, to reel it in. Guide them, but let them experience the process. Celebrate every catch, big or small. Take pictures, but don't forget to be in them—because someday, they'll look back at those moments and remember not just the fish, but the person who stood beside them. Teach ethical catch and release, showing how to handle fish gently and return them properly.

Fishing shouldn't be a one-time event. The key to passing it on is making it a tradition. A yearly fishing trip builds anticipation and creates lifelong memories. The first trout, the first time using a fly rod, the first night fishing trip—these moments deserve recognition. A simple fishing journal, where kids can record their catches, draw pictures, and note their observations, can turn each trip into a lasting memory. But the lessons should go beyond the fish—identify birds, explore aquatic insects, and learn knots together. Fishing is a gateway to understanding the natural world.

At its core, fishing isn't about the fish. It's about what happens in between the casts—the laughter, the quiet moments, the stories told, and the memories made. By taking a child fishing, you're not just teaching them how to catch fish. You're showing them a way to connect with nature, to build patience, to appreciate the simple, timeless joys that come with standing beside a stream.

Maybe, years down the line, when they take their own child to the water's edge, they'll remember the day you stood beside them and passed it on. Because fishing isn't just something we do in the moment.

It's something we leave behind.

And that brings us to trout themselves. Ever wonder where the fish in your favorite river started their journey? Before they ever rise to a dry fly or disappear into the current, many of them begin in a place few anglers ever think to visit—the hatchery

Chapter 56: The Hatchery

Beyond the River: The Hidden World of Trout Hatcheries

Most anglers think of a trout hatchery as just a place where fish are bred, raised, and released. But a hatchery is much more than that. It's the foundation of modern trout fishing, a behind-the-scenes look at the delicate balance between conservation, recreation, and science. If you've never stepped foot inside a hatchery, you're missing out on a chance to understand where trout come from, how they are managed, and why they matter.

A trout hatchery is part science lab, part fish farm, and part conservation hub. It's where trout eggs are collected, fertilized, hatched, and raised in carefully controlled environments before they are released into lakes, rivers, and streams. Some hatcheries focus on restoring native trout populations, while others exist to support recreational fishing by stocking hatchery-raised trout in popular waters. These facilities, run by state fish and wildlife agencies, federal conservation programs, and private organizations, play a critical role in ensuring trout populations remain healthy and sustainable.

The process starts with egg collection and fertilization, carefully selecting adult trout to provide eggs, which are then fertilized and incubated under precise conditions. Once hatched, tiny trout emerge, still attached to their yolk sacs for nutrients, before progressing to the fingerling stage, where they begin swimming freely in rearing tanks. As they grow, they are moved to larger raceways or outdoor ponds, developing the strength and instincts needed for release. Eventually, when they reach the right size, these trout are transported to lakes, rivers, and streams where they will become part of the ecosystem—or the next fish on an angler's line.

Without hatcheries, many trout fisheries across the U.S. would struggle to exist. Some waters lack natural reproduction, meaning stocked fish are the only way to sustain a fishery. Others focus on bringing back native species that have been outcompeted or wiped out due to habitat destruction. Hatcheries also serve as an insurance policy for trout species. In places where wild populations have collapsed, hatcheries have played a crucial role in reintroducing species like the greenback cutthroat in Colorado or the Lahontan cutthroat in Nevada.

The debate over hatchery trout versus wild trout has been going on for years. Some argue that stocking hatchery fish dilutes wild genetics, creating trout that lack the natural survival instincts of their wild-born counterparts. Others argue that without hatcheries, many beloved trout streams wouldn't hold fish at all. The reality is that both hatchery and wild trout have their place. Hatchery trout provide accessible fishing opportunities, ensuring more people can experience the joy of catching a trout, while wild populations represent the long-term health of our rivers and deserve protection. The key is balance—knowing when to use hatcheries and when to let nature take its course.

I remember the first time I visited a trout hatchery. I wasn't expecting much—just some fish in concrete tanks, maybe a few signs explaining how they got there. But what I found was something far deeper.

The first thing that hit me was the sound—the constant rush of flowing water, the hum of aerators, the quiet movements of the workers tending to the tanks. I watched as thousands of tiny trout, no bigger than my fingertip, darted through the water. I saw trucks lined up, preparing to stock rivers I had fished before, and suddenly, I understood. These weren't just fish in tanks. These were the trout that anglers dream about, that kids would catch for the first time, that would bend rods and break lines. Every stocked fish was an opportunity for someone—maybe an experienced fly angler, maybe a first-timer who just wanted to feel the pull of a fish on the line.

Most hatcheries are open to the public, and if you've never been to one, you're missing out on an incredible experience. Watching thousands of trout at different life stages gives you a deeper appreciation for the species we chase. It's not just about seeing fish—it's about understanding the work that goes into keeping fisheries alive. Hatcheries aren't just raising trout; they're restoring native populations, protecting ecosystems, and ensuring that the waters we fish today will be just as full of life for the next generation. If you've ever wondered why some rivers are stocked while others remain wild, hatchery workers have the answers. If you've never tossed fish food into a raceway and watched hundreds of trout explode at the surface in a feeding frenzy, you've missed one of the simplest joys of visiting a hatchery.

The people who run these hatcheries are some of the most dedicated in the fishing world. Part scientist, part caretaker, part angler—they work long hours, battling disease, predation, and shifting water conditions, all to ensure that these fish have a fighting chance once they leave the hatchery. Their work isn't glamorous, but their passion is undeniable. They care about the fish, and they care about the anglers who chase them. They know their work keeps fisheries alive, keeps traditions going, and gives people a reason to get out on the water.

After visiting a hatchery, you never look at trout fishing the same way again. When you release a fish back into the river, you think about the journey it took to get there. When you catch a hatchery trout, you appreciate the effort it took to raise, transport, and stock that fish so you could have a chance to hook it. And maybe, just maybe, you start paying a little more attention to where your fish come from, how your waters are managed, and what role you play in keeping the sport alive.

A trout hatchery isn't just a fish farm. It's a lifeline for fisheries, a tool for conservation, and a glimpse into the future of trout fishing. It's where science meets tradition, where anglers and conservationists work together, and where the next generation of trout—and anglers—begins.

If you haven't been to one yet, go. Take your kids. Take a fellow angler. Walk through the tanks, watch the trout swim, talk to the people who run the place.

Because understanding where your fish come from makes every cast, every rise, and every catch that much more meaningful.

There are places where the world feels closer to its original design—where time slows, noise fades, and the mind becomes as clear as the water flowing over smooth stones. A trout stream is one of those places. It's where man meets the wild, not as a conqueror, but as a visitor.

Fly fishing isn't just a sport. It's a practice in patience, humility, and reverence. You don't command the river. You don't dictate to the fish. You step into moving water with open hands, knowing that what you seek isn't about what's caught—it's about what's given.

A river moves like the unseen hand of something greater—shaping the landscape without force, yet with certainty. It carves rock, shifts mountains, and still, when you kneel beside it, it speaks in whispers. I believe God moves this way. Always shaping. Always present. Working in ways we don't always see but always feel. Standing in a stream, feeling its quiet rhythm, is itself a kind of prayer.

Gratitude comes naturally in the current. There's no entitlement here. Every rise to a dry fly, every flash of silver beneath the surface, every mist-covered morning on the water—

it's all a gift. The best anglers understand this. They leave the river richer, not because of what's in their net, but because of the stillness they've borrowed for a time.

Some days, the fish never come. Some days, the wind howls, the water runs high, and the cast feels clumsy. But even then, the river offers something—a lesson, a moment of silence, a reminder that perfection is never the point. The flow continues, indifferent to success or failure. There's wisdom in that.

Fly fishing strips everything away. Here, you're just another figure in the current, learning to move with it rather than against it. The greatest anglers return to the same waters year after year—not to master them, but to learn from them. Because the river, like faith, is never conquered. It's experienced. It's understood in small moments—in glimpses, in the way the light catches the surface at dusk. It is, and always will be, something greater than ourselves.

Maybe that's why fly fishing and faith are so often intertwined. Both require trust. Both require surrender. Both remind us that we are never in control. But if we're willing—if we're present—if we let the current move as it must—there is grace in the drift.

And yet, we return. Again and again.

Maybe it's instinct. Maybe it's obsession. Or maybe, at its core, it's something deeper.

Because fly fishing was never just about the fish.

Chapter 57: Why We Keep Chasing Trout

There are easier ways to catch fish. If it were just about numbers, we'd all be out with spinning rods, trolling deep lakes, or setting bait rigs that do the work for us. But we don't.

We pick fly rods. We choose moving water. We chase trout.

And that choice says something about us.

Ask a hundred fly anglers why they do it, and you'll get a hundred different answers. Some say it's the challenge. Others, the escape. Some do it to be outdoors. Some to be alone. Some to feel connected to something bigger than themselves.

But underneath it all is a simple truth: we chase trout because trout live in the kind of places we want to be.

A Creek Runs Through It... Even on a Ski Trip

I was riding the chairlift, taking in the mountain views, when I saw it—the creek. A ribbon of clear water cutting through the valley, winding past snow-covered pines like something out of a painting.

And just like that, the idea shot through my mind: I need to fish that.

I told myself I'd just take a look. Five minutes.

Three hours later, my ski pass was still in my pocket, my fingers were half-frozen from brushing snow off rocks, and my friends were probably wondering if I'd gotten lost between the rental shop and the lift.

That night, I made a quick stop at Walmart and picked up the cheapest fly rig they had. It didn't matter. The fish didn't care what brand was on my rod, and neither did I.

The next morning, while my friends carved down the slopes, I took a different route—down to the banks of that creek, high rubber boots on, fly rod in hand. I spent the next three days doing an even split—50% skiing, 50% fishing, and 100% knowing I had a problem.

And I wouldn't change a thing.

I never caught a trout. Not one.

But I didn't need to. Just standing there, casting into that icy water, watching the drift, feeling the cold air settle into the canyon—I was completely happy.

I also learned an important lesson: never share your fishing ideas with ski buddies. I made that mistake once, and the looks I got told me all I needed to know. If I wanted future ski trip invites, it was best to keep my winter fly fishing thoughts to myself.

The Challenge of the Unseen

Unlike bass fishing or deep-sea trolling, trout fishing doesn't guarantee a catch. Some days, the river gives freely. Other days, it doesn't.

That unpredictability makes it special.

We read the water. We change our flies. We adjust our approach. And still—trout are indifferent to our plans. They remind us that effort doesn't always equal reward. But when it does, it means something.

Trout Are Beautiful, But Their World Is Even More So

No one denies that trout are stunning—golden browns, iridescent rainbows, brookies painted like an autumn forest. But as much as we admire the fish, we admire where they live even more.

We chase trout because they lead us to places untouched by time—high alpine meadows, deep canyons, mist-covered streams where the only sounds are the rush of water and the occasional splash of a rising fish.

No one ever fished a city drainage pond and felt closer to nature.

The Ritual of the Chase

There's a rhythm to fly fishing that makes the process as rewarding as the outcome. The careful selection of a fly. The tie of a knot. The arc of a cast. The way time slows when you mend the line just right.

Even the failures—hooking a tree branch, slipping on wet rocks, losing a fish at the net—become part of the experience.

A trout fisherman isn't just after a fish. He's after a perfect moment. A cast made well. A drift that looks real. A take he knew was coming before it even happened.

An Excuse to Be Somewhere Better

Fly fishing gives us a reason to wake up early. A reason to explore places we might otherwise never visit. A reason to unplug.

I could have spent that entire ski trip racing downhill, chasing adrenaline. Instead, I spent half of it pacing the banks of a frozen creek, rod in hand, chasing something different. A slow moment. A challenge. A connection.

Why We Keep Coming Back

We chase trout because something about the pursuit changes us. It teaches patience. Sharpens focus. Reminds us that the best things in life aren't always the easiest.

And if that means skipping a few ski runs, so be it.

Because once a river gets into your blood, it never really lets go.

You can fish a hundred streams, travel thousands of miles. But there's always that one stretch of water that calls you back—again and again.

Chapter 58: The Magic of Returning to a Stream

There's something about a familiar trout stream that never gets old. No matter how many times you've walked its banks, studied its currents, or cast into its pools, it still holds the power to surprise you.

A bend in the river reveals a fallen tree that wasn't there last time. A flood reshapes a gravel bar. The water carves a new pocket where a trout might be waiting. The light hits the surface just right, making the entire place feel brand new.

Some anglers chase the new—the untouched, the undiscovered. But for many of us, there's something even more magical about returning to a place we already know and seeing it with fresh eyes.

The Upper Nantahala and an Unforgettable Waterfall

I was fishing the Upper Nantahala, drifting flies through a stretch of pocket water I knew well. A deep pool sat just upstream, nestled below a spectacular waterfall partially hidden by the trees. I'd seen it plenty of times before.

But that day, something about it felt different. The way the mist rose. The golden light cutting through the canopy. It caught me off guard.

A fellow angler stood nearby, watching me take it all in. Sensing my awe, he chuckled. "First time here?"

I hesitated. I had been here before—many times—but in that moment, it felt new again. A little embarrassed, I nodded and said, "Yeah, first time."

He gave me a knowing smile, like he'd heard that answer before. And maybe, in a way, it was my first time. Because every return to a beloved stream is its own kind of discovery.

The Upper vs. Lower Nantahala

The Nantahala River is really two rivers in one.

The Upper Nantahala is a classic mountain stream—steep,

rocky, and lined with thick rhododendron, where wild rainbows and browns dart between boulders. It's the kind of place where a delicate cast matters, where every pocket of water holds a surprise. You won't find many big fish here, but the ones you do catch fight like they don't know their size.

Then there's the Lower Nantahala, a completely different beast. Once the dam releases, the river transforms into a wide, powerful flow—drift boat country. The water runs deep and cold, stocked with large, aggressive trout. If you want size, this is where you go. But if you want intimacy—the feeling of having a river to yourself—the Upper Nantahala is hard to beat.

The Changing River

I've fished the Upper Nantahala in the early morning when the mist clings to the surface like a ghost, the only sound the rhythmic tumbling of water over stone.

I've fished it in the midday sun when the water turns a clear emerald, revealing trout holding in impossible places, tucked against ledges and behind fallen logs.

I've fished it at dusk, when the light fades and the air cools, and suddenly, fish begin rising in places that seemed lifeless just hours before.

But no matter when I come, it's always different.

One season, a flood uproots a massive tree, rerouting the current entirely. Another year, a drought lowers the flow, exposing hidden rock ledges that change how the river fishes. The water is always moving, always shaping itself into something new.

And sometimes, it just comes to life in a way you don't expect. I've seen slow, sleepy water suddenly turn into a surging rush of pocket water after a hard rain, the kind of current that tests your balance and forces you to fish differently. , the kind of current that tests your balance and forces you to fish differently. You can never take a river for granted. It moves at its own pace, changes on its own terms. And that's what keeps us coming back.

The Pull of Familiar Waters

I could fish anywhere. I could chase new rivers, seek out undiscovered waters, put pins on a map of the world. But somehow, I keep coming back here.

Maybe it's because this river has a way of teaching me something new each time. Maybe it's because I've built memories in its currents, ones I don't want to forget.

There's comfort in knowing where a certain pool is, in understanding how the river bends and where a trout might rise. But there's also excitement in the unknown—because no matter how well you know a river, it still has secrets to reveal.

A One-Lane Bridge and the Stream That Hooked Me

There's another stream that calls me back time and time again—one that runs beneath a narrow, one-lane bridge near Banner Elk.

It's not the kind of place that makes magazine covers or Instagram feeds. But it's where my obsession with trout fishing started.

The first time I stopped there, I barely knew how to cast. I fumbled through knots, lost flies in overhanging branches, and spooked more fish than I care to admit.

But there were always trout here. Always.

Some days, I'd hook into a few, but often, they were too smart for me. These fish had seen it all. They knew every bad drift, every poorly presented fly.

But I kept coming back.

Even when I didn't catch anything, just standing on that bridge, looking down into the clear water, watching trout hold effortlessly in the current, was enough.

This place made me a fly fisherman.

And no matter how many miles of river I've waded since, I still find myself coming back to that same stretch, standing in the same spot, wondering if those same fish are still there.

Why Do We Keep Coming Back?

Some streams call us back time and time again.

Maybe it's because they hold good memories.

Maybe it's because they've never let us down.

Or maybe it's because, like us, they are always changing—never the same river twice.

Chapter 59: Why Fly Fishing is a Lifetime Pursuit

The One That Stays With You

Fly fishing isn't just something you do—it's something that becomes part of you, woven into your best memories. Other hobbies come and go, burning hot and fading out. But fly fishing? It stays. It gets into your bones.

It's there when you're young, casting with more enthusiasm than skill. It's there when you're older, appreciating the rhythm of the river, the sound of the line unrolling, the sheer joy of just being on the water.

And it's always there, waiting.

The Evolution of an Angler

There's a predictable arc to how a fly fisher changes over time.

We all start in the same place—obsessed with catching a fish, any fish. Numbers matter. Walking away without landing something feels like failure.

Then, at some point, it shifts. The obsession with numbers fades, replaced by the need for a challenge. Now, it's not just about catching a fish—it's about catching the right fish. A wild fish. A wary fish. One that makes you work for it.

And finally, when enough time passes, even that fades. The last phase of an angler is the one who just wants to be on the water. No stress. No rush. Just fishing for the sake of fishing, knowing that the next cast might be the one that lingers in memory forever.

Why We Keep Casting

The perfect cast to the perfect spot is almost as satisfying as catching a fish. There's a quiet pleasure in watching your line unroll flawlessly, the fly landing like a whisper exactly where you meant it to. It's the kind of precision that makes you nod to yourself, even if no one else is watching.

Every angler has had that moment—the one cast, the one take, the one fish that rewires something in their brain.

Maybe it was a perfect drift, a dry fly vanishing in a slow, deliberate take, as if time itself had paused. Maybe it was an explosion—a strike so violent you thought you'd hooked a freight train.

Whatever it was, it left a mark.

That's why we keep coming back.

It's not about filling the net. It's about the next perfect cast. The one that lands just right, that connects you, even for a second, to something bigger than yourself. It's about that electric feeling—that fleeting, charged moment when the world disappears and it's just you, the water, and the fish.

The Story That Stays

Every fly angler has one. A day, a moment, a fish that never really leaves them.

Maybe it was a golden afternoon on a favorite river, the kind of day where every cast felt effortless. Maybe it was a spontaneous road trip to fish unfamiliar waters, ending with an unforgettable battle against a trout that seemed to know exactly how to outsmart you.

Or maybe, it was a moment of absolute stillness—standing waist-deep in a cold mountain stream, not needing to catch anything at all, just soaking it in.

The stories we remember aren't always about the biggest fish. They're about the experience. The feeling. The realization that you're exactly where you're supposed to be.

Fishing with Generations

One of the greatest gifts of fly fishing is how it connects generations.

A father teaching his son how to mend a drift. A grandfather passing down an old bamboo rod, one that's caught more fish than anyone can remember. A daughter outfishing her dad for the first time, grinning ear to ear.

Fishing is a thread that runs through time. The rivers don't change. The flies may evolve, the gear may improve, but the feeling? The feeling is timeless.

Whether you're six years old catching your first trout or sixty-five with a lifetime of casts behind you, that tug on the line still sends the same shockwave of joy through your veins.

There Is No Last Cast

Every angler talks about their "last cast."

But here's the truth—there never really is one.

No matter how many seasons pass, no matter how many fish we've caught, we always come back.

Maybe not to the same river. Maybe not with the same rod.

But the need to cast, to feel the line unroll, to watch the water move—that never leaves us.

Chapter 60: Final Cast: The Stream Keeps Flowing

It was one of those days.

The kind where you wake up already regretting the decision to go fishing. The kind where the wind is relentless, the rain cuts sideways, and the water is too high, too fast, too damn cold. I had one day off, just one, and I was determined to make the most of it. I was going to catch trout, rain or shine, and nothing was going to stop me.

Except, apparently, everything.

The wind howled down the valley, sending my fly line in directions I wasn't even casting. The rain soaked through every layer of gear I had. The river—usually so familiar—felt like it had turned against me. Drifts wouldn't hold, flies wouldn't land, nothing looked right.

For the first hour, I stayed hopeful. It'll pass. The fish will turn on. It's gotta get better.

By hour three? I was done.

I started muttering under my breath, then I just started swearing. At the wind. At the rain. At the flies that refused to cooperate. At the trout—wherever the hell they were. And at myself—for even coming out here.

"This sport is stupid," I muttered. "I could've been warm and dry at home. I could've slept in. I could've—"

Just then, my line finally straightened. A take.

I set the hook like I had been waiting for this moment my entire life. The rod bent, the fish held deep—finally, finally, I had one on. Then, just as quickly as it happened, the line went slack. I stood there, rod still raised, watching as my strike indicator continued its useless drift downstream.

That was it. The breaking point.

I stomped out of the river, threw my rod in the truck, and swore—I was done. I wasn't just done for the day. I swore I wouldn't fish the rest of the season.

Done. Over it. No more.

I meant it, too. I drove home, peeled off my wet layers, and convinced myself that I was done wasting time chasing trout in the wind and rain.

Then, a week later, I was back on the water.

Why We Always Come Back

This sport has a way of breaking you down and bringing you back in equal measure. One day, you swear you'll never fish again. The next, you're tying flies at the kitchen table, already making a plan for next weekend.

I don't know why we do it.

Maybe it's the stubbornness—the idea that next time will be different.

Maybe it's the addiction to the unknown—because every cast is a question waiting to be answered.

Maybe it's because we know, deep down, that the hard days make the good ones even better.

The Days That Break Us

Every angler has a story like mine. The trip where nothing worked. The trip where the weather turned on you. The trip where the fish refused to play along. And every single one of us has sworn off fishing at some point.

That's it. I'm done.

But we never mean it. Not really.

Because for every miserable, fishless day, there's a day when everything clicks. The cast lands perfectly. The drift is flawless. The take is exactly how you imagined it. And suddenly, all the bad days are worth it.

The Best Days Come After the Worst Ones

If I've learned anything from this sport, it's that the best days often come right after the worst ones. The first time I ever caught a wild brown trout, it came the morning after I had spent six straight hours getting skunked. I almost didn't go back. I almost gave up.

Then, on a whim, I decided to fish one last run before leaving. That's when it happened.

A perfect drift.

A slight pause in the line.

A hook set so automatic, I barely thought about it.

And then—the fight.

That fish ran me all over the river before I finally netted it. I remember everything about it. The cold of the water against my legs. The golden-brown color of the fish in the net. The way it kicked free when I released it.

If I had let my bad day win, I never would've had that moment. That's the lesson.

Fishing is like life—sometimes you just have to keep showing up.

The Stream Keeps Flowing

There's something humbling about rivers.

They don't care about your frustration.

They don't care if you're having a bad day.

They don't owe you a fish.

They just keep flowing. With or without you.

When you think about it, fly fishing isn't really about catching fish. It's about:

Being there, even when it's hard. Learning to enjoy the process, not just the outcome. Understanding that some of the best moments come when nothing goes as planned.

That's why I came back a week later. Not because I forgot how miserable I was, but because the river doesn't hold grudges. It just keeps moving. And if you give it another shot, it just might remind you why you love this sport in the first place.

Final Thoughts: The Last Cast is Never Really the Last

If you're anything like me, you've had your own version of "I'm done" days.

You've fought the wind. You've been soaked to the bone.

You've walked off the river thinking, I don't even like this sport.

But you'll be back. We always come back. And if you ever say out loud that you're done with the sport, be careful—someone in your house might actually believe you. Then, the next time you mention sneaking off for a 'quick morning on the river,' you might get a reminder about how you swore off fishing forever—right before you're volunteered to stay home and entertain the neighbors instead. Because fly fishing isn't something we do—it's something we live. And no matter how many times we leave, the river will always be there, waiting.

And if you're looking for new waters to explore, some of the best are hidden in plain sight—in the wild, protected landscapes of America's national parks.

Part 7: Exploring New Waters: Adventures Beyond Home

Chapter 61: The Top 10 National Parks for Fly Fishing

Trout fishing in national parks is about more than just catching fish. It's about standing knee-deep in pristine, untamed waters, casting into places where the wild still rules. The best trout fishing in America happens in the parks that have protected these rivers, lakes, and streams for generations. If you're looking for world-class fly fishing, these ten national parks should be at the top of your list.

1. Yellowstone National Park (Wyoming, Montana, Idaho)

Yellowstone isn't just the best national park for trout fishing—it might be the best place on the planet. This park is home to legendary waters like the Yellowstone River, Firehole River, and Slough Creek. You'll find native Yellowstone cutthroat trout, along with browns, rainbows, and brook trout. The Lamar Valley is where dreams are made—crystal-clear waters, big rising trout, and bison grazing in the background. While stocking was historically used in Yellowstone, the park has since shifted to a wild trout conservation focus—meaning the fish you catch here are as wild as the landscape around them.

Best Time to Fish: Late June through September

2. Great Smoky Mountains National Park (Tennessee, North Carolina)

Home to some of the last wild Appalachian brook trout, this park is an East Coast fly fishing paradise. The Little River, Deep Creek, and Abrams Creek are prime spots. Historically, stocking introduced non-native rainbows and browns, but today, conservation efforts focus on restoring native brook trout populations. The fishing here is technical and rewarding, making every catch feel like a small victory.

Best Time to Fish: Spring (March-May) and Fall (September-November)

3. Rocky Mountain National Park (Colorado)

A high-altitude haven for anglers, Rocky Mountain National

Park offers pristine alpine lakes and small streams filled with greenback cutthroat trout—a species once thought extinct. The Big Thompson River, Glacier Creek, and Dream Lake offer incredible scenery and wild fish that smash dry flies in the summer months. The park stopped stocking fish in the 1970s to protect native species, so all trout here are wild.

Best Time to Fish: June through September

4. Glacier National Park (Montana)

Remote, rugged, and breathtaking—Glacier National Park offers solitude and serious trout fishing. The Flathead River system (North, Middle, and South Forks) is cutthroat country, with wild fish that haven't seen every fly in the book. Stocking was discontinued decades ago to preserve native populations, making this a true wild fishery.

Best Time to Fish: Late June through early October

5. Yosemite National Park (California)

Yosemite isn't just for climbers and hikers—its high-country lakes and rivers hold some of California's best trout fishing. The Merced River, Tuolumne River, and Tenaya Lake offer rainbows, browns, and brook trout, often in breathtaking alpine settings. Some waters here were historically stocked, but today's fisheries are self-sustaining and wild, offering anglers a glimpse into California's native trout waters.

Best Time to Fish: July through September

6. Shenandoah National Park (Virginia)

For anglers on the East Coast, Shenandoah's small, intimate mountain streams offer classic brook trout water. The Rose River, Rapidan River, and Whiteoak Canyon are legendary among dry fly purists. The park no longer stocks its waters, focusing instead on restoring native brook trout to their historical range.

Best Time to Fish: Spring and Fall

7. Grand Teton National Park (Wyoming)

Sitting in Yellowstone's shadow, Grand Teton often gets overlooked—but that's a mistake. The Snake River, Pacific Creek, and Jackson Lake hold huge Snake River cutthroat trout. While the park itself does not stock fish, some nearby state-managed waters still receive stocking to enhance fishing opportunities. The wild cutthroat populations here are thriving, making for some of the best dry fly fishing in the West.

Best Time to Fish: June through October

8. North Cascades National Park (Washington)

For those who like hiking deep into the backcountry, North Cascades offers alpine lakes filled with wild rainbow, cutthroat, and brook trout. Thunder Creek, Ross Lake, and Diablo Lake are top destinations. Some high-elevation lakes in the North Cascades still receive stocked trout under state programs, making this park a rare case where both wild and stocked fish coexist in a national park setting.

Best Time to Fish: Late July through September

9. Acadia National Park (Maine)

A hidden gem for anglers, Acadia offers a mix of sea-run brook trout, wild landlocked salmon, and native brookies. The park's Jordan Pond, Eagle Lake, and streams like Hunters Brook provide unique fishing opportunities. Some of the waters here are still stocked by the Maine Department of Inland Fisheries and Wildlife, making it one of the few national parks where anglers can target both wild and stocked fish.

Best Time to Fish: May through October

10. Olympic National Park (Washington)

Few places in the world offer the variety of Olympic National Park. Here, you can catch wild steelhead, cutthroat trout, and even salmon in pristine rivers like the Hoh, Sol Duc, and Queets. The park itself does not stock fish, but surrounding waters managed by Washington State still receive hatchery support, particularly for steelhead recovery programs. This is a park where you can truly test yourself against some of the strongest fish on the planet.

Best Time to Fish: September through March (Winter steelhead season)

Final Thought: A Balance Between Wild and Stocked

Fisheries

National parks are more than just fishing spots—they are sacred places, where nature is left alone to thrive. While most national parks have moved away from stocking to protect native fish, some still allow limited stocking in certain waters, balancing tradition with conservation. Whether you're targeting pure wild trout in Rocky Mountain National Park or enjoying the mix of wild and stocked fisheries in Acadia, the experience remains unparalleled.

If you haven't fished a national park yet, start planning your trip. Because once you experience it—once you watch a wild trout rise in a place untouched by time—you'll understand why anglers never stop coming back.

But national parks aren't the only places where trout fishing reaches legendary status. Across the country, entire states are defined by their waters—their rivers, their streams, their hidden gems known only to those who seek them.

Some states are obvious choices. Others might surprise you. But no matter where you go, if you're chasing trout, you're in the right place.

Chapter 62: The 15 Best States for Trout Fishing

If you're looking to chase trout across America, you're in luck. The country is laced with some of the finest trout waters in the world, from legendary Western tailwaters to wild, untamed streams in the East. The beauty of trout fishing is that every region has its own character, its own soul. Some states have big, sprawling rivers that feel endless. Others have tucked-away streams where you might not see another angler all day. But here's the truth—plan a fishing trip to any of these 15 states, and you can't go wrong.

These aren't just great places to catch trout. These are places to experience fly fishing at its best, where you'll wake up before dawn, feel the crisp mountain air, and step into the kind of water that stays with you for life.

1. Montana – The Crown Jewel of Trout Fishing

Montana is where fly fishing legends are born. The Madison, the Yellowstone, the Missouri—just the names alone carry weight. Picture yourself knee-deep in the Madison River, golden light spilling over the valley, and trout rising in rhythmic cadence. This isn't just a fishing destination; it's the Mecca.

Must-Fish Rivers: Madison, Yellowstone, Missouri, Big Hole

2. Idaho – Wild and Remote Waters

Idaho often gets overshadowed by its big brother Montana, but the trout fishing here is just as good, and the crowds are thinner. The Henry's Fork is the kind of river that makes you earn your fish—technical, demanding, but deeply rewarding. Then there's the Salmon River, where you can feel like an explorer in untouched water.

Must-Fish Rivers: Henry's Fork, Salmon, Big Lost, Silver Creek

3. Wyoming – Big Sky, Big Trout

Trout fishing in Wyoming is about space. The North Platte's tailwaters offer huge browns and rainbows, while the Snake River runs wild through the Tetons. The best part? You might just have it all to yourself.

Must-Fish Rivers: Snake, North Platte, Wind River, Green River

4. Colorado – Gold Medal Waters

Colorado's trout streams are as diverse as they come. The Fryingpan, the South Platte, the Gunnison—each offers its own unique challenge. Whether you're casting dries to picky fish on the "Pan" or swinging streamers on the Gunnison, Colorado's waters will test your skills.

Must-Fish Rivers: Fryingpan, South Platte, Gunnison, Blue River

5. Alaska – The Untamed Frontier

If you want big trout, Alaska is where you go. The Kenai holds some of the largest rainbows on the planet, and the remote streams of Bristol Bay are untouched by time. This is where fly fishing is still wild, raw, and unforgiving.

Must-Fish Rivers: Kenai, Kvichak, Naknek, Copper River

6. California – The Land of Giants

California may not be the first place you think of for trout fishing, but it should be. The McCloud River, birthplace of the world-famous McCloud rainbow trout, runs cold and clear. And if you're after monster browns, the Upper Sacramento delivers.

Must-Fish Rivers: McCloud, Upper Sacramento, Hat Creek, Owens River

7. Oregon – Wild Rainbows and Steelhead Dreams

The Deschutes River is the stuff of legend, with aggressive native redband trout that will test your skills. But Oregon is more than just one river—its remote creeks and coastal steelhead runs make it a year-round trout paradise.

Must-Fish Rivers: Deschutes, Metolius, McKenzie, Rogue

8. Pennsylvania – America's Fly Fishing Birthplace

The streams of Pennsylvania are where fly fishing in America began. The limestone creeks hold wild browns that are as smart as they are beautiful. Fishing here is about precision, tradition, and history.

Must-Fish Rivers: Penns Creek, Letort Spring Run, Yellow Breeches, Spring Creek

9. Michigan – Brook Trout Heaven

Michigan is where the brook trout still reigns. The Au Sable's dark waters hide wild fish that take dry flies like it's still 1890. And the Pere Marquette? That's where steelhead and big browns lurk.

Must-Fish Rivers: Au Sable, Pere Marquette, Manistee, Muskegon

10. New York – The Catskills and Beyond

The Catskills are hallowed ground for fly anglers. The Beaver Kill, the Delaware—these are the rivers where American fly fishing took shape. But the Adirondacks offer their own wild, remote waters that hold native brookies.

Must-Fish Rivers: Beaver Kill, West Branch Delaware, Esopus Creek, Ausable River

11. Utah – The Hidden Gem

Utah flies under the radar, but its waters are spectacular. The Green River below Flaming Gorge is as good as trout fishing gets—thousands of trout per mile, crystal-clear water, and scenery that stops you in your tracks.

Must-Fish Rivers: Green River, Provo River, Logan River, Weber River

12. Washington – Blue Ribbon Trout and Steelhead

The Yakima River is Washington's crown jewel for trout, but the real magic happens when you go searching for wild steelhead. The state's mountain-fed streams hold fish that are as tough as they are beautiful.

Must-Fish Rivers: Yakima, Spokane, Skagit, Hoh River

13. Wisconsin – The Driftless Region's Spring Creeks

The Driftless Area is one of the most unique trout fishing destinations in the country—spring-fed streams full of wild browns, rolling hills, and a feeling like you've stepped into a different time.

Must-Fish Rivers: Kickapoo, Timber Coulee, Black Earth Creek, Kinnickinnic River

14. North Carolina – Southern Trout at Its Best

The rivers of North Carolina's mountains hold strong populations of wild and stocked trout. The Davidson is known for its finicky, big fish, and the Nantahala provides deep pools and technical pocket water.

Must-Fish Rivers: Davidson, Nantahala, South Toe, Linville River

15. Georgia – Big Browns and Deep Pools

The Peach State has some seriously good trout water. The Chattahoochee below Buford Dam is loaded with fish, and the Toccoa produces some of the biggest browns in the Southeast.

Must-Fish Rivers: Toccoa, Chattahoochee, Chattooga, Tallulah River

Plan Your Trip – You Won't Regret It

Trout fishing is not the same everywhere. Chasing trout will take you to a lot of varied places. Every one of these states offers something special. Whether you're looking for wild cutthroat in Wyoming, spring creek browns in Pennsylvania, or steelhead in Washington, the adventure is out there.

So grab your gear, book the trip, and hit the water. You won't regret it. And if the fish don't cooperate? Well, that's just part of the game.

But what if the adventure takes you beyond the familiar rivers of the U.S.?

Fly fishing isn't just an American pastime—it's a global pursuit. Some of the world's most breathtaking waters lie far beyond our borders, waiting for those willing to explore. Whether it's the wild browns of Patagonia, the gin-clear creeks of New Zealand, or the icy flows of Iceland, one thing is certain: the thrill of the catch knows no boundaries.

Chapter 63: Exploring International Fly Fishing

Fly fishing is a universal pastime, offering unique challenges and opportunities across diverse landscapes. While the USA boasts some of the best fly fishing in the world, international destinations provide a fresh perspective, different species, and techniques that expand an angler's skillset. Whether casting in crystal-clear New Zealand streams, battling monster browns in Patagonia, or exploring the volcanic rivers of Iceland, these waters offer adventures worth experiencing.

New Zealand: The Land of Giants

If there is a holy land for trout fishing, New Zealand is it. The South Island, with its crystal-clear rivers, large, wild brown trout, and technical sight-fishing, is the ultimate test of skill. The trout here require stealth, precise presentation, and a near-perfect drift.

Many New Zealand anglers swear by large dry flies like the Cicada, especially in the summer months when trout key in on these high-protein meals. But when conditions change, tiny nymphs like the Pheasant Tail and Hare's Ear become the go-to weapons.

Key Rivers: Mataura River, Oreti River, Ahuriri River

Prime Season: November – April

Patagonia: The Wild Frontier

Trout fishing in Patagonia, Argentina, and Chile feels like stepping back in time—untouched waters, massive trout, and the kind of rugged beauty that makes you forget the modern world exists. Here, rivers twist through the Andes, lakes sit beneath snow-capped peaks, and anglers target rainbows and browns that grow to ridiculous sizes.

One of the greatest joys of fishing Patagonia is the variety. One day, you might be swinging streamers in deep glacial rivers, the next, casting dry flies in remote mountain lakes that have rarely seen a human footprint.

Key Rivers: Rio Limay, Rio Grande, Futaleufú River

Prime Season: December – March

Iceland: The Land of Fire, Ice, and Monster Trout

In Iceland, fly fishing feels almost mythical. The landscape is raw—volcanic rock, black sand beaches, and glacial rivers—and the trout are just as wild. Anglers here chase massive brown trout in the highlands, but the real trophy is the Arctic char and sea-run browns that migrate through Iceland's rivers.

The fishing here is dictated by the elements. Wind, rain, and sudden shifts in weather make every cast a test of patience and adaptability. If you can master the conditions, the rewards are unreal—browns pushing 10+ pounds, sometimes caught on tiny black gnats.

Key Rivers: Laxá in Ásum, Tungufljót, Lake Thingvallavatn

Prime Season: June – September

Kamchatka, Russia: The Last Truly Untouched Trout Waters

Kamchatka is what Montana must have been 200 years ago—untouched rivers, no crowds, no pressure, just pure wilderness. The rivers here hold giant, unpressured rainbow trout, and fishing them feels like discovering fly fishing for the first time. The rainbows are aggressive, fearless, and often take mouse patterns off the surface.

Fishing Kamchatka isn't for the faint of heart. The logistics are tough—getting there requires floatplane access, guides, and a deep love for adventure. But once you're on the river, it's worth every effort.

Key Rivers: Zhupanova River, Savan River, Two Yurt River

Prime Season: July – September

Mongolia: The Hunt for Taimen, the River Wolf

If you think trout are the pinnacle of fly fishing, Mongolia might change your mind. The taimen—a prehistoric cousin of trout that can grow over 50 inches long—is the ultimate predator. Fishing for taimen isn't about finesse; it's about power and aggression. These fish crush giant streamers, smash surface flies, and fight with the fury of a wild animal.

While Mongolia has its share of trout and lenok (a native salmonid), taimen are the main event. They require patience, dedication, and a willingness to throw huge flies all day—but landing one is a lifetime achievement.

Key Rivers: Eg-Uur River, Delger Murun River

Prime Season: June – October

Europe: The Old World, the New School

Trout fishing in Europe is a mix of history and modern technique. Rivers like the River Test in England hold centuries of fly-fishing tradition, while places like Slovenia's Soča River feel like they belong in a fantasy novel—turquoise waters, massive marble trout, and nearly untouched landscapes.

Czech nymphing was born in the fast waters of Central Europe, where anglers developed the tight-line nymphing technique that has since become a dominant strategy worldwide. If you want to test technical small fly fishing, the chalk streams of England and the Alps of Austria are the proving grounds.

Key Rivers: Soča River (Slovenia), River Test (England), San River (Poland)

Prime Season: March – October

What International Waters Teach Us

Fishing in foreign waters expands an angler's perspective, offering new species, techniques, and challenges. It's about learning new techniques, adapting to new challenges, and immersing yourself in fly fishing culture worldwide.

New Zealand rewards patience and precision. If you can fool a Kiwi brown trout, you can fool any trout in the world.

Patagonia demands adaptability. The rivers change every day, and success comes from reading the water, not just sticking to a plan.

Iceland tests resilience. The weather is brutal, but the fish are worth every bit of the struggle.

Kamchatka delivers pure, unfiltered joy. Trout should not be this aggressive—but they are, and it's incredible.

Mongolia puts anglers to the test against the ultimate predator. Taimen aren't trout. They're something bigger, meaner, and wilder.

Europe preserves tradition and refines technique. The old-world rivers still hold lessons for modern anglers.

Every fly fisherman should experience at least one of these legendary destinations. Not just for the fish, but for the knowledge, the culture, and the adventure that comes with it.

(And if nothing else, it's a great excuse to tell your family you need a "once-in-a-lifetime" fishing trip… every year.)

But in every legendary destination, there are legendary anglers—those who don't just fish the waters but redefine them.

Some changed the sport forever. Others remain local legends, known only by those who share the river with them. Yet all of them left behind something more than just stories. They left a legacy.

Chapter 64: The Legends of Fly Fishing

Some fly anglers are more than just good—they become legends. Their names are whispered on riverbanks, their casts spoken about with reverence, their understanding of the water almost supernatural. Some were pioneers who changed the sport forever, designing flies, revolutionizing casting, or redefining conservation. Others remain local heroes, known only in their home waters but capable of catching fish where everyone else comes up empty.

And then there are the stories—half-truth, half-myth, passed down like old fishing secrets.

I've spent years chasing that level of mastery, reading the water, refining my cast, tying my own flies. For all the practice and days spent waist-deep in moving water, I've only ever touched that perfection once.

And just like that, it was gone.

The Moment I Fished Like a Legend

Every fly angler has heard about the perfect cast—the one where the line unfurls like silk, the leader extends effortlessly, and the fly drifts down like a feather falling from the sky. The old-timers talk about it as if they do it every day, and maybe they do. I had heard the stories—the legends of anglers who could place a dry fly so softly that trout below never suspected a thing. I had seen the videos, read the books, and tried again and again to achieve that cast myself.

Then one day, it happened.

It wasn't planned. It wasn't calculated. Maybe it was the perfect wind, maybe it was a gift, or maybe, just for a moment, I had tapped into something I wasn't supposed to.

I made my cast, and the fly rolled out in a way I had never seen before. The leader extended smoothly—no abrupt snap, no awkward drop. It landed perfectly on the water—delicate, natural, flawless.

I stood there watching it, mesmerized. I had done what the

legends do on every cast.

And in that moment of awe, I lost track of everything else.

The current caught me, pushing me toward an overhang. I scrambled, but it was too late. My fly snagged on the low-hanging branches, my leader tangled in the limbs, and I was left standing knee-deep in the water, staring at the mess I had made.

I had done it. For one brief, fleeting moment, I had cast like a legend.

But I've never been able to replicate that cast again.

Maybe it was a trick of the wind. Maybe it was pure luck. Or maybe, just for a moment, the river let me borrow something that didn't belong to me.

Whatever it was, I keep chasing it.

Because that's what the legends do.

The Pioneers Who Shaped Fly Fishing

Some legends weren't just good anglers—they changed the sport forever. They designed flies, taught casting techniques, and spread fly fishing from mountain creeks to saltwater flats.

Lee Wulff believed a trout was too valuable to be caught only once. He designed the Royal Wulff, a fly still found in every serious angler's box today, and advocated catch-and-release long before it was widely accepted. His books and films inspired generations.

Joan Wulff, often called the First Lady of Fly Fishing, shattered expectations in a sport dominated by men. She won multiple casting championships, competing on equal footing, and wrote books on casting techniques that are still studied today. Her school of fly fishing has trained thousands of anglers, proving that timing, not strength, is what makes a great cast.

Lefty Kreh changed the game entirely. His smooth, effortless casting stroke became the gold standard, and his book Fly Fishing in Saltwater revolutionized how we approach big fish on the fly. He designed the Lefty's Deceiver, one of the most versatile and effective flies ever created, and introduced thousands of anglers to a looser, more natural style of casting.

Norman Maclean didn't invent a technique or design a famous fly, but he did something just as important—he made fly fishing immortal. A River Runs Through It romanticized the sport like no other work ever had, capturing the soul of fly fishing and ensuring it was seen as an art, not just a technique.

Some legends refined the craft in other ways. Ed Shenk mastered spring creeks and designed flies like the Letort Hopper, while Joe Humphreys spent decades teaching and mastering night fishing for trophy trout. Gary LaFontaine studied trout vision, designing flies based on science rather than tradition. Dave Whitlock championed warm-water fly fishing, proving that bass could be just as rewarding as trout.

Others carried the torch in specific regions, becoming legends in their own right. Sylvester Nemes revived soft-hackle flies, Charlie Brooks pioneered deep-water nymphing, and Jim Casada documented the traditions of Southern Appalachian fly fishing. Mark Cathey, the Dean of Smoky Mountain Anglers, was revered for his uncanny ability to find wild trout in the park's toughest waters.

I admit I'm biased toward those last two names—I spend more than half my fishing time in the Smokies. But their legacy is part of the river itself. Their techniques, their stories, their understanding of these waters—they all live on, whether we realize it or not.

What We Can Learn from the Legends

Some legends are real people whose skills became legendary. Others take on mythical status over time. But the reason they matter is simple: fly fishing is more than just a sport.

It's a craft, a lifelong pursuit, and a tradition passed down through stories. It's about pushing limits, learning from experience, and respecting those who came before.

Each of these pioneers had a different approach. Wulff taught us that sometimes less gear means more skill. Joan proved that fly fishing is about rhythm, not brute force. Lefty showed that a loose grip and relaxed casting stroke can make all the difference. Maclean reminded us that at the end of the day, fly fishing is about storytelling.

But the real lesson? Consistency beats talent.

The legends didn't just fish casually—they obsessed. They studied, practiced, and experimented until they became masters of the craft. If you want to improve as a fly angler, don't just fish on weekends. Get out there as much as possible.

Even the greats didn't become legends overnight.

They earned their skill one cast at a time.

The Forgotten Waters Still Hold Lessons

Not every lesson is learned on a famous river or under the guidance of a legend. Some of the best teachers are the waters no one talks about—the streams that don't make magazine covers or top ten lists, yet still hold wild, willing trout.

The forgotten waters. The hidden gems. The places waiting to be discovered.

Part 8: The Past, Present and Future of Fly Fishing

Chapter 65: Rediscovering the Forgotten Streams

The Forgotten Streams

There are rivers that make magazine covers, rivers that fill Instagram feeds, and rivers that see more anglers in a week than some see in a decade. And then, there are the forgotten trout streams—the hidden gems that don't make the lists, don't have the fame, but hold trout just as wild, just as beautiful, and often, even more willing to take a fly.

The Lost Waters of the Great Smoky Mountains

The Great Smokies are a maze of blue lines on a map, many of them unnamed or barely spoken of outside small circles of dedicated anglers. While places like Deep Creek and Abrams Creek get attention, there are countless tiny streams tucked deep in the hills where brook trout, the true natives of the region, still thrive.

Some of these streams require a steep hike into the backcountry, others demand nothing more than curiosity and a willingness to ignore the more popular pull-offs. The waters are often no wider than a car, winding through rhododendron tunnels, their depths hidden beneath overhanging branches. These are streams where a 12-inch trout is king, where dry flies land without spooking the entire pool, where the solitude is as much a reward as the fish.

Yellowstone's Forgotten Cutthroat Streams

Most anglers visiting Yellowstone National Park race to the Madison or Firehole, hoping to hit a famous hatch. But the park holds a network of small, hidden tributaries where native Yellowstone cutthroat trout still rise eagerly to well-placed flies. Creeks like Slough Creek's upper reaches or the more remote Lamar tributaries offer pristine, untouched water where the trout haven't been pressured into graduate-level selectivity.

The cutthroat here are survivors. Decades ago, non-native species were introduced into many of their waters, pushing them out of their historic range. But in the tucked-away pockets of

Yellowstone's high-country streams, they persist, wild and unspoiled. Fishing these waters feels like stepping back in time, casting to fish that evolved in this very place before fly rods even existed.

The Unmarked Streams of the Adirondacks

New York's Adirondack Mountains are better known for their lakes and larger rivers, but the real magic lies in the unmarked streams that tumble down the mountainsides. These streams are narrow, sometimes barely wider than a rod length, yet they hold wild brook trout untouched by stocking trucks and hatchery genetics.

These are the waters where old-time anglers fished with cane rods and hand-tied wet flies, where access is still earned rather than given. Finding them requires more than just a map—it takes a willingness to hike off-trail, to push through thick underbrush, to step carefully on moss-covered boulders. But the reward? Trout that have never seen a fly, waiting in clear, ice-cold water, feeding in perfect rhythm with the current.

How Forgotten Streams Stay Forgotten

There's a reason these streams remain overlooked. Some are too remote, too difficult to reach without serious effort. Others are overshadowed by their more famous neighbors. And then there's the most important reason: those who fish them don't talk about them.

In today's world of geotagging and online fishing reports, true solitude is a rarity. The anglers who know these waters keep them quiet, sharing their locations only with those they trust. These are places where the code of silence is stronger than any fly pattern advice.

How to Find Your Own Hidden Gems

If you want to fish a stream that hasn't been written about, photographed, or pressured into submission, you have to know where to look. The best waters aren't found in guidebooks. They're discovered by those willing to explore.

Start with the maps. Look for blue lines that don't have names, those tiny tributaries that snake away from well-known rivers. If a stream doesn't appear in a guidebook, that's a good sign. Follow those blue lines, especially if they originate in high country or flow through dense forest cover.

Stay off the beaten path. If a stream has a parking lot and an official trailhead, you're probably not the first one fishing it that day. Instead, look for places where the only access is by foot, bushwhacking through thick brush or wading upstream into the unknown.

Ignore the stocking reports. Hatchery trout bring crowds. Wild trout keep secrets. If a stream isn't on the stocking list, there's a chance it holds a naturally reproducing population, undisturbed by the weekly truckloads of fish dumped into more popular waters.

Talk to the old-timers, not the internet. The best knowledge isn't always online. Sometimes, the guy at the local fly shop, the one who's been fishing the area for fifty years, holds the real secrets. Buy him a coffee. Ask the right questions. And listen closely—not just to what he says, but to what he doesn't.

It's easy to be drawn to the rivers that everyone talks about, the ones with the biggest fish, the most famous hatches, the perfect water conditions. But the best trout fishing isn't always where the crowds go.

Sometimes, it's where no one goes at all.

It's in the forgotten creeks, the hidden blue lines, the places without a name but with plenty of fish. And the best part? If you find one of these places, you might just get to keep it for yourself.

But there's another kind of hidden magic that only a select few get to master—something that transforms the pursuit of trout into an art form.

Chapter 66: Can Trout Remember? The Science of Trout Memory

Do Trout Learn From Their Mistakes?

Every angler has wondered it. That moment when a trout rises, inspects your fly, and then, at the last possible second, refuses it. Or worse—when a trout takes the fly, you set the hook, feel the head shake, and then... nothing. The fish is gone.

You tie on the same pattern, make another cast, land it in the same drift line. The fly floats perfectly. You hold your breath. But the trout? Nowhere to be seen. Did it learn? Did it recognize danger? Or was it just bad luck?

The answer, like most things in nature, is complicated. But one thing is clear: trout remember more than we think.

The First Mistake: A Too-Perfect Fly

Sometimes, a fly that looks too perfect is the problem. Hatchery fish—those raised in tanks and stocked in streams—fall for bright, oversized flies. But wild trout? They've seen the real thing. They know the way an insect moves, how it lands, how it struggles. If your fly is too stiff, too symmetrical, too artificial—it raises alarms.

A trout may rise once to inspect it, but if something feels wrong—an unnatural silhouette, a suspiciously stiff hackle—it commits your fly to memory as something to avoid.

The Hook and Release Memory

There's an old saying that trout only get caught once. Anyone who has fished long enough knows this isn't true—some trout seem to have a death wish, getting hooked multiple times in a single day. But bigger, older trout? They get smart.

Studies have shown that fish retain negative experiences for weeks, even months. A trout that gets hooked and released may become more cautious, rejecting flies it once took without hesitation. It may retreat to deeper water, refuse to rise to dry flies, or feed only under the cover of darkness.

The Missed Strike: When a Trout Gets a Free Lesson

Perhaps the most frustrating mistake is the one that never fully happens—the missed strike. The trout takes the fly, but you set too early, too late, or too aggressively. The hook never finds home, and the fish swims away.

What happens next? More often than not, that trout will not fall for the same trick twice. It may still feed but will likely ignore any pattern that resembles the one it just mouthed. It knows something was wrong, even if it doesn't understand exactly what.

Selective Feeding: The PhD-Level Trout

In heavily pressured waters—where trout see hundreds of artificial flies a week—fish develop near-impossible selectivity. They learn to reject flies with micro-imperfections. Hackle that is too stiff or too sparse. Flies that float too high or too low. Colors that don't match the exact hatch. Unnatural movement caused by drag in the current.

On famous spring creeks, like Silver Creek in Idaho or the Henry's Fork in Montana, trout become professors of deception. They study flies like examiners looking for forgeries. Some even learn to recognize monofilament leaders glinting in the sun, rejecting any drift that has a visible tell.

The Spooked Trout: Learning the Sound of Danger

Trout don't just learn from flies—they learn from their environment. A splashy cast, an approaching shadow, the vibration of footsteps on the bank—all of these signal danger.

A trout that is spooked doesn't just bolt blindly downstream. It often remembers the exact source of the disturbance. If an angler splashes through a pool too carelessly, the fish may abandon that feeding lane for the rest of the day, even after the danger is gone.

The Hatchery Fish vs. Wild Fish Experiment

Science has tried to answer this question in controlled settings. In one study, researchers stocked a stream with hatchery fish and monitored their behavior over time. At first, the stocked fish were reckless, eating anything that hit the water. But after just a few encounters with anglers, they became skittish, preferring deep cover, refusing easy meals.

Wild trout, by contrast, showed a lifetime of learned caution. Even after a long winter, they remembered feeding patterns, the safest times to rise, and how to avoid risky scenarios.

Can Trout Be Trained?

There are stories—rare but real—of trout recognizing individual anglers. In small streams with resident fish, some trout develop a bizarre familiarity with human presence. A person who feeds them regularly can elicit feeding responses just by walking to the water's edge. But an angler who has caught and released the same fish multiple times may find that trout disappearing at the mere sight of a rod.

The Broken Code: When Trout Forget

But trout do not have perfect memories. While they learn caution, they also have short windows of forgetfulness—especially after long winters or disruptions to their environment.

A sudden flood can erase feeding lanes, forcing trout to relearn where and how to eat. A new generation of insects can reset their feeding preferences. And sometimes, simply surviving a season overwrites past mistakes—allowing an old fish to make the same error once again.

How Anglers Can Adapt

So, how do you beat a trout that learns from its mistakes? Change flies frequently. A fish that refused your fly once will likely refuse it again. Try a different size, a different color, a different silhouette. Fish smarter, not harder. Instead of repeatedly casting to the same fish, change angles, drift direction, and presentation. Use lighter tippets and natural drifts. In selective waters, trout recognize drag, glare, and anything unnatural. A longer leader and a gentler approach increase success rates. Rest the pool. If you spook a trout or miss a strike, step back and wait. Sometimes, giving it ten or fifteen minutes can reset the moment. Vary retrieval speeds. If a fish rejects your nymph or streamer, a slight change in movement can trigger a reaction strike.

Final Thought: Do They Learn or Do They Survive?

The real question isn't just whether trout learn. It's why they learn. In the wild, survival depends on remembering danger. A trout that forgets what a heron's shadow means will not live long. A trout that rises recklessly at every insect silhouette will eventually meet an angler's hook.

Yet, even the smartest fish make mistakes. Even the oldest trout, the ones that have seen it all, sometimes rise at the wrong moment, chase the wrong meal, and find themselves in the angler's hands once more.

So, do trout learn from their mistakes?

Yes.

But sometimes, just like us, they forget just long enough to get caught again.

And maybe that's part of the magic of fishing—the unpredictability, the quiet battle between the angler and the trout. But the river offers something more than just sport. It offers something that goes deeper.

There are places in this world that heal. Rivers, in particular, have a way of washing away more than just dirt and debris. They carry with them the power to cleanse, to restore, to offer a quiet escape from the pressures of life.

Chapter 67: Why Rivers Heal Us

Rivers do not require an appointment. They do not ask for insurance. They ask only that you show up, step into the water, and let the current carry something away—stress, regret, grief, doubt. A river does not judge. It does not hurry. It does not care who you are. It simply flows. And that, in itself, is the therapy so many of us need.

The River as an Escape

When the world is too loud, when the weight of life presses just a little too hard, there is a pull—a whisper that calls you back to the water. The river asks for nothing in return. It offers a place to slow down, to exist outside the noise, to be in a moment where the only thing that matters is the drift of a fly, the rise of a trout, the rhythm of breath in sync with moving water.

Some people run. Others meditate. Some lift weights or sit in therapy offices, untangling the knots in their minds. And then there are those of us who fish. Not always to catch, but to lose ourselves in something bigger, something older than any of our worries.

The Ritual of Casting Away Stress

The act of fly fishing is therapy in motion. The steady rhythm of the cast, the slow loop of the line, the connection between angler and river—it is impossible to stand in moving water and not feel a shift. Your body finds a cadence. Your mind narrows its focus. There is no past, no future. There is only now. The water. The fly. The possibility of a strike.

Science backs this up. Studies show that time spent in nature lowers cortisol levels, reduces anxiety, and improves mental clarity. Fly fishing, in particular, engages both body and mind, forcing an angler into a meditative state of focus. The casting stroke requires precision. The reading of the water demands attention. And the simple act of being surrounded by moving water forces the brain to recalibrate, to let go of the static that hums through modern life.

Why Water Heals

There is something about water that speaks to us on a primal level. Maybe it's because we are mostly made of it. Maybe it's because our ancestors lived and died by rivers, relying on them for food, for movement, for survival. Or maybe it's something deeper, something we cannot fully explain.

Wallace J. Nichols, in his book Blue Mind, explores the idea that simply being near water can trigger a sense of calm and well-being. It is why people are drawn to the ocean, to lakes, to rivers. The sight of flowing water, the sound of it, the feel of it rushing against our legs—it resets us. It reminds us that we are small, that the world will keep moving, that whatever burdens we carry will be washed away in time.

The River as a Mirror

A river is both a reflection and a lesson. It moves forward, always, yet never in a straight line. It carves its own path, adapts to obstacles, wears down even the hardest stone. There is wisdom in that. The river does not resist change. It bends, it shifts, it finds a way.

Fishing forces you into that same state of mind. The trout do not wait for you to figure things out. The river does not care that you are frustrated, that your mind is somewhere else. If you want success, you must be present. You must watch, adjust, move with the current instead of against it. And in doing so, you find clarity.

Grief, Loss, and the Water's Embrace

Many who fish do so not just for sport, but for something deeper. They come to the water in times of loss, in moments of struggle. They step into the current when they don't know where else to go. Because the river listens, even when no one else does.

There are stories—so many stories—of anglers who have cast flies in memory of those they have lost. Fathers who taught them how to tie a knot. Grandfathers who took them to their first trout stream. Friends who waded the same waters but are now only present in echoes and photographs.

Fly fishing is a way to connect with something beyond ourselves. To speak without words. To grieve without breaking. To heal without force.

The Therapy of the Chase

Some might argue that fishing is not about peace, but about pursuit. About the chase, the tension of the fight, the satisfaction of landing a wild fish. But that, too, is its own kind of therapy. The moment when a trout takes the fly, when the line goes tight, when adrenaline surges—that is the exhale, the release. A reminder that life is still thrilling, still unexpected, still full of moments that make the heart race.

And then, just as quickly, it is over. The trout slips back into the current. The water swallows the memory. And you are left standing there, smiling, feeling lighter than before.

A Memory That Will Never Leave Me

There are days when fly fishing is meditation, when it brings stillness and clarity. And then, there are days when the river reminds you that life is still full of surprises.

One afternoon, I took my daughter fishing. The water was perfect, the sky clear. I had spent the entire day casting, drifting, adjusting—without a single take. The river was winning. And then, finally, a fish. A beautiful brown trout, flashing golden in the current.

The fight was on. The kind that demands full attention, the kind where every movement matters. And then—

"Daddy! Daddy! Come see this lobster!"

I tried to ignore her at first. I had a fish on. The first fish of the day. But she was insistent. "Daddy, come now!"

I glanced over, torn between landing my trout and whatever had captivated her so completely. I tried to do both—walk toward her while keeping pressure on the line. You can guess how that ended.

The brown trout vanished, lost to the river. My one fish of the day, gone. And the "lobster"? A two-inch crawfish she had found under a rock, pinching the air like it was ready for battle.

She was beaming. She didn't care about my lost fish. She cared about that crawfish, about the wonder of what she had discovered. And in that moment, I realized something: maybe this, too, was therapy.

It wasn't about the fish. It never was. It was about being there, about the moment, about the memory. And that memory, unlike my trout, is something I will never lose.

Final Thought: The River is Always Waiting

Fishing may not solve every problem. It won't fix a broken heart, erase stress, or bring back what is lost. But it will always be there. The river is always waiting. The current always moves forward. And sometimes, that is enough.

So if you ever feel lost, if you need a place to reset, to breathe, to let go—go to the river.

Step in.

And let the water do what it does best.

But the river is only there for us because someone recognized the river's value before it was too late.

Chapter 68: The Impact of Conservation Laws on Fly Fishing

The best trout waters in America exist today because someone had the foresight to protect them. It wasn't always this way. In the early days of the sport, rivers were treated as infinite resources, fish as limitless commodities. It took decades—centuries, even—for anglers, lawmakers, and conservationists to realize that without protection, these waters and their trout would be lost.

The Early Days: Before Conservation

There was a time when catching 100 trout in a day wasn't just possible—it was expected. Streams were stuffed with wild fish, and no one thought twice about taking home a stringer full. There were no creel limits, no seasonal restrictions. If you wanted to fish, you fished. If you wanted to keep what you caught, you kept it.

But nature has limits, and as human pressure grew, trout populations declined. Logging operations stripped banks of shade, turning once-cold rivers into warm, sterile waters. Industrial runoff poisoned streams. Dams blocked migration routes, and hatcheries became a desperate attempt to replace what had been lost.

The Laws That Saved Trout Fishing

Regulations didn't happen overnight. They were hard-fought battles, often led by anglers themselves—people who saw firsthand what was happening and demanded change. Some of the most important conservation laws include:

The Lacey Act (1900) – One of the first major pieces of U.S. conservation law, it banned the transport of illegally caught fish and game across state lines. This stopped commercial poachers from wiping out native trout populations.

The Clean Water Act (1972) – Perhaps the single most important law for protecting trout waters, this act regulated pollution in rivers and lakes, forcing industries to clean up their waste and ensuring water quality remained high.

Wild and Scenic Rivers Act (1968) – This law designated certain rivers as protected from development, preventing dams, diversions, and destruction of key trout habitats.

Catch-and-Release Regulations – While not a federal law, many states implemented mandatory catch-and-release zones, allowing fish populations to rebound and ensuring wild trout remained a resource for future generations.

The Hatchery vs. Wild Trout Debate

One of the biggest conservation battles in fly fishing is the role of hatcheries. In the early 20th century, hatchery fish were seen as a solution to declining trout numbers. Stocking trucks dumped thousands of trout into rivers every year. But over time, biologists and anglers realized that stocked fish weren't a solution—they were part of the problem.

Hatchery fish are weaker – Born in tanks, raised on pellets, and dumped into streams, they lack the survival instincts of wild trout.

They compete with native fish – Stocked trout often push out wild populations, reducing genetic diversity and disrupting natural ecosystems.

Some states have reversed course – Many fisheries now focus on habitat restoration instead of stocking, helping wild populations return naturally.

Modern Conservation Efforts

Thanks to decades of work, fly anglers today fish healthier waters than generations before us. But the fight isn't over. Some of today's biggest conservation challenges include:

Environmental Changes & Water Temperatures – Trout thrive in cold, oxygen-rich water. Rising temperatures threaten fisheries worldwide. Many organizations work to plant trees along riverbanks to keep water cool.

Public Land Protections – Laws protecting national parks, forests, and wild rivers are constantly under political threat. Without them, prime trout habitat could be lost to development.

Overfishing & Illegal Harvesting – Poaching and ignoring

regulations still exist. Strong enforcement and education are key to protecting fisheries.

How Anglers Can Help

The government can only do so much—real conservation happens on the water, with the anglers who love these rivers. Every fly fisher has a responsibility to protect what they fish. Here's how:

Follow the regulations – Know the laws, respect them, and educate others.

Practice ethical catch-and-release – Handle fish properly, keep them in the water, and use barbless hooks when possible.

Join conservation groups – Groups like Trout Unlimited, Bonefish & Tarpon Trust, and Wild Salmon Center actively fight to protect our waters.

Support habitat restoration – Volunteer for stream cleanups, tree planting, and river restoration projects.

Advocate for conservation laws – Call representatives, sign petitions, and vote for policies that protect natural waters.

The Unexpected Consequences of Conservation

While conservation laws have been a lifeline for trout fisheries, they've also led to some unintended consequences. For example, in catch-and-release-only waters, some trout have grown so accustomed to being released that they seem to play along with the game. There are stories of the same fish being caught multiple times in a single day, almost as if they've figured out that the worst thing that happens is a quick photoshoot before being sent back home.

Then there are the so-called "educated trout"—fish in heavily regulated waters that have seen so many flies drift by that they've developed a Ph.D. in refusing artificial patterns. Anglers who've spent days on waters like the Henry's Fork or the Delaware River can attest: these fish have zero tolerance for sloppy presentations. It's as if they've formed a union and agreed to ignore 90% of what's offered to them.

Final Thought: The Future of Fly Fishing Depends on Us

If there's one truth in fly fishing, it's this: we do not inherit these waters; we borrow them from future generations.

Every trout we release, every piece of trash we pick up, every conservation effort we support ensures that the next generation of anglers will have the same rivers to wade, the same fish to chase, and the same stories to tell. Because a river only stays wild if we fight to keep it that way.

And if we do it right, maybe one day, the trout will finally forget what a dry fly looks like—just in time for us to fool them all over again.

But protecting the future of fly fishing isn't just about what we do today. It's about looking at the rivers that were nearly lost—rivers that were saved by the tireless efforts of those who refused to let them disappear.

Some rivers seemed doomed. But with the right action, the right people, and the right mindset, they came back.

Chapter 69: Success Stories of Rivers That Were Nearly Lost but Brought Back

Trout streams aren't invincible. While some waters have flowed steadily for millennia, others have nearly disappeared—victims of pollution, overuse, and human neglect. Thankfully, some of these rivers have been rescued through dedicated conservation efforts, passionate anglers, and organizations like Trout Unlimited, which works tirelessly to restore and protect fisheries across the country.

The Henry's Fork – Saved by Science and Stewardship

The Henry's Fork of the Snake River in Idaho is legendary now, but it wasn't always the pristine fishery it is today. Decades ago, water diversions, habitat destruction, and irrigation demands pushed its wild trout populations into decline. Low flows, rising temperatures, and dwindling resources left anglers wondering if the Henry's Fork could ever recover.

That's where The Henry's Fork Foundation came in. This group of conservationists and anglers took action, using scientific research, habitat restoration, and improved water management policies to breathe new life into the river. Today, the Henry's Fork is celebrated as one of the country's most cherished wild trout fisheries, drawing anglers from around the world to its thriving populations of rainbow and brown trout.

The Clark Fork – From Toxic Waste to Wild Trout Revival

Montana's Clark Fork River once suffered the devastating impact of over a century of mining and smelting operations. Toxic metals leached into the water, leaving the river nearly devoid of life. With its contaminated waters and nearly vanished fish populations, many believed the Clark Fork was beyond saving.

Then came the massive Superfund cleanup. Millions of cubic yards of toxic sediment were removed. Dams were dismantled. Native vegetation returned to the banks. The results were astounding. Wild trout reappeared, insect hatches improved, and the Clark Fork evolved into a thriving fishery once more. Anglers casting into these waters today are part of a remarkable comeback story.

The Au Sable River – Fighting for a Classic Trout Stream

Michigan's Au Sable River is legendary among fly anglers, but not long ago, its future was in jeopardy. Logging operations, pollution, and unregulated development led to eroded banks, heavy sedimentation, and declining trout populations. The river's historic reputation seemed at risk of fading forever.

But local conservation groups and Trout Unlimited joined forces to defend and restore the Au Sable. They opposed harmful construction projects, rehabilitated habitats, and implemented better fishing regulations. Thanks to these efforts, the Au Sable's wild brook and brown trout are once again flourishing in its cold, clear waters.

The Penobscot River – A Victory for Cold-Water Fish

Maine's Penobscot River faced a dire situation. Dams blocked the migration routes of native Atlantic salmon and wild trout. Poor water quality and disrupted habitats left the river's fish populations in serious decline. For years, it seemed that these cold-water species might disappear entirely from the Penobscot's waters.

The Penobscot River Restoration Project turned things around. By removing several dams and creating bypasses, the project opened more than 1,000 miles of cold-water habitat. Trout and salmon numbers rebounded, and the ecosystem began to heal. Today, the Penobscot stands as one of New England's best cold-water fisheries, a triumph of collaborative conservation efforts.

Trout Unlimited: Protecting Waters for Future Generations

While some rivers have seen incredible turnarounds, others still face threats. Trout Unlimited (TU) remains at the forefront of protecting and maintaining these waters. Through habitat restoration, policy advocacy, and educational outreach, TU ensures that future generations can enjoy the same trout streams we do today.

TU's approach is simple yet powerful: Protect, Reconnect,

Restore, and Sustain. This philosophy drives their volunteer efforts, which range from trash cleanups to native vegetation planting to dam removals. TU's work extends beyond improving the health of rivers; it creates a legacy of stewardship that benefits both fish and people.

What We Can Learn from These Success Stories

The revival of these rivers proves that damaged fisheries can recover. It takes dedication, science, and a collective commitment, but it's possible. However, these victories aren't permanent. Every river requires ongoing care and vigilance.

Anglers have an essential role to play. Volunteer for a cleanup day. Support conservation initiatives. Become a Trout Unlimited member. By taking action, we ensure that our favorite trout streams continue to flow, supporting the fish we love to chase.

A New Era of Fly Fishing

The fight to protect rivers isn't confined to the water's edge. Fly fishing is evolving. It's no longer just about solitude on the stream; it's also about connecting a new generation to the sport. Today's anglers not only fish—they capture moments, share stories, and inspire others to care about these waters.

The rivers we fish tomorrow depend on what we do today. Let's ensure they remain places of beauty, adventure, and thriving trout populations.

Chapter 70: The Rise of Fishing in the Digital Age

There was a time when fly fishing was an unplugged experience, where the only sounds were the rush of the river, the whisper of a cast, and the occasional shout of triumph (or frustration). But step onto the water today, and you might hear something else—a GoPro beeping as it starts recording, a phone buzzing with a live-stream notification, or a drone humming overhead capturing cinematic footage of the day's adventure.

The younger generation views the outdoors through a different lens—literally. They see fly fishing not just as an experience to be had, but as one to be documented, shared, and even curated. For them, it's not just about catching fish; it's about telling the story in real-time.

I remember taking a younger friend fishing, only to realize he spent more time adjusting his drone for the perfect river shot than actually casting his line. It was fascinating and frustrating at the same time. I'll admit—I wanted to roll my eyes.

But then, later that night, he sent me the footage. Seeing the river from above, watching a trout glide through crystal-clear pools—it gave me a new perspective, too. Well, at least I think it was a trout. On the drone footage, it was so small I thought he had accidentally filmed a water bug on a solo adventure. I squinted, paused, rewound—nope, still looked like a speck of lint drifting downstream. But hey, if he says it was a trout, who am I to crush his dreams?

Technology isn't just changing how we document the outdoors; it's changing how we experience it. Modern anglers can check water conditions from an app, use GPS to locate new fishing spots, and even buy gear with a single tap on their phones. In some ways, the new tools make anglers more informed and prepared than ever before. But in other ways, it creates a new kind of distance—one where the experience risks becoming secondary to the documentation of it.

The Shift from Solitude to Social Connection

For past generations, fly fishing was a quiet pursuit—a time for reflection, patience, and an escape from the world. Today, it's often a social event. Fishing trips are organized through group chats, photos are instantly uploaded, and success is measured by likes, shares, and digital engagement. Some might argue that this diminishes the soul of the sport, but there's another way to look at it.

Instead of resisting change, we have to ask: What's actually being lost, and what's being gained?

There's something powerful about the way younger anglers build communities through fishing. Social media groups connect beginners with seasoned pros, and YouTube tutorials offer casting lessons to anyone willing to learn. While older anglers might have learned from their fathers, uncles, or a few good books, new anglers have entire digital libraries at their fingertips.

The Rise of the "Conscious Angler"

One major shift in the younger generation's approach to fly fishing is their heightened awareness of conservation. Decades ago, anglers rarely questioned keeping a full limit of trout. Today, catch-and-release is not only common but often expected. Younger fishermen are more educated on sustainability, and they often see themselves as stewards of the water rather than just users of it.

For many, fishing isn't just a sport—it's an extension of environmental activism. Conversations about barbless hooks, trout-safe handling, and river restoration are far more common among younger anglers than they were in past generations. Some even forgo fishing certain rivers during extreme heat to prevent stress on the trout population.

It's easy to dismiss younger anglers as glued to their phones, but the truth is, they are more engaged than ever in protecting the resource. They use social media to raise awareness, sign petitions, and advocate for better fisheries management. The river isn't just a place to fish—it's a place to defend.

The Disconnection from the Wild

But with all this connectivity, there's also a loss—a fading sense of true solitude. Many younger anglers never experience the feeling of being completely alone on the river, untethered from notifications and updates. That's a kind of magic that can't be replicated with an Instagram post.

I once watched a group of young anglers set up a tent next to a pristine backcountry stream, only to spend the first hour of their trip troubleshooting their Wi-Fi hotspot so they could stream a live fishing session. I couldn't help but wonder: If you're always connected, do you ever truly escape?

While previous generations of anglers found solitude without effort, today's fishermen have to actively seek it out—turning off phones, leaving the camera behind, and stepping into the river just to fish, not to record.

Bridging the Generational Gap

So where does that leave us? Are these changes ruining the essence of fly fishing, or are they simply evolving it?

The answer, as always, is somewhere in between. The truth is, every generation has put its own stamp on the sport. The older generation once scoffed at graphite rods replacing bamboo, just as some anglers today roll their eyes at the GoPros and TikTok clips of modern fishing culture.

The key isn't in resisting change but in making sure that the core of fly fishing remains intact. That means:

Passing down knowledge in a way that resonates with younger anglers. That might mean teaching on the water and online.

Encouraging both tradition and innovation—new tools should complement, not replace, time-tested skills.

Making sure the experience matters more than the digital proof of it—reminding new anglers that some moments are better left unposted.

Fishing with a Foot in Both Worlds

I'm not against technology. I own a GoPro. I check river gauges on my phone before heading out. I even enjoy watching high-quality fly fishing videos when I can't be on the water myself. But I also know this: no picture, no video, no live stream will ever capture the feeling of being there.

The rush of cold water against your legs. The silent moment before a trout takes. The deep inhale of mountain air when you step into a river valley at sunrise.

You can capture the image, but you can't capture the moment. Ultimately, that's the lesson we need to pass on.

Fly fishing isn't 100% about the fish or the size of the fish. It's about the connection—to the water, to the wild, and to something that can't be measured in likes or comments. The next generation may see the river differently, but as long as they feel it, we haven't lost anything at all.

But just like everything else in fly fishing, the tools we use are constantly changing. What started as a simple stick and string has evolved into a high-tech marvel—one that blends craftsmanship, innovation, and a bit of clever marketing.

Chapter 71: The Evolution of Fly Rods

A Stick, Some String, and Centuries of Obsession

Fly rods have come a long way. From the first primitive sticks used by ancient anglers to today's ultra-light, high-tech marvels, the evolution of fly rods is a story of craftsmanship, science, and—let's be honest—some very persuasive marketing. If you've ever walked into a fly shop and been told that the latest rod is "stronger, lighter, and more sensitive than ever before," congratulations—you've experienced firsthand how the fly fishing industry keeps us all perpetually one purchase away from the perfect cast.

The Golden Age of Bamboo: When Fly Fishing Was an Art Form

Once upon a time, if you wanted a fly rod, you got a bamboo rod. Not just any bamboo—Tonkin cane, harvested from China, hand-split, planed, glued, and wrapped in silk thread. These rods were beautiful, deeply personal, and slow as molasses. The casting stroke required patience, a rhythm closer to poetry than sport. Every movement felt intentional, every bend in the rod a lesson in finesse.

But bamboo rods weren't for the impatient. They were heavier than modern rods, expensive to produce, and heartbreakingly fragile if mistreated. Snap one in a car door, and you'd feel the kind of sorrow usually reserved for the loss of a beloved family heirloom. Yet, for those who fished them, bamboo wasn't just a tool—it was an experience, a connection to a bygone era where fly fishing felt more like art than engineering.

Fiberglass: The Forgotten Middle Child

Then came fiberglass, the great democratizer of fly fishing. Affordable, nearly indestructible, and with a buttery-smooth action that made even an average cast feel elegant, fiberglass revolutionized the sport in the mid-20th century. Suddenly, fly fishing wasn't just for those who could afford custom cane rods—it was for everyone.

Fiberglass had its quirks. The action was soft, sometimes too soft, turning tight loops into wide, lazy arcs. But it had soul. Anglers who fish fiberglass today—many of whom prefer it for small stream fishing—tend to view graphite rods the way vinyl record collectors view MP3s: technically superior, but lacking a certain depth of character.

Graphite: The Industry Standard

Then, in the 1970s, everything changed. Graphite fly rods hit the market, and suddenly, anglers could cast farther with less effort. These rods were lighter, stronger, and more responsive. They were also faster—meaning a quicker recovery time, tighter loops, and more control. Graphite didn't just replace bamboo and fiberglass; it redefined the sport.

For years, graphite rods got progressively better. Every new model promised increased sensitivity, more power, and improved accuracy. And they delivered—mostly. But there was a catch. High-modulus graphite, the kind used in the best rods, was also notoriously brittle. The stronger the rod became, the more likely it was to shatter when it met an unexpected rock, car door, or angler who forgot it was leaning against the tailgate.

Graphene: The Future of Fly Rods?

Now we have graphene—the so-called "miracle material." Stronger than steel, lighter than graphite, and theoretically capable of delivering the most efficient energy transfer of any rod ever made, graphene is being marketed as the next great leap forward. Fly rod manufacturers are rolling out models that boast insane durability and near-telepathic sensitivity.

But here's the thing: if you think graphite rods are expensive, graphene rods will make you reconsider your financial priorities. They come with price tags that make you wonder if they also pay your mortgage. And while they might offer some real performance benefits, the question remains—how much of it is genuine innovation, and how much is just another excuse to convince anglers they need another new rod?

The Marketing of Fly Rods: Why You're Always One Purchase Away from Perfection

Fly rod companies are masters of persuasion. Every year, a

new model is released that promises to be "stronger, lighter, and more sensitive" than the last one. And every year, we believe it.

The rod you bought three years ago? The one you swore was the best rod you'd ever owned? Well, guess what—it's outdated. Too heavy. Too slow. Not nearly as responsive as the new model. And just like that, you're convinced that you need an upgrade.

But here's the hard truth: no rod can make up for bad casting. If you're out there flailing your line like you're trying to scare the trout away, even a $1,500 rod won't save you. A tight loop isn't built into the blank—it's built into the angler.

Why I Haven't Bought the Expensive Rod Yet

Every year, I make a deal with myself. If I can go an entire season without snapping the tip off my rod, I'll consider investing in a high-end model. And every year, I fail. I've broken rods in every way imaginable—caught in doorways, slammed in car trunks, crushed under wading boots. If rod manufacturers keep records of frequent offenders, I'm probably on a list somewhere.

So, for now, I stick with what works. A solid mid-range graphite rod that I don't have to treat like a newborn baby. Because if I ever do buy that $1,500 graphene rod, you better believe I'll be walking through doorways sideways, carrying it like it's made of spun glass.

Still, Some Things Never Change

No matter how advanced rods become, no matter how much technology gets packed into the blank, some things remain constant. A bad drift is still a bad drift, no matter how expensive the rod. The river still demands patience. And fly fishing will always be more about the angler than the gear.

But if history has taught us anything, it's that innovation won't stop. New materials will emerge. Rod companies will continue finding ways to convince us that we need the latest and greatest. And we'll keep buying into it—because deep down, every angler believes that just maybe, the next rod will be the one that finally makes the perfect cast.

And maybe it will.

Or maybe, just like always, it'll still be up to us.

But rods aren't the only thing surrounded by myth in this sport. Walk into any fly shop, spend enough time swapping stories on the riverbank, and you'll hear them—rules, theories, and half-truths that have been passed down for generations. Some hold water. Others? Well, let's just say it's time to separate fact from fiction.

Chapter 72: Fly Fishing Myths

Because the River is Full of Fish… and Bad Advice

Every sport has its legends, and fly fishing is no exception. Passed down from generation to generation, whispered in fly shops, and repeated in online forums, these "truths" become gospel—until, of course, you actually put them to the test.

The problem? Most of them aren't true.

Fly fishing is already challenging enough without carrying a bag full of outdated myths and half-baked wisdom. So, let's set the record straight and bust some of the most persistent fly fishing myths that refuse to die, no matter how many trout try to prove them wrong.

Myth #1: Trout Are Leader Shy

The Truth: Trout Are More Worried About the Fly Than the Leader

How many times have you heard someone say, "If you're not using 7X tippet, you're scaring all the fish away"? Somewhere along the way, anglers became convinced that trout were part-time optometrists who could measure line diameter down to the micron.

Sure, trout can see tippet—but they're far more concerned about how your fly behaves in the water. A drag-free drift, the right size and movement, and a convincing presentation matter way more than whether you're using 5X or 6X. In fact, some of the biggest trout ever caught were fooled on shockingly thick tippet.

When leader size matters: In slow, crystal-clear water where trout have all the time in the world to inspect your fly.

When it doesn't: In fast, turbulent water where trout have half a second to decide before their meal disappears downstream.

Moral of the story: Presentation beats tippet size. Always.

Myth #2: Big Flies Only Catch Big Fish

The Truth: Big Trout Eat Tiny Bugs, Too

It's easy to think that a 24-inch brown trout wouldn't bother with something as small as a size 20 Blue-Winged Olive. After all, shouldn't a beast like that be eating baby ducklings and terrified mice?

While big trout can be aggressive predators, they spend most of their lives eating what's most available—which, in most trout streams, means small aquatic insects. Tiny midges, mayflies, and caddis make up the bulk of their diet.

That's why some of the biggest trout ever landed have been caught on flies so small they could fit on a grain of rice. So if you're only throwing articulated streamers the size of a squirrel, you're missing out on a whole world of selective big trout slurping midges like fine wine.

Myth #3: Trout Always Face Upstream

The Truth: Trout Face Wherever the Food Is

This is a classic piece of fly fishing wisdom: "Always cast upstream because trout only face into the current." Except... they don't.

Yes, most trout prefer to face upstream because that's where the majority of their food drifts from. But when insects emerge from the bottom, trout turn in all directions—sometimes even drifting backward to chase rising bugs.

Not to mention, in still water, lakes, or slower currents, trout move constantly, hunting for food instead of waiting for it to come to them.

Why this myth matters: If you're only fishing upstream presentations, you might be missing opportunities to catch fish that are looking in another direction.

Myth #4: If You're Not Matching the Hatch, You Won't Catch Anything

The Truth: Sometimes, Trout Just Want Something Different

There's an old saying: "Match the hatch or go home." While hatch-matching is important, it's not the only way to catch fish.

Trout are opportunistic eaters, and sometimes, throwing

something completely different from what's on the water can trigger an instinctual response. That's why attractor patterns like the Royal Wulff, Stimulator, and Purple Haze work even when nothing like them is hatching.

In other words, when your perfect mayfly imitation gets ignored for the fifteenth time, maybe it's time to try something that doesn't look like everything else floating downstream.

Myth #5: The More Expensive Your Gear, the More Fish You'll Catch

The Truth: Expensive Gear Catches More Ego Than Fish

The fly fishing industry wants you to believe that a $1,200 rod will make you a better angler. And hey, high-end gear is nice—but it won't make up for bad casting, poor presentation, or lack of water-reading skills.

A good angler with a $100 rod will outfish a bad angler with a $1,000 setup every single day.

Yes, quality gear matters, but technique, knowledge, and time spent actually fishing matter way more. So if you're debating whether to upgrade your fly rod or spend that money on a weekend fishing trip, take the trip.

Because trout don't check price tags.

Final Thought: Don't Let These Myths Hold You Back

Fly fishing is full of traditions, but not all traditions hold up under scrutiny. The truth is, the best way to learn is to experiment for yourself. Try the unconventional. Fish at odd hours. Throw a size 22 fly at a monster brown.

Because trout don't read fly fishing books. They don't visit online forums. And they definitely don't care about your expensive new rod.

Somewhere, two trout are sitting in the deep pool, watching another fly drift by.

"Yeah," says the second. "Like I don't hear them tripping over rocks the whole way down."

Then they both laugh and go back to ignoring your perfect

drift.

But even if the trout are laughing, the truth remains—there's always something new to try, and sometimes, it's the forgotten techniques that are the most effective. Wet fly fishing might have been left in the dust, but it's making a comeback—quietly, without fanfare—waiting for those who dare to rediscover it.

Chapter 73: Reviving The Lost Art of Wet Fly Fishing

Wet Flies: The Greatest Comeback Story That Never Happened

Somewhere along the way, wet fly fishing got ghosted. Once the undisputed champion of trout fishing, it was slowly abandoned like an old MySpace account. Dry-fly anglers sneered, nymphers got scientific, and streamer junkies started swinging meat the size of squirrels. Meanwhile, wet flies sat in the corner, quietly collecting dust in forgotten fly boxes.

But here's the secret: wet flies still work, and trout still love them. In fact, they might just be the most effective flies you're not using. So before you go all-in on euro-nymphing or sell your soul to the dry-fly gods, let's take a trip back in time and rediscover the trout-catching magic of the wet fly.

What the Heck Is Wet Fly Fishing?

Wet flies are like the middle child of the fly fishing family—not quite a nymph, not quite a dry fly, and completely underappreciated. They're lightweight, soft-hackled flies that drift just beneath the surface, imitating insects that are struggling, drowning, or otherwise failing at life (which, let's be honest, is when trout really take notice).

Before modern fly fishing became a contest of who can tie the tiniest fly on the lightest tippet with the most Latin-sounding bug name, wet flies were the go-to method for catching trout. Anglers fished multiple flies at once, swinging them across the current like a Victorian gentleman with too much free time. And it worked.

And guess what? It still works.

Why Wet Flies Are the Underdog You Should Bet On

They're Easy to Fish – No need to perfectly match the hatch, high-stick your way into a back injury, or false-cast until your arm falls off. Wet flies are low-maintenance and get the job done.

They Cover More Water – Unlike dry flies that require pinpoint accuracy or nymphs that demand a drag-free drift, wet flies swing, drift, and move naturally—doing most of the work for you.

They Trick Trout with Motion – Dead-drifted nymphs just sit there. Dry flies rely on trout being in a picky mood. But wet flies? They flutter, pulse, and scream, "Eat me!" in trout language.

They Make You Look Like a Fishing Hipster – Nothing says "I knew about this before it was cool" like tying on a soft-hackled fly and outfishing everyone on the river.

How to Ask for a Wet Fly at the Local Fly Shop (Without Getting Laughed At)

Asking for a wet fly at a modern fly shop can go one of two ways:

You get an old-school, bearded shop guy who nods approvingly and says,

"Ah, a man of culture! Let me show you my finest soft hackles."

You get a 20-something guide bro who looks at you like you just asked for a rotary phone.

"Uh… you mean a streamer?"

So how do you ask for a wet fly without getting weird looks? Here's the play:

Be Specific: Instead of saying, "Got any wet flies?" (which might make them think you're just describing the weather), ask for soft hackles or a specific pattern, like a Partridge & Orange or a March Brown Spider.

Mention Your Strategy: Say something like,

"I'm looking to swing some soft hackles in the riffles today—what do you recommend?"

Now you sound like a pro, not a time traveler from 1894.

Lean Into It: If they give you a funny look, just say,

"Hey, trout have been eating wet flies since before dry flies even existed. You got any or not?"

(Bonus points if you add, "G.E.M. Skues would be rolling in his grave right now.")

Embrace the Laughs: If they chuckle, own it. Wet fly fishing is like vinyl records—it's old-school but still awesome. Just smile and say,

"That's fine, I'll just be over here catching fish while you guys argue about tippet diameter."

Will They Actually Laugh at You?

Maybe. But the real question is: will the trout?

(Answer: No. They'll just eat your wet fly while the nymph guys are still adjusting their indicators.)

How to Fish Wet Flies Without Looking Confused

Fishing wet flies isn't rocket science (which is why it's perfect for people like me). Just let the current do the work and avoid overthinking. Here are some basic strategies that even the fishiest of trout snobs would approve of:

The Swing – Cast down and across, let the fly swing naturally through the current, and prepare for a violent strike that will make you question your reflexes.

The Lift – Let your fly drift, then give it a little lift at the end of the swing. This mimics an insect rising toward the surface, which triggers an automatic "MUST EAT" response from trout.

The Two-Fly Setup – Feeling spicy? Tie on a second wet fly a foot above the first one. Twice the temptation, twice the fun.

The "I Forgot What I Was Doing" Drift – Just cast it out and let it drift naturally while you daydream about lunch. Sometimes, that's all it takes.

Classic Wet Flies That Still Slay Trout

These flies have been fooling trout for generations—and they don't even require the use of a magnifying glass to tie on:

The Partridge & Orange – Simple, elegant, and as old-school as it gets.

The Soft Hackle Pheasant Tail – A pheasant tail nymph with some fancy soft hackle? Yes, please.

The March Brown Spider – Works like magic during mayfly hatches, or when you want to pretend you're in a 19th-century English novel.

The Greenwell's Glory – If you like catching fish and sounding sophisticated, this one's for you.

The Leadwing Coachman – Looks fancy. Works everywhere. Trout can't resist.

Bringing Wet Fly Fishing Back—One Cast at a Time

The modern fly fishing world might be obsessed with the latest trends, but wet fly fishing remains one of the most effective, stress-free, and flat-out fun ways to catch trout. No complicated rigs, no fancy casts, no heartbreaking refusals—just simple, effective fishing that still works after all these years.

Trends come and go, but the river stays the same. Somewhere out there, a trout is waiting for a classic wet fly to drift by, just as it did a century ago.

Will you be the one to remind it?

Next time the fish ignore your dry flies and laugh at your nymphs, tie on a wet fly, swing it through the current, and get ready.

While the world may have forgotten wet fly fishing, the trout never did.

The river never forgets. It remembers the past and waits patiently for those who understand its timeless rhythm.

But while you're out there reconnecting with the classics, don't get bogged down by unnecessary gear. The river doesn't care how much you bring—it cares about what you do with the gear you have.

Chapter 74: The Bare Necessities

Pack Light, Fish Hard

If you've been fly fishing long enough, you've seen it: the guy who looks like he raided an outdoor store five minutes before hitting the river. A vest packed with 37 fly boxes, a wading staff, a bear whistle, three different tippet spools, a flask of whiskey (okay, maybe that one's necessary), and enough gadgets hanging off him to make a Swiss Army knife blush.

Here's the truth: you don't need all that crap.

Fly fishing isn't about carrying half of your garage into the water. It's about efficiency—having exactly what you need and nothing more. The guy with the simplest setup often catches just as many fish, if not more, than the one loaded down like a pack mule.

A 9-foot, 5-weight rod covers nearly everything. Unless you're chasing steelhead or tiny brook trout, you don't need seven different rods. A good, smooth reel is important, but let's be real—unless you're fighting big fish, your reel is just a glorified line holder. A weight-forward floating line does the job 90% of the time. If you're swapping lines every few minutes, you might be overcomplicating things.

And flies? You don't need 500 of them. If it doesn't fit in a small fly box, it's probably excess. A Parachute Adams, a Pheasant Tail, a Woolly Bugger, and a Hopper will catch trout almost anywhere. If you find yourself carrying five boxes of flies, ask yourself—how many of these do I actually use?

Tippet? One spool. Leader? One or two, max. If you're switching leaders every few casts, you might need to focus more on your drift than your gear. Forceps, nippers, and clippers—these are the only tools you actually need. Everything else—the zingers, gadgets, and accessories—just gets in the way.

And let's talk about vests. They're fine, but let's be honest—they make you look like you're wearing tactical gear for a trout battle. A small sling pack or waist pack is lighter, more functional, and forces you to carry only the essentials.

Now, do you really need waders? Not always. Wet wading in summer is one of the best ways to experience a river. Quick-dry pants, a good pair of wading boots, and a willingness to embrace the cold are often all you need. If you're spending more time adjusting your waders than fishing, it might be time to rethink things.

I used to bring way too much gear. I thought I needed options, backups, and tools for every possible situation. But over time, I started stripping things down, removing what I didn't need, simplifying my approach. And what happened? I started fishing better. I was more focused on the water, on my drift, on the rhythm of the cast—because I wasn't distracted by gear.

One Last Thing

Fly fishing doesn't have to be complicated. Some of the best days on the water happen when you strip everything down and focus on what matters. The gear you need is simple. The skills you require are timeless. And the connection you make with the river is what lasts.

It's easy to get caught up in the latest gadgets or to think you need a mountain of gear to catch a trout. But in the end, it's the simplicity of the experience—the quiet moments, the thrill of a good cast, and the satisfaction of a successful drift—that define fly fishing.

So, next time you head out, keep it light, keep it simple, and fish hard.

For me, fly fishing has always been about getting back to basics. Whether I'm standing in a creek or sitting at my desk writing, the goal is the same: to keep learning, keep improving, and keep chasing that quiet peace the river offers.

My kids get it, too. They ask me constantly when we're going back to the creek, even when our vacation is still months away. Their excitement builds with every passing week, as if time moves too slowly when water, fish, and adventure are waiting. And honestly, I feel the same way. No matter how many times I step into a stream, the anticipation never fades.

Because the river is always there, waiting.

And maybe that's the real lesson fly fishing teaches us—not just about catching fish, but about showing up. About patience. About slowing down enough to notice the small things. And, most of all, about returning to the places that make us feel alive.

This book is my way of sharing that journey with you. But the conversation doesn't have to stop here.

Fly fishing has a way of stirring something deep within us—memories, new perspectives, or simply the pull of the water. There's always more to learn, more to discover. That's what makes this pursuit so special.

I'm excited for whatever comes next—whether it's another chapter, another cast, or another stream waiting to be explored.

And if you ever find yourself standing at the edge of a river, listening to the current, feeling the weight of the moment before your first cast—know that I'll be out there too, somewhere, doing the same.

Appendix:

What Every Angler Should Know- A Fly Fishing Q&A

The Art of Fly Fishing

Q: What's the single most important thing to learn in fly fishing?

A: Control. The guy who controls his cast, his line, his drift—he catches fish. The guy who doesn't? He's just standing in a river waving a stick.

Q: Why do trout sometimes refuse a perfectly presented fly?

A: Because they're trout. Sometimes they eat a speck of dust off the water and ignore your masterpiece. The lesson? Don't take it personally. Adjust. Change flies. Try again.

Q: What does "reading the water" really mean?

A: It's like walking into a party and knowing exactly who's up to something. The river has tells. Slow seams? A trout's hiding. Riffles? They're feeding. Deep pools? That's where the big one waits. Learn to read the water, and the fish stop being a mystery.

Q: What's the best way to improve your fly cast?

A: Take the water out of the equation. Perfect your cast on the lawn, in a park, wherever. The best casters make the motion second nature before they ever step into a river.

Q: What's the biggest mistake new fly anglers make?

A: They rush. Fly fishing isn't about brute force. Slow down. Your cast, your approach, your hook set—everything gets better when you stop trying to muscle it.

Q: How important is fly selection?

A: More important than people think. You can have the best cast in the world, but if your fly is wrong, you're just playing fetch with the river.

Q: Should I always match the hatch?

A: No. Sometimes trout want something different. If everyone's throwing the same fly, switch it up. Be the angler who stands out.

Q: Is nymph fishing really just "bait fishing with fur and feathers"?

A: Only if you have no soul. Nymphing is an art—knowing where fish hold, how currents affect your drift, and how to feel a strike you can't even see. It's fly fishing at its purest.

Q: How do I get better at detecting strikes?

A: Pay attention. Trout don't always slam a fly. Sometimes it's just the slightest pause, a flicker of movement. If you think, "Was that a strike?"—it was.

Q: How does fly fishing compare to other types of fishing?

A: It's chess versus checkers. Sure, you can catch fish with any method, but fly fishing is about craft, patience, and problem-solving. You're not just fishing—you're decoding a river.

Q: What's the best way to fight a big trout?

A: Stay calm. Let it run when it wants to, keep steady pressure, and don't force it. Trout are like stubborn dogs—pull too hard, and they'll pull back harder.

Q: Why do some anglers fish bamboo rods instead of graphite?

A: Because they're romantics. Bamboo isn't just a rod—it's a feeling. It bends differently, responds to the river in a way that modern rods don't. It's slower, but that's the point.

Q: What's the biggest myth in fly fishing?

A: That expensive gear makes you a better angler. It doesn't. Skill, knowledge, and patience do. A thousand-dollar rod won't fix a bad cast.

Q: Why do some people prefer wet flies over dry flies?

A: Because most of a trout's diet is underwater. Dry flies are flashy, but wet flies match what fish actually eat most of the time.

Q: How do I know when to switch flies?

A: When what you're using isn't working. If you haven't had a bite in 20 minutes, change something—fly size, color, or type.

Q: What's the best way to mend a fly line?

A: Lift the line with a smooth motion, then reposition it upstream without disturbing the fly. A good mend lets your fly drift naturally—bad mends scare fish.

Q: How can I improve my accuracy when casting?

A: Pick a target—a leaf, a ripple, a shadow—and hit it every time. Precision in fly fishing is about consistency, not power.

Q: What's the secret to a perfect drift?

A: Eliminate drag. Your fly should move at the same speed as the water. Any unnatural movement tips off the trout.

Q: How do I avoid spooking fish?

A: Move slow, stay low, and make every step count. Trout feel vibrations. If you stomp around like a linebacker, they'll be gone before you even make a cast.

Q: What's the best way to land a trout?

A: Keep its head up and guide it toward you. If it's thrashing, let it tire out. Net it quickly, keep it in the water, and handle it like a priceless artifact.

Q: How do I know if my fly is too big or too small?

A: If fish are rising and ignoring your fly, it's too big. If they're interested but hesitant, try one size smaller.

Q: Why do some anglers use barbless hooks?

A: Because they care. Barbless hooks cause less damage, make for easier releases, and keep the sport about skill—not brute force.

Q: What's the best way to wade in a river?

A: Slow and steady. Watch your footing, use a wading staff, and never assume the riverbed is solid—it shifts more than you think.

Q: How do I keep my fly from getting tangled?

A: Stop false casting so much. The more you whip it around, the more knots you'll get. Smooth, controlled motions prevent headaches.

Q: What's the best way to store fly fishing gear?

A: Dry it out. Wet gear grows mold and rust. Take care of your flies, rods, and reels—this isn't cheap stuff.

Understanding Trout & Their Habitat

Q: What are the four main types of trout streams?

A: Spring creeks, freestone rivers, tailwaters, and headwaters. Each one offers a different challenge. Spring creeks are clear and technical, freestones are wild and unpredictable, tailwaters are stable but require precision, and headwaters are small, intimate waters often teeming with wild trout.

Q: How do headwaters differ from freestone rivers?

A: Headwaters are the birthplaces of rivers—narrow, shallow, and often found high in the mountains. The water is cold, oxygen-rich, and filled with small but aggressive trout. Freestone rivers, on the other hand, are larger, more unpredictable, and shaped by seasonal runoff, making them dynamic and ever-changing.

Q: How does water temperature affect trout?

A: It's their life force. Trout thrive between 50-60°F. Too hot, and they get sluggish—or worse, they die. Too cold, and they become finicky, waiting for the right moment to feed.

Q: Where do trout hide in a river?

A: Look for the seams. Where fast and slow water meet, that's their buffet line. Deep pools, undercut banks, behind boulders—trout want to expend the least energy for the most reward.

Q: What's the best way to locate trout in a new river?

A: Think like a predator. Watch for rising fish, look for structure, and scan the water for shadows and movement. Slow water means easy meals. Fast water oxygenates. Learn to read the river, and you'll find the fish.

Q: How do seasons affect trout behavior?

A: Each season rewrites the script. Spring means fresh hatches and aggressive fish. Summer makes them cautious, retreating to deep, cool water. Fall triggers pre-spawn feeding frenzies, and winter slows everything down to a chess game.

Q: Do trout see color?

A: They see contrast more than color. In low light, they pick up silhouettes. In clear water, they notice fine details. That's why an old-school black fly can outfish the most realistic pattern.

Q: What's the best time of day to catch trout?

A: Early morning and late evening are magic. Midday sun makes them skittish, but cloudy days can extend the bite window. Watch the bugs—when they hatch, trout are on.

Q: How do trout react to weather changes?

A: Like gamblers reading the odds. Before a storm, they feast. After, they sulk. On bright sunny days, they hunker down. Overcast skies? That's when they feel bold.

Q: What's the role of oxygen in trout habitat?

A: Oxygen is life. Fast-moving water, riffles, and waterfalls keep it high. Stagnant pools get low, making fish sluggish. Cold water holds more oxygen—that's why trout crave it.

Q: What insects do trout eat?

A: Mayflies, caddisflies, stoneflies—the holy trinity. Midges in the winter, terrestrials in summer. If it's in the water and it moves, they'll consider it food.

Q: How does river depth affect trout feeding?

A: Deeper water keeps them safe. Shallow water makes them nervous but is prime for feeding, especially in the early morning and evening.

Q: Why do trout stay near logs and boulders?

A: Cover equals survival. These spots provide shade, break the current, and offer ambush points for food. If you were a trout, you'd hide there too.

Q: How do hatch cycles influence trout feeding?

A: It's their meal plan. When a hatch happens, they key in on it—sometimes to the exclusion of everything else. That's when matching the hatch becomes an obsession.

Q: Do trout migrate?

A: Some do. Brown trout move upstream to spawn. Some cutthroats travel between rivers and lakes. Rainbows follow food. It's all about survival and opportunity.

Q: How does water clarity impact fishing?

A: Clear water makes trout cautious—they see everything. Murky water gives you an edge; they have to rely more on feel than sight. Adjust your approach accordingly.

Q: How do different species of trout behave differently?

A: Rainbows are aggressive and acrobatic. Browns are moody and calculated. Cutthroats are opportunistic and wild. Brook trout? They're ghosts of the forest, small but fierce.

Q: Why do trout sometimes refuse perfectly good flies?

A: Because they can. They're survivors, trained by nature to be skeptical. If something's off—the drift, the size, the silhouette—they'll ignore it.

Q: What's the best way to stalk trout without spooking them?

A: Move slow. Stay low. Approach from downstream. Blend in with your surroundings. If you look like a predator, they'll treat you like one.

Q: Why do some rivers produce bigger trout than others?

A: It's all about food, water temperature, and genetics. Rich insect life, stable water flow, and good cover produce giants. Some rivers have the right combination—others don't.

Q: How do dams affect trout habitat?

A: They create tailwaters, which can be great fisheries. But they also disrupt natural flows, limit migration, and alter water temperatures. It's a double-edged sword.

Q: Why do trout sometimes stop feeding suddenly?

A: Something changed. A shadow passed overhead. A water level dropped. A pressure shift signaled caution. They're always tuned into survival mode.

Q: What's the best way to predict where trout will be in a river?

A: Think like a hunter. Where's the cover? Where's the food? Where's the least resistance in the current? Find those spots, and you'll find fish.

Q: How do floods impact trout populations?

A: They can be a disaster, washing away eggs and changing streambeds. But sometimes, they refresh a river, carving out new holding spots and improving habitat.

Q: How can you tell if a river is overfished?

A: Smart fish, empty riffles, and spooky behavior. If trout refuse everything, they've seen it all before. That's when presentation becomes everything.

Q: How do trout survive harsh winters?

A: They slow down, conserve energy, and find deep pools where water stays stable. Ice-covered rivers still flow underneath—trout are just waiting for the right moment to move.

The Philosophy of the Stream

Q: What does "the calling of the creek" really mean?

A: It's that pull you feel deep down, the one that makes you leave the house before sunrise just to stand in moving water. It's not about the fish—it never was. It's about something older, something primal.

Q: How does fly fishing teach patience?

A: Because you're going to fail—a lot. You'll get tangled, miss strikes, spook fish. But the only way to succeed is to keep casting. Life works the same way.

Q: Why do some anglers say, "You never step into the same river twice"?

A: Because rivers change. So do you. The water moves, the fish shift, and the angler who fished here last year isn't the same person who wades in today.

Q: What can fly fishing teach you about resilience?

A: It humbles you. It makes you work for every success. The river doesn't care how much gear you own—either you adapt, or you don't catch fish.

Q: Why does fly fishing feel meditative?

A: Because it forces you to be present. The rhythm of casting, the flow of water, the focus on the drift—it shuts out the noise and locks you into the moment.

Q: What's the connection between fly fishing and storytelling?

A: Every cast writes a new chapter. Some are triumphs, some are lessons, but they all become part of the story you tell when you step out of the river.

Q: How does fly fishing shape your perspective on time?

A: It slows it down. You stop counting minutes and start measuring life in casts, rises, and sunsets over the water.

Q: Why do veteran anglers talk about "the one that got away"?

A: Because it's not just about the catch—it's about the chase, the mystery, the moment you were inches away from perfection.

Q: How does fly fishing teach humility?

A: Because you can't cheat nature. The fish don't care who you are. The river doesn't owe you anything. You earn every success.

Q: What can fly fishing teach us about letting go?

A: You learn to accept the things you can't control. Sometimes the fish rises and refuses your fly. Sometimes a storm rolls in. You adjust, you cast again, you move forward.

Q: How does fly fishing mirror the challenges of life?

A: It's all about reading the water, adjusting your approach, and staying patient. Just like in life, the best opportunities come when you least expect them.

Q: Why do anglers keep coming back to the same river?

A: Because it's never the same twice. The water changes, the fish change, and so do you.

Q: What is the real reward of fly fishing?

A: It's not the fish—it's the experience. The quiet, the challenge, the connection to something bigger than yourself.

Q: Why do some people call fly fishing an art?

A: Because it requires creativity, skill, and intuition. No two casts are ever exactly the same, and mastery comes through practice and adaptation.

Q: How does fly fishing test your ego?

A: Because the river will humble you. The fish don't care how many books you've read or how much money you spent on gear. They teach you real skill, not borrowed confidence.

Q: What makes fly fishing a lifelong pursuit?

A: Because you never truly master it. There's always a new river, a smarter fish, a better cast to perfect. It's a craft that grows with you.

Q: Why do some anglers release every fish they catch?

A: Because it's not about possession. It's about respect, about knowing that the experience itself is enough.

Q: What can fly fishing teach us about focus?

A: If your mind drifts, your cast suffers. If you're distracted, you miss the rise. Fly fishing demands full attention—just like the best things in life.

Q: Why do so many fly fishers prefer solitude on the water?

A: Because the river is honest company. No distractions, no

expectations—just you, the fish, and the endless rhythm of the stream.

Q: What's the biggest lesson the river can teach you?

A: That everything moves forward. The current doesn't stop for anyone. You can fight it, or you can learn to move with it.

Q: How does fly fishing cultivate gratitude?

A: It makes you appreciate the small things—the bend of a rod, the flash of a fish, the way sunlight dances on the water.

Q: Why is the first fish of the day always special?

A: Because it validates everything. The early wake-up, the miles driven, the hours of patience—it all comes together in that one perfect moment.

Q: What makes fly fishing an escape?

A: It's a world away from deadlines, noise, and pressure. The only thing that matters is the cast, the water, and the pursuit.

Q: How does fly fishing change the way you see the world?

A: It makes you look closer. You notice the insects, the currents, the subtle movements of fish. You start seeing patterns where others see chaos.

Conservation & Ethics

Q: Why does conservation matter in fly fishing?

A: Because without healthy waters, there's no fishing. The river gives, but only if we respect it. Conservation isn't optional—it's the cost of admission.

Q: What is the golden rule of catch and release?

A: Handle the fish as little as possible, keep it wet, and release it gently. A careless release is no better than keeping it.

Q: Why should anglers use barbless hooks?

A: Less damage to the fish, easier removal, and a cleaner fight. If you think you need a barb to land a fish, you need to improve your skills.

Q: What's the best way to revive a trout before release?

A: Hold it gently facing upstream, let the current run through its gills, and wait until it kicks away on its own. Forcing it back too soon is a death sentence.

Q: Why do some rivers have special regulations for trout fishing?

A: To protect fragile populations, prevent overfishing, and keep the experience intact for future generations. If a river has rules, they exist for a reason.

Q: What's the impact of stocking trout in rivers?

A: Stocked trout can help put fish in the water, but they can also disrupt native populations. A wild fish in a wild river is always the better experience.

Q: How do dams affect trout populations?

A: They change water temperature, block migration, and disrupt natural flows. Some tailwaters thrive, but many rivers pay the price.

Q: Why is habitat restoration crucial?

A: Because trout need more than just water—they need clean, cold, oxygen-rich environments. Every fallen tree, restored bank, and protected riffle makes a difference.

Q: What role do insects play in a healthy river?

A: They are the foundation of the food chain. If the bugs disappear, so do the fish. Pay attention to the insect life, and you'll know the health of the water.

Q: How can anglers reduce their environmental impact?

A: Pack out what you pack in. Stay on designated trails. Respect the river like it's your own backyard—because it is.

Q: Why is ethical angling more than just following the rules?

A: Because rules are the bare minimum. True ethics mean respecting the fish, the water, and the experience—whether anyone's watching or not.

Q: What's the biggest mistake anglers make when handling

fish?

A: Taking them out of the water too long. A trout can't breathe air. If you need a photo, keep it brief and keep it wet.

Q: Why should you avoid fishing for trout in high water temperatures?

A: Because warm water stresses them out. If the river is too warm, give the fish a break. If you care about trout, you'll wait for better conditions.

Q: How does overfishing affect trout populations?

A: It depletes numbers, reduces genetic diversity, and makes fish more wary. The best anglers take only what the river can afford to lose—or nothing at all.

Q: Why is supporting conservation groups important?

A: Because they fight for the waters we love. Every river needs a guardian, and groups like Trout Unlimited make sure these places survive.

Q: What's the best way to educate others on conservation?

A: Lead by example. Preaching rarely works. Show respect for the water, and others will follow.

Q: Why do some anglers remove invasive species?

A: Because non-native fish can outcompete, overpopulate, and destroy delicate ecosystems. Protecting native trout means keeping their waters in balance.

Q: How do plastics and pollution affect trout waters?

A: Microplastics end up in the fish. Trash chokes the river. Every bottle left behind is an insult to the place that gives us so much.

Q: What's the most underrated aspect of conservation?

A: Advocacy. Healthy rivers don't happen by accident. Speak up, support policies that protect watersheds, and let your voice count.

Q: What does "leave no trace" really mean for anglers?

A: It means leaving the river better than you found it. Pick up trash, respect wildlife, and be the kind of angler that future generations will thank.

Q: How does climate change impact trout fishing?

A: Rising temperatures mean warmer rivers, fewer fish, and disrupted hatches. If we don't act now, future anglers won't have the same waters to enjoy.

Q: Why should catch limits be respected?

A: Because they aren't suggestions. They are designed to keep fish populations stable. If you care about the future of fishing, you'll follow them.

Q: What's the single best thing an angler can do to help conservation?

A: Care. Truly care. If you love the water, you'll do whatever it takes to protect it. That's the difference between a fisherman and a steward of the river.

Q: How do human activities outside the river impact trout?

A: Deforestation, pollution, urban runoff—all of it affects the water. What happens miles away still finds its way to the river.

Q: What's the best way to ensure future generations can fish these waters?

A: Teach them. Show them how to fish responsibly, respect the river, and appreciate the experience beyond just catching fish.

Q: Why should anglers participate in stream cleanups?

A: Because it's not just about fishing—it's about stewardship. If you love a river enough to fish it, love it enough to protect it.

Q: What can be done to combat habitat destruction?

A: Support conservation efforts, vote for policies that protect watersheds, and educate others. The fight for healthy rivers is never over.

Q: How does responsible angling contribute to conservation?

A: Every ethical decision—catch and release, proper fish

handling, using barbless hooks—keeps the fish population thriving. Conservation starts with the individual angler.

Practical Skills & Troubleshooting

Q: What's the best way to tie a secure knot for fly fishing?

A: Learn the clinch knot first, then the loop knot. If you can tie those in the dark, you'll never lose a fish to a bad knot.

Q: How do I properly rig a dry-dropper setup?

A: Tie your dry fly onto the leader, then attach a short section of tippet to the bend of the dry fly's hook, where you'll tie on a nymph. It covers two feeding zones at once—trout love options.

Q: What's the best way to deal with line tangles on the water?

A: Stay calm. Jerking at the knot makes it worse. Find the loop that started it, work backward, and if needed, snip it and retie—better to lose a few inches of tippet than waste half an hour fighting a mess.

Q: How do I keep my fly from dragging unnaturally?

A: Mend your line. If you don't, the current grabs your fly like a puppet on a string. A good mend lets the fly drift free—just like the real thing.

Q: How do I adjust my casting in windy conditions?

A: Lower your cast and tighten your loops. Use more power on the forward stroke and less on the backcast. If the wind is really bad, sidearm casting can save your day.

Q: What's the easiest way to change flies quickly?

A: Use a tippet ring or a quick-change snap. If you're old school, practice tying knots fast—speed and efficiency mean more time fishing.

Q: How do I wade safely in fast-moving water?

A: Move slow, use a wading staff, and keep your feet shoulder-width apart. Always angle upstream when moving—it gives you more control.

Q: How do I cast in tight quarters with trees and brush behind me?

A: Learn the roll cast and bow-and-arrow cast. If you're getting tangled in branches all day, you're not adapting to the river—you're fighting it.

Q: What's the best way to store my flies to keep them in good shape?

A: Dry them out before putting them back in your box. Wet flies rust, and a rusted hook won't hold. Use a patch on your vest or a drying pad before reboxing.

Q: How do I dry out a soaked fly on the water?

A: Shake it hard, squeeze it with a drying cloth, then use desiccant powder. If you don't have any, false cast a few times and let the wind do the work.

Q: What's the best way to pack my gear for a day trip?

A: Essentials first—flies, leader, tippet, nippers, forceps, floatant. Layered clothing, water, and snacks. Keep it light—if your pack weighs you down, you'll regret it by noon.

Q: How do I choose the right leader and tippet size?

A: The general rule—match the tippet size to the fly size. Small flies need finer tippet, big flies need heavier. If in doubt, err on the side of stealth.

Q: What's the difference between fluorocarbon and monofilament?

A: Fluorocarbon sinks and is nearly invisible underwater—great for nymphing. Monofilament floats better—perfect for dry flies. Knowing when to use each gives you the edge.

Q: What's the best way to detect a subtle strike while nymph fishing?

A: Watch for the slightest pause in the indicator, the tiniest twitch in your line. If you think, "Was that a strike?"—set the hook. It probably was.

Q: How do I find trout when the water is high and muddy?

A: Look for structure—trout hold tight to banks, behind rocks, and in slower pockets. Darker, larger flies work better in stained water.

Q: What's the best way to fight and land a big trout?

A: Keep side pressure, let it run when it wants to, and don't panic. When it tires, guide it toward your net smoothly—rushing this part loses more fish than bad knots.

Q: How do I prevent my fly line from sinking when fishing dry flies?

A: Dress it with floatant before hitting the water. If it starts sinking mid-session, clean it and apply more floatant—it makes all the difference.

Q: What's the best way to handle a trout for a quick release?

A: Keep it wet, handle it gently, and never squeeze. If you must touch it, cradle it with wet hands and get it back in the water fast.

Q: How can I improve my accuracy in fly casting?

A: Pick a target—a leaf, a ripple, a shadow. Cast to it. Miss? Try again. Accuracy isn't about magic; it's about repetition.

Q: What should I do if my fly keeps getting ignored?

A: Change something—fly size, color, presentation. Sometimes the tiniest adjustment turns rejection into a strike.

Q: How do I prevent line twist when using streamers?

A: Use a loop knot or a small swivel to let the fly move naturally. If your line is twisting like crazy, your presentation is suffering.

Q: What's the best way to cast longer distances?

A: Tighten your loops, increase line speed, and double haul. Power isn't the key—efficiency is.

Q: How can I practice fly casting at home?

A: Set up targets in your yard and practice landing the fly on them. The more precise you are on land, the better you'll be on the water.

Q: What's the biggest mistake anglers make when setting the hook?

A: They either wait too long or rip it too hard. With dry flies, set fast. With nymphs, set at the first sign of a pause. And never "trout set" a streamer—strip set instead.

Q: How do I fish a tight mountain stream with little casting room?

A: Get low, use a bow-and-arrow cast, and be stealthy. These streams demand precision and patience, not long casts.

Q: What's the best way to fish under overhanging branches?

A: Sidearm casts, roll casts, and accurate short presentations. If you try to force a normal cast, you'll spend half the day untangling from trees.

Q: How can I make my fly look more natural?

A: Focus on the drift. The best presentation is one that mimics real insects—dead drifting nymphs, twitching streamers, and delicate dry fly landings.

Q: What's the best way to fish a deep pool?

A: Let your fly sink naturally, use a longer leader, and be patient. Trout in deep pools won't waste energy chasing a bad drift.

Q: How do I manage my fly line better to avoid tangles?

A: Keep extra line off the water, strip it in smoothly, and avoid coiling it too tight. Messy line management leads to lost fish.

Acknowledgments

This book wouldn't exist without the unwavering support of my wife, Waewdao, whose patience and encouragement made it possible for me to spend countless hours writing, revising, and chasing the perfect words. Thank you for always believing in me and giving me the space to bring this book to life.

To Katie and David, my greatest adventure partners—may you always hear the call of the creek and never lose your sense of wonder in the wild.

A special thanks to the friends, fellow anglers, guides, fly shops, hatchery keepers, Coweeta Lab Ecologists, and mentors who have shaped my understanding of fly fishing over the years. Whether on the water or around the campfire, your stories and wisdom have left a lasting impression.

And finally, to the creeks and rivers themselves—places of peace, challenge, and endless discovery.

About the Author

James Salas was born to chase moving water. He's not a professional guide, he doesn't spend his days on private waters, and he never claimed to be a world-class fly caster. But for years, he's answered the call of the creek—wading into mountain waters, casting to wild trout, and learning the unspoken rhythms of a life spent on the stream.

He lives in South Florida—a place more famous for yachts and sandy beaches than mountain streams—but his second home in western North Carolina, bordering the Nantahala National Forest and near the Great Smokies, keeps him close to the waters that call him back. His journey into fly fishing wasn't born out of tradition but obsession—an unshakable need to understand what makes a trout vanish as quickly as it appears: the sudden flash, the ripple, the ghost in the current.

When he's not on the water, he's with his wife, the steady current in his life, whose love for the outdoors runs as deep as his own. Together, they've passed down that same wild-hearted spirit to their two children, Katie and David, who would rather wade in a creek, chase minnows, and skip rocks than stare at an iPad all day—something James considers a small victory.

He's also the designer of Made-in-America e-stick fishing rods, built to introduce young anglers to the thrill of casting a line. A devoted explorer of creekside lore, fishing techniques, and outdoor adventure stories, he's spent years immersing himself in the wisdom of classic fly-fishing books and modern storytelling. His stories are shaped by trial, error, lost fish, and lessons learned the hard way. He's made more bad casts than good and spent enough time on the water to know that no one ever truly masters the stream—but maybe that's the point.

A Small Favor Before You Go

You made it to the end. That means either you enjoyed this book, or you just have an obsessive need to finish what you start. Either way, I respect it.

Here's the deal—books live or die by word of mouth. And in today's online world, that means reviews matter. If this book made you see a trout stream differently, gave you something to think about, or just made you want to grab your rod and disappear into the woods for a few hours, I'd love to hear about it.

No need to overthink it. Just a line or two:

"Good book."

"Made me want to sell everything and move to a cabin."

"Dude really likes trout."

That's all it takes.

The river doesn't care about opinions, but reviews help keep books flowing. If The Call of the Creek deserves a spot in the current, your words help keep it there.

So drop a few thoughts, then go find some moving water. The next perfect cast is out there waiting.

www.ingramcontent.com/pod-product-compliance
Lightning Source LLC
Chambersburg PA
CBHW020532030426
42337CB00013B/815